ActionScript
for Multiplayer Games
and Virtual Worlds

Learn multi-user interaction concepts from the experts

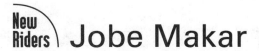

New Riders   Jobe Makar

ActionScript for Multiplayer Games and Virtual Worlds

Jobe Makar

New Riders
1249 Eighth Street
Berkeley, CA 94710
510/524-2178
510/524-2221 (fax)

Find us on the Web at www.newriders.com
To report errors, please send a note to errata@peachpit.com
New Riders is an imprint of Peachpit, a division of Pearson Education

Copyright © 2010 by Jobe Makar

Acquisitions Editor: Wendy Sharp
Project Editor: Wendy G. Katz
Production Editor: Cory Borman
Composition: Danielle Foster
Indexer: Emily Glossbrenner
Cover and Interior Design: Mimi Heft
Cover Production: Andreas DeDanaan
Cover art: Robert Firebaugh, Cyril Guichard, and Karl Prewo

Notice of Liability

The information in this book is distributed on an "As Is" basis, without warranty. While every precaution has been taken in the preparation of the book, neither the author nor Peachpit shall have any liability to any person or entity with respect to any loss or damage caused or alleged to be caused directly or indirectly by the instructions contained in this book or by the computer software and hardware products described in it.

Trademarks

Many of the designations used by manufacturers and sellers to distinguish their products are claimed as trademarks. Where those designations appear in this book, and Peachpit was aware of a trademark claim, the designations appear as requested by the owner of the trademark. All other product names and services identified throughout this book are used in editorial fashion only and for the benefit of such companies with no intention of infringement of the trademark. No such use, or the use of any trade name, is intended to convey endorsement or other affiliation with this book.

ISBN-13: 978-0-321-64336-0
ISBN-10: 0-321-64336-4
9 8 7 6 5 4 3 2 1
Printed and bound in the United States of America

Acknowledgments

Writing this book was a tremendous amount of work and a lot of fun. This was more of a collaborative effort than any other book that I've been a part of. I'm very lucky to have had a brilliant group of contributors to help me create the book I've wanted to write for years!

Mike Grundvig, Mike Bowen, and the renegade Matt Bolt were generous enough to author chapters. The quality of this book is greatly increased by the addition of their works. Thanks also to Grundvig for writing the complete server-side code for Old World.

This book has a ton of great example files. Thanks to Teresa Carrigan for developing the server code for most of them, as well as writing actual words here and there to talk about how to use them. Scott Smith did a fantastic job programming the server portion of Super Blob Bros., the multiplayer coop game, while Robert Firebaugh created the adorable art for that game—thanks Robert! And also thanks to Cyril Guichard for the richly detailed art of Old World.

Annika Hamann did an amazing job translating my kindergarten-style sketches into clean and attractive diagrams!

On the rare occasion that I don't know what I'm talking about (extremely rare ☺), Clint "Maverick" Little and Joel Stewart help keep me in line with their insightful tech editing. Thanks guys!

Thanks to Wendy Katz for making me sound smart, and to the New Riders production team for turning a large pile of words and pictures into a very coherent (if I do say so myself) and good-looking "reading experience."

I have to thank Mother Nature for the gorgeous spring weather here in Elm City, NC that allowed me to author much of this book on the porch or in the gazebo. And to my wife Kelly: thanks for putting up with months of trying to sleep through the soft glow of my laptop screen. Seriously, if I turn it away from the French doors you can't even see it!

I can't forget the biggest support group of all—our animals. Our mew of cats are a constant source of entertainment and keep me sane. My fluffy dog Free takes me for walks to the pond to make sure I work my legs out once in a while. And the 250,000 honeybees—well, they're just plain evil. But I do have to thank the lone exotic-sounding bird that shows up this time of year for continually intriguing me.

And thanks mom, for giving birth to me!

Contributors

The creation of this book would not have been possible without the generous contributions of the following people:

MIKE GRUNDVIG

Mike wrote Chapter 3, *Security: You vs. Everyone Else*. In addition, he wrote the server-side code and did the database work for Old World, which is used in several chapters.

TERESA CARRIGAN

Teresa wrote the complete server-side code for the tank game in Chapter 9 as well as the server-side code for every example in the book except for Old World and the coop game. Teresa also wrote most sections of the book where server code or the deployment of the applications is discussed.

MIKE BOWEN

Mike Bowen wrote Chapter 11, *Cooperative Game Play*, and coded the client-side portion of the game Super Blob Brothers, which was used in that chapter.

MATT BOLT

Matt Bolt wrote chapter 16, *User Homes*. Matt created the sprite sheets used for the avatars in Old World. He also created the sprite sheet used for the NPC found in the inn in Old World.

ANNIKA HAMANN

Annika created the 60+ diagrams found throughout the book.

ROBERT FIREBAUGH

Robert created the artwork for the Super Blob Brothers coop game found in Chapter 11. He also created the bridge seen in the tank game.

CYRIL GUICHARD

Cyril created all of the world artwork seen in Old World and most of the user interface. Cyril also created the menu screen for the tank game found in Chapter 9.

SCOTT SMITH

Scott programmed the complete server code for the Super Blob Brothers game found in Chapter 11.

BRUCE BRANSCOM

Bruce created the map editor as an AIR application for Old World. It is discussed in Chapter 14.

TOM McAVOY

Tom programmed the vendor user interface for purchasing furniture items in Old World, discussed in Chapter 14. He also programmed the buddy-list user interface code found in Chapter 15.

MIKE PARKS

Mike wrote about the ElectroServer administration pages in Chapter 4. In addition, he did some sprite sheet work to rearrange the order of the rows. Mike also took some of the screenshots found in the book.

JONATHAN WAGNER

Jonathan contributed to Chapter 5 by writing about chat filtering. He also reviewed Chapter 3.

PAT MAKAR

Pat created the background music found in Old World.

SHANNON KOZLOWICZ

Shannon prepped the layered animation files for avatars found in Chapter 13.

PETER ROYAL

Peter provided consulting via email and reviewed Chapter 3.

KARL PREWO

Karl created most of the artwork for the tank game seen in Chapter 9.

RENEE SHERBO

Rene created the user interface artwork seen in the chat example in Chapter 5.

KELLY GOODNOW

Kelly created the icons used in the Old World map editor.

Table of Contents

INTRODUCTION

There are some things you should know before getting started with this book. In this section we introduce you to the tools that are used in this book, where you can find the files, and how to use them. If you need more information, feel free to contact me at jobe@electrotank.com.

This book discusses multiplayer concepts and how to apply them with ActionScript. We assume that you are already familiar with ActionScript and with Flash fundamentals.

ActionScript 3 and Flash Develop

All client code discussed and found in the example files in *ActionScript for Multiplayer Games and Virtual Worlds* is ActionScript 3, targeting Adobe Flash Player 10. Know that Adobe Flash CS4 or newer is *not* required for this book. All projects are compiled using the Flex compiler. Project files created in Flash Develop (a free editing tool, available at www.flashdevelop.org, that uses the Flex compiler) are provided for all examples. If you install Flash Develop, you'll be able to easily open and compile all projects. To use the example code with Flex Builder, you will need to import the files into a Flex Builder project.

ElectroServer

This book uses ElectroServer 4.06 (www.electro-server.com) as the socket server to power all multiplayer examples. ElectroServer is one of the most-used socket servers for powering Flash, Shockwave, and Unity multiplayer games and virtual worlds. It is formally introduced in Chapter 3, and then used throughout the book.

Where to find the example files

NOTE *To gain access to the zip file via the Peachpit/New Riders site— www.peachpit.com/ actionscriptformpgs—you'll need to sign in and enter the ISBN. After you register the product, a link to the additional content will be listed on your Account page, under Registered Products.*

All the example and game files that go along with this book can be found in a zip file (gamebook.zip) that you can downloaded from one of two places:

- My website (www.electrotank.com/gamebook)
- The publisher's website (www.peachpit.com/actionscriptformpgs)

In either location, download the gamebook.zip file and unzip it. It contains subfolders that break up the information according to the relevant chapters.

Directory structure for the examples

Many examples have been created for this book. There is a very big example virtual world created called Old World, which can be found in the old_world folder once you've downloaded the gamebook.zip file. All other client example files can be found under directories named for the chapter they are in. Throughout the book, each example location is referred to as it comes into play.

Most examples also make use of server code. The server code used to run all of the client examples except for Old World can be found in the book_files/examples_extension folder. All of the code used to install and run Old World can be found in the book_files/old_world/server_extension folder. The details on installing and running those files can be found in the Appendix (starting on page 277).

CHAPTER 1

Web Game Landscape

QUITE SIMPLY, a web game is a game hosted on a website and played through a web browser. With tens of thousands of them on the Internet, one thing is clear: web-based games are tremendously popular. If you have so much as opened a web browser in the last ten years, then you have run across them. And if you are like most of us, you have found a few addictive gems and allowed them to chew up many hours.

Games are fun to play, and even more fun to create!

In this chapter, we briefly explore client-side technology choices, typical goals of web games, and how this all relates to multiplayer games.

Client-side Technology

Web-based games are created using a number of different platforms. The platform provides you with a programming language and a way to compile it into game content publishable to the web. To interact with the game through a web page, the *virtual machine* for that compiled content needs to be installed on the client machine. A virtual machine is software that your web browser uses to know how to run compiled content. Adobe's Flash virtual machine is just called Flash Player.

Top platform choices for web-game development

	DEVELOPER LEARNING CURVE	RUN-TIME PERFORMANCE	VIRTUAL MACHINE INSTALLATION BASE	DEVELOPER BASE	EASE OF DEVELOPMENT
Java	High	Fast	Medium	Large	Moderate
Shockwave	Medium	Fast	Medium	Medium	Moderate
Unity	Medium	Fast	Small	Small	Moderate
Flash	Low	Moderate	Large	Large	Easy

While Java, Shockwave, and Unity are more powerful than Flash when it comes to capabilities and run-time performance, Flash is the most-used platform for creating web-based games. This is because Flash has a much lower learning curve, bridges the gap between artist and programmer very well, and has the widest installation base for its virtual machine. For these reasons, Flash is generally the target for new games.

In this book, we assume that the games and virtual worlds are played through the web browser. However, they do not need to be. Flash content can be downloaded and run outside of the web browser from your hard drive. Flash content can be compiled in three separate ways to achieve this:

- SWF—A SWF file can be downloaded and run from a user's hard drive. This isn't ideal, because the typical user doesn't have a way to run the SWF file, and the default security settings block interesting things from happening, like talking to a remote server.

- EXE—(Windows only) A SWF can be converted to an EXE file called the Flash Projector. It contains Flash Player within it, so that it can play the Flash content without the user having to install anything.

- AIR—Adobe AIR is the preferred way to prepare Flash content that will run on a user's machine. The user must have the AIR runtime installed, which can be easily done through Adobe's website. Flash is able to do many things through AIR that it cannot do under normal circumstances, such as write files to the hard drive.

Where Multiplayer Fits In

While web games have been popular for as long as the web has been popular, *multiplayer* web games took a lot longer to grow in numbers and coolness. This isn't because users were unwilling to play them—users are happy to try *anything* new!—it was due to a combination of factors. Flash was by far the most-used platform to develop web games. However, not many Flash developers knew how to program a multiplayer game, and those who did may not have had the server-side technology available or the time required to do so. Because of these factors, there was little multiplayer Flash content out there.

Multiplayer games have been possible in Flash since Flash Player 4 (1999). I programmed my first multiplayer Flash game (chess) using a client-server polling technique—bleh! (See Chapter 2 for more about that.) Flash Player 5 introduced the ability to establish a socket connection with a remote server, which was exactly what we needed to really kick-start multiplayer game development. A few companies, including my own, developed commercial servers to support multiplayer Flash games starting around 2001.

In early 2006, multiplayer game development in Flash seemed to finally start taking hold. More clients were asking for them, and more developers were learning how to produce them. There was a small handful of Flash-based virtual worlds starting development around this time, and a few experimental ones that had already been created.

2007 and 2008 saw an explosion of demand for multiplayer Flash games and virtual worlds.

So where do multiplayer Flash games and virtual worlds fit into the web-game landscape now? Right in the middle of it! Nearly every development request that I see today has a multiplayer component to it. There is much more demand for multiplayer content than there are companies who can provide it.

Typical Goals

This section classifies most web games into some general categories that attempt to answer the question, *why was this game made*? These answers do not drive anything else in this book, so it is brief. However, you should keep these goals in mind when designing a game, so that your game design supports what you are trying to achieve.

In each of the categories, a multiplayer perspective is added that can help support the goal.

GENERATING BANNER AD REVENUE

The goal here is to earn revenue through ad impressions. You try to attract as many people to your site as possible, and keep them on it as long as possible, to generate a large number of ad impressions. Many sites rotate banner ads at the top of the web page while the game is in play. In the last few years, it's become common for games to display an ad within the game for a few seconds before you start playing.

How multiplayer can help. If keeping users around longer is the goal, then giving users the ability to chat adds a new layer to your site that will give users another reason to stick around.

MAKING YOUR SITE EVEN STICKIER

Sometimes games are created and put on non-game websites in an attempt to get visitors to stay longer. The idea is that if a user stays on your website to play a game, then maybe that user will exercise other aspects of the website when not playing the game. There is debate about the efficacy of this approach.

How multiplayer can help. In this particular instance, the goal is to get users to use the game for a while and then browse the site. Since the goal isn't longer game play, it's tough to see how multiplayer would help. There are likely creative ways to get "planted" users to communicate to the game players about the rest of the website.

MARKETING

Games are often created to promote things like movies, TV shows, consumer products, and events. Most of the games that my company creates fit this category. The game is usually loosely tied to the thing it is promoting. Sometimes this approach is mixed with ad banners.

How multiplayer can help. The multiplayer possibilities here are endless. There are websites that make use of simple things, like MTV's Back Channel (http://backchannel.mtv.com), which allows for text chatting during TV shows. Or Mattel's Rebellion Race game (www.hotwheels.com/games/rebellion/index.aspx), which allows the real-time multiplayer car-racing game to promote the company's toy cars.

DRIVING DOWNLOADS

The casual game download market is huge and very successful. Sites like Real Arcade (www.realarcade.com) and Big Fish Games (www.bigfishgames.com) promote many of their downloadable games with free lightweight web games. The idea is that the web game is a sample of what you would download. You get hooked with the web game, and then download and pay for the full game.

How multiplayer can help. This is an area where there is currently no multiplayer component at all. The target game downloads are largely simple puzzle games that allow for many hours of solitary play. As such, it is difficult to see how multiplayer can help here.

EDUCATION

If you assume that games are fun and education isn't, then the goal here is to make education more fun by creatively weaving it into game play. This is a difficult task, because you run the risk of making a game that is not fun at all—which won't keep the user engaged (and hence not learning).

How multiplayer can help. Educational games can greatly benefit from multiplayer concepts. There are many possibilities here, such as driving the desire to learn more through competition, giving learners assistance in real time, or providing one-on-one creative training approaches.

PROVIDING SUBSCRIPTION VALUE

By paying a monthly subscription, users gain access to regular new features and content. This approach is used successfully by many virtual worlds, such as Club Penguin (www.clubpenguin.com) and Faraway Friends (www.farawayfriends.com).

How multiplayer can help. Most sites like these are virtual worlds. One of the most attractive parts of a virtual world is the social aspect. Providing more multiplayer content gives user the ability to interact with friends in new settings as well as simply giving them something fresh to do.

BECAUSE I CAN

This is one of the most common motivations for creating games—developers just want to create something. They tinker, experiment, and see where that goes. They may create a personal website to display their game or upload it to community game sites such as New Grounds (www.newgrounds.com) or Kongregate (www.kongregate.com).

How multiplayer can help. If the goal is to experiment and create something innovative, then making the game multiplayer opens up a new dimension for creativity. Developers can try new things and learn what is fun to program and what is fun to play.

Last Words...

Multiplayer Flash content is fun to create and is in high demand. Using concepts found in this book combined with your own creativity, you will be able to achieve amazing results!

CHAPTER 2

Connecting Users

THINK ABOUT THE multiplayer application that you want to create, and how popular you hope it becomes. What probably comes to mind is a virtual world or game lobby system that is bustling, alive with constant activity. Users are joining and leaving frequently, chatting, and interacting with each other.

How do these users get information about each other? Are they directly connected to each other, or is something else going on? This chapter answers those questions and describes the most common way this interaction is handled. We'll wrap up by choosing a technology that we'll use for the rest of the book.

Connection Techniques

In order for anything multiuser to take place, clients have to be able to get information about other clients, and to send information that is destined to be "seen" by other clients. Typically, clients can interact with each other in one of two primary ways:

- **Peer to peer.** Information is transferred between clients without the use of a server.

- **Client-server.** A client sends information only to the server. The server then transfers information to clients. This category has two primary approaches: *polling* and *persistent socket connections*. A persistent socket connection, through the use of a socket server, is the most common approach, for reasons explained soon.

In a fully connected peer to peer setup, all clients connect to each other.

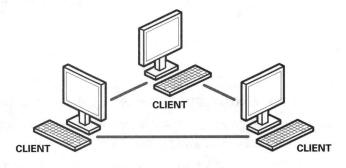

In a client-server setup, clients communicate with the server to exchange information.

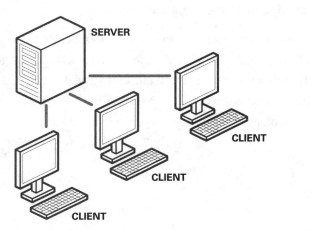

We'll describe these techniques in the following sections.

Peer to Peer

NOTE *Before we go any fur-ther, I should make it clear that this technique is not possible in Flash Player 9 or earlier. There is some support for it starting in Flash Player 10. (More on that below.)*

Peer to peer is when two or more clients communicate without the use of a server. A server may have been used to allow them to find each other in the first place, but is not used after that. Clients can exchange information by having every client connect to every other client (this is a *fully connected* topology) or by information passing through one or more other clients on its way to you (this is a *ring* topology). In this chapter, when we refer to peer to peer, we assume the fully connected topology.

Generally speaking, peer to peer is not used much in gaming. In many cases, a game may appear to be using peer to peer, but in reality, one of the players is designated as the host and acts as the server (this is discussed in more detail in the following section). However, peer to peer is alive and well for file-sharing networks, and is also being used successfully to distribute patches for games like World of Warcraft. This reduces the load on the web servers while speeding up the patch download for the players.

The peer to peer technique has a couple of clear advantages over client-server, as well as some major disadvantages. Let's start with the advantages.

PEER TO PEER ADVANTAGES

NOTE *The lower the latency, the more real-time the game play can be.*

Lower latency. *Latency* is the amount of time it takes for a message to get where it's going. In a client-server model, the message moves from one client to the server, and then from the server to another client. Compare that with peer to peer, where the message goes directly from one client to another, effectively cutting the travel time in half.

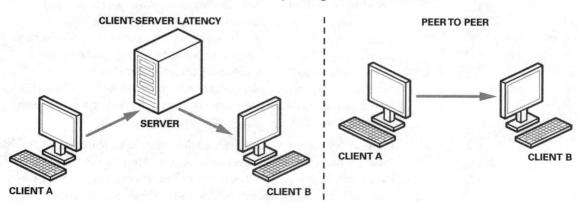

The latency in a peer to peer setup is approximately half of that in a client-server setup.

No server needed. Since peer to peer is made up completely of clients, no server is necessary. Game developers and game publishers would like this because they wouldn't need to pay hosting and administration fees to keep the centralized game servers up and running.

Now that we have looked at a couple of the advantages of peer to peer, let's look at some of the disadvantages.

PEER TO PEER DISADVANTAGES

Scalability in gaming. When you're talking about games with a fairly small number of clients, you can make a case for using peer to peer, because of the lower latency and no need for a server. But when it comes to larger numbers of clients, let's say hundreds or thousands, then peer to peer is just not feasible. It requires that an individual connection be made between one client and every other client. If there are 1,000 clients, then each client must establish and maintain 1,000 open connections in the fully connected topology. This also results in a client receiving everything from everyone, as opposed to a client just receiving intelligently chosen and aggregated messages from a server.

You'd also have to give some thought to where this network will exist. Imagine that you had 1,000 clients, but they were all within a school's subnet. Having 1,000 clients each connected to everyone else results in *1,000,000 connections*. That could present a strain on a network. If, instead, this number of connections is over the Internet, then it doesn't present a problem.

Decision-resolution logistics. Imagine a two-player peer to peer game. Each player controls a mouse and is trying to eat the cheese. Player A approaches the first block of cheese and determines that he is close enough to eat it. Player A awards himself with points for eating the cheese, and sends a message to Player B, indicating that the cheese has been eaten. Player B receives and processes this message, removes the cheese from the screen, and updates Player A's score. Life is good, and both clients agree on the state of the game.

But now Player A and Player B are headed toward the second block of cheese. Within a few milliseconds of each other, Player A and Player B both individually determine that they have eaten the cheese. They award themselves with points for having done this, and send information to the other player indicating the eaten cheese. The two players now do not agree on the state of the game.

This illustrates a problem with a peer to peer setup—no central brain for making decisions. Here are some quick examples:

- Two kill shots are fired at the remaining players. Who died first?

- In a racing game, who crossed the finish line first?

- Players are racing to grab a key on the ground. Who grabbed it first?

The best solution is to use a client-server approach. Let the server maintain the important bits of the game states and be the decision-maker to resolve all important conflicts.

To be fair to peer to peer, one of the clients *can* be designated as the host to resolve conflicts. But this introduces two new problems:

1   If all important decisions are to be run through a specific client, then you start to lose the lower-latency benefit of this approach. A message goes from a client to the controller and then from the controller back out to clients.

2   Peer to peer games naturally have security concerns, because all of the important logic is run on the client machines with no validation in a central location. But if on top of that you move *all* important decisions to a single client machine, then that client is presented with a theoretical advantage (read: hacking opportunity) in the ability to control, or at least to know, all game decisions.

FLASH PLAYER 10 SUPPORT FOR PEER TO PEER

Flash Player 10 introduced a new communications protocol called RTMFP (Real-time Media Flow Protocol), which is used in peer to peer message transfer. This means that developers now have the ability to connect Flash clients directly to each other. The Flash clients must first connect to a RTMFP-capable server such as the Adobe Stratus server, which is in beta at the time of this writing. The Stratus server aids in connecting Flash Player end points (Flash clients) with each other. An end point must maintain a connection with the server to also be allowed to maintain connections with other end points.

Using the Stratus server, in addition to creating games, Flash developers should be able to create audio or video chat applications that have much lower latency.

Polling

Polling is an approach that rarely makes sense to use. We describe it here to be complete and to illustrate the downsides. Over the years, on message boards, I have seen developers try this approach time and again. It will work with some success for low numbers of users—and breaks down quickly under load.

Polling is the act of a client making a request to the server on a timed interval to check for updates. Take a chat room, for example. The clients in this chat room would probably be set to poll the server approximately two times per second to check for updates. A client polls the server and gets a response. The response may be formatted in a way that indicates there are no updates, or the response may contain an update that says there is new information. This new information could indicate that users have joined or left the chat, or that new chat messages have been added.

A client is polling the server repeatedly looking for updates, and usually there are none.

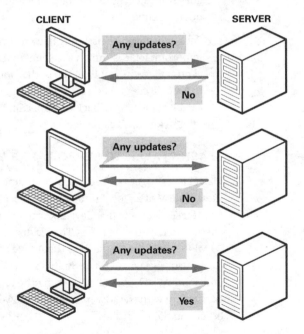

CLIENT   **SERVER**

Any updates?

No

Any updates?

No

Any updates?

Yes

At first, polling may not seem like that bad of an idea. But when you start to look at it more closely and imagine how it would scale, some problems come to light. First, imagine that you had a popular chat, game, or virtual world that had 10,000 concurrent clients. Assuming that each client polls the server twice per second, well, let's just do the math on how much work the server would be doing—two calls per second—that would come out as 20,000 total server requests and 20,000 server responses per second! That's a tremendous amount of bandwidth and server resources being used constantly, even if there are no updates.

In reality, you will likely start to run into performance problems at a few hundred to 1,000 requests per second.

There are two more major downsides to this approach that need mentioning before we move on.

First, there's the latency between when an event happens and when a client is informed of the event. If the client polls the server every 500ms, then the client can learn of an event that happened as much as 500ms + normal Internet latency after it happens. Let's assume a reasonable Internet latency of 100ms. Depending on where in the poll cycle the event occurs, the client will learn about it 100ms to 600ms after it happens. For a chat application or turn-based game, this amount of latency variation is acceptable, and won't be noticeable. But for many other types of games, this variation would cause problems. For example, if the latency varies between 100–600ms with every server request in real-time games, that's harder to deal with.

The second significant problem is in determining when a client is no longer there. With polling, a client is never connected to the server; the client makes quick calls on timed intervals. So, how can the server tell when the client is no longer around? The only way is by "noticing" that the client isn't polling any more. It may take a delay of up to several seconds before the server registers the fact that someone has left.

Socket Servers

This is the technique we've been working up to—socket servers. A socket server is a program running somewhere (typically on a remote physical server), listening for connection attempts. It accepts connections from clients, manages them, and intelligently routes messages between clients. Socket servers exist at an IP address or hostname and listen for connections on at least one port (for example: hostname: electrotank.com port: 9899).

When a client establishes a connection with a socket server, they have opened up a persistent socket connection with the server. Using this open socket, the client can send information to the server, or the server can send information to the client, without being asked! There is no need for polling or anything like it. Since the socket is open and ready to be used, information is passed back and forth quickly.

Assuming that the socket server has enough intelligence built in, the system can be set up in such a way to minimize the amount of data transferred. Some servers can also be used to aggregate client-bound messages (which has benefits discussed later in the book). Aggregated messages are messages that are grouped together and sent as one. To be fair, message aggregation can be used in peer to peer networks too. Some commercial socket-server products, such as ElectroServer, discussed below, allow message aggregation to be turned on so that you don't have to program this feature yourself.

To get a sense of the event-driven nature of socket-server applications, imagine that you have a chat application running. If nothing happens for five minutes, then no information is transferred from the clients to the server or from the server to the clients, and no bandwidth is used. (Compare that to the polling example, where every connected client is constantly hitting the server, no matter what.) When something does happen in the chat, such as a user joining or leaving, or a chat message is sent, information is then pushed to all of the connected clients that need to receive this update.

Updates are event-driven and are real-time. Internet latency is still something to be dealt with in some games.

Socket Server Choices

When it comes to choosing a socket server for your project, you have several to choose from. We list three here, and we then choose one to use for the rest of the book. The multiplayer concepts illustrated in following chapters are not tied to any specific server or implementation, but when it comes to actually showing by example, we have to choose a specific server to work with. The concepts are the same, but the details of how they are used may vary depending on the server chosen.

Developing a socket server that is feature-rich, highly scalable, and actively maintained is a costly effort and typically requires a multi-year commitment from the server developers. Because of this, most companies choose to use an existing one rather than building their own. There are not many choices, and most are commercial. You can achieve most of what you would want to with any of the three listed below. They do have their differences for ease of use, scalability, and video streaming abilities.

Adobe Flash Media Interactive Server

Adobe has several variations of their media server. One in particular (www. adobe.com/products/flashmediainteractive) is intended to allow for greater interactivity between connected clients. The others are more geared toward streaming media.

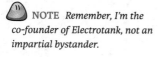

NOTE *Remote shared objects are data containers that can include objects of type Object, arrays, numbers, string, Booleans, and a few other data types. A client can modify a property in a shared object, and it is synchronized on all connected clients that see that object.*

The server version we're going to concentrate on allows for custom server-side scripting to extend the functionality of the server. It also allows for streaming of audio and high-definition video. It uses remote shared objects to synchronize data on connected clients.

Adobe Flash Media Interactive Server is free for up to five connected clients. To enable more connections than that, a license is required. Visit the Adobe website for more information.

Red5

Red5 (http://osflash.org/red5) is an open-source server product, intended to be a direct replacement for Adobe's media servers. Red5 supports media streaming, remote shared objects, and nearly every other feature provided by the Adobe servers.

As an open-source project, Red5 is free. As with all open-source software, you just have to be willing to fix any bugs you find—or wait for the authors to get around to it.

ElectroServer 4

NOTE *Remember, I'm the co-founder of Electrotank, not an impartial bystander.*

ElectroServer 4 (www.electro-server.com) is a product of Electrotank. It is free for up to 25 concurrent users, and requires a license for use above that.

ElectroServer has been around longer than any other socket server used for Flash games—even longer than the Adobe products—and is used for a significant number of the virtual worlds and multiplayer Flash games out there. It benefits from being refined over the years to contain features useful for game development. It also has support for audio and video streaming, though not to the level of the Adobe servers.

One of the primary advantages to using ElectroServer is the massive scalability it allows for—it can scale to hundreds of thousands of connected clients.

Any of these servers would work for building multiplayer games and virtual worlds. If you are looking to scale, you'd want to put some thought into scalability and project budget.

For this book, not surprisingly, we will be using ElectroServer 4. ElectroServer 4's concepts are easy to understand, and its API is straightforward.

CHAPTER 3

Security: You vs. Everyone Else

WHEN CREATING A multiplayer game or virtual world, you end up also creating a hidden social game—you vs. the world. The only rule for this social game is that you'll never know what "they" are going to try until after they've done it. Your only defense is to be armed with knowledge and proactive in development. That doesn't mean you are sure to lose—it just means you need to keep on your toes and roll with the punches. In other words, *security* is a word with many contexts and meanings when it comes to multiplayer content.

Before you decide to simply skip this chapter, thinking that your virtual world won't get hacked, know that you are completely wrong. If your world is popular enough for people to play, it's popular enough for people to hack. For many people, the fun in your world isn't the game itself, but the challenge of ruining the game for others. The fun for them comes from breaking the rules.

In this chapter, we discuss a variety of security topics, from keeping the application safe to keeping children safe.

By applying the information provided in this chapter, you will be able to dramatically harden any application (virtual world, game, or otherwise) and protect yourself from malicious users. You will be able to identify when they are acting up and know how to address the most common attacks. Forewarned is forearmed, and this is a fight you don't want to lose.

Logical Security

Ask programmers about security, they will talk about securing code. Ask parents about security, you will get a completely different answer. Most of this chapter is going to discuss physical application security, but first we'll take a step in a different direction, talking about logical security—more specifically, about making a virtual world a secure environment for the participants.

In this context, security and privacy go hand in hand. The best way to maintain security is to provide anonymity to the participants. This often goes against the goals of the project, though, as it dramatically limits the usefulness of the world as a marketing platform.

Unfortunately, this entire topic gets into a lot of potential legal concerns and issues, so rather than get into specifics, this section is going to lay out the various concepts and things to be aware of, without providing specific advice. You should seek legal counsel from an online privacy specialist concerning your specific project.

COPPA and Data Capture

Any discussion concerning securing online activities for kids in the United States has to take COPPA into account. COPPA (the Child Online Privacy Protection Act) is legislation intended to protect children when they are on the Internet. The law is targeted most directly, though not exclusively, at companies providing online activities (chat, games, articles) for kids.

The main push of the law is around collecting data and parental approval. In general, it's best to avoid collecting anything personally identifiable. At the simplest level, this means you shouldn't ask for a full name, address, or phone number during account registration, though that's just an example. In general, the less you capture, the safer you are. It's important to seek legal counsel to ensure you are protected.

CHATTING AND COMMUNICATION

Socializing is a huge aspect of virtual worlds, but it's also considered a large risk factor. The ability for players to chat directly with each other makes the world more immersive and fun at the same time as it exposes users to potential abuse. Parents are always concerned about their children being brought into contact with online predators.

NOTE We'll further discuss these two types of chatting in Chapter 5.

The most common and simplest way to eliminate this risk is to remove open chat and support only list-based chat. *Open chat* is the ability to simply type a message and send it. *List-based chat* allows the user to select and send a prewritten message from a list of possible messages, thereby preventing the user from sending or receiving information he shouldn't.

That's really the crux of the problem: how do you prevent predators from getting information (names, addresses, phone numbers—any personally identifiable information) from the other players that they shouldn't have?

If the world supports open chat, then protection comes down to chat filtering, moderation, and parental approval. In some worlds, parents approve who their child can talk to via an admin panel. And in some worlds, parents approve if the child can use open chat at all. In almost all cases, filtering plays a huge role.

Physical Security

Physical security is the process of actually preventing hackers from getting at your data or damaging the application or user experience for others. There are many layers to application security, with each layer protecting different parts of the system. In this section, we will cover general security rules and practices as well as dig into the specific attacks that are common against a Flash application.

The Problem and Its Solution

The problem ultimately is a simple one to express: how do you create a virtual world in Flash that is hack-proof? The short answer isn't one that most people want to hear: you simply can't do it. If your world is on a server that's connected to the Internet, it's vulnerable to hacks. The trick isn't to shoot for hack-proof; it's to shoot for making it as hard and unrealistic to hack as possible. The vast majority of exploits and hacks come from simple oversights which, if addressed, immediately make your world dramatically harder to hack. With a few precautions and a little knowledge of what can be done, you will be able to ensure your world is as protected as it can reasonably be.

For the rest of this section, we'll explore the basic tenets and rules for building a secure virtual world or multiplayer game. You should consider each of these rules when building a new piece of functionality, and apply them as aggressively as you are able. Doing so will dramatically strengthen your project.

MINIMIZE THE SURFACE AREA

The idea behind attempting to minimize the surface area for hackers is a simple one. You want to reduce what they can access and use against you. This is an overarching concept that you apply to everything in your world—servers, code, and data.

For instance, let's say you are passing data about users from the server to the client—some of that data is required, and some might not be, but it's easiest for a developer to just send everything. That's a bad idea—who's to say that the data you send back doesn't provide the final key the hacker needed for an exploit against your system? Not only are you wasting bandwidth, you are needlessly providing data that could potentially be used against you.

Need a more concrete example? The original Asheron's Call game used to send all information from the server to the client about collectible items spawning in the map for a large area surrounding that user. This allowed the game client to properly render the items on the ground when you got close to them. The problem was that the server sent the information for a large area rather than only for the immediate area around the player. That was a mistake—hackers created tools that would show where all the spawned items were on your mini-map and make it easy to find and collect them. The hackers were rewarded with a glut of items because they didn't have to look for them; they already knew where they were as soon as they appeared.

Minimizing your surface area is critical to ensuring that there's as little as possible available to use against you. If you don't need it, don't include it.

OBSCURITY IS NOT SECURITY

This is a common misconception that leads to a huge number of problems. Just because something is complicated doesn't make it secure. When writing code to secure a score, for instance, you should not assume that doing a few passes around adding and multiplying numbers to the score achieves the same results as real encryption. Flash is easily decompiled, and once someone has decompiled the application, it's trivial to work your algorithm backwards to break it. True security is when the hacker knows exactly how it works and still can't break it.

TRUST NO ONE

As previously stated, Flash is easily decompiled or reverse-engineered. When writing your application, you should assume a hacker can figure out how the Flash client is doing things (such as submitting scores), so you've got to protect the client. Allowing the server to help with validation of data or handling the data in the first place is the best choice. You will see examples of this throughout the book.

A good real-world example of this is a chat client developed at Electrotank years ago. It used HTML to display the chat text in various colors, based on who was talking and if the messages were public or private. To ensure the HTML was well formatted, the Flash client provided some level of validation to chat messages before they were sent.

Not good enough! Some hackers created a version of the client they could run locally that removed the HTML validation check. Since the server assumed good behavior by the client, it let the hacked text through. The hackers then did any number of things to cause problems in the chat room. They sent HTML that embedded images into the text field, formatted hyperlinks that took users to inappropriate sites, changed the text size to something ridiculously huge, or just malformed the HTML so that the text field would not render correctly. Providing server-side validation of the chat messaging, rather than trusting the client to do it, would have prevented this.

VALIDATE EVERYTHING

This goes hand in hand with the previous entry. Do not trust the client—you need to verify everything it sends to the server to make sure it never breaks the rules and causes problems. This validation is useful in general, as it will also assist you in finding errors with client/server communication.

A good example of the importance of validation is with combat. Let's say I have a gun in the game that can fire one shot per second. Each shot sends a message to the server, which is then broadcast to everyone around me. The client code uses a timer to handle sending each shot when I hold down the trigger. A hacker could simply remove the delay per shot on the client, and they'd have an instant machine gun! The solution is to validate the number of shots being fired over time, and to log any violation on the server.

It's also important to note that validation can occur on the client as well as the server. In a multiplayer game, the client is in a position to detect erroneous messages from the server and ignore them. We'll go into an example of this in a bit.

TRAP IT ALL

Simply validating is a huge step in a more secure direction, but you should also code defensively. Assume the client will send data at the wrong time, or formatted incorrectly. To this end, you should trap errors on the server and log them with as much information as possible. This will be your "hacker early warning system." Odd entries and errors in the logs give you something to either fix or harden as needed.

IF YOU DON'T NEED IT, REMOVE IT

This goes along with minimizing your surface area. There are many tools installed on a physical server by default that give server administrators lots of functionality. But most of this (the tools *or* the functionality) is not needed to host a game or virtual world. If you leave all of the default installed applications on the server, you might be exposing the server to hacks (and in any case, you're taking up space unnecessarily). The tool the hacker needs might be there because you didn't remove it. If you don't need it, remove it.

Here's a real-world example of this that we experienced a few years ago with ColdFusion (a server product from Allaire, then Macromedia, and now Adobe). When installed, ColdFusion included a nice little set of examples along with the server; they were made available automatically over the Internet when ColdFusion was installed. One of them gave the ability to run arbitrary code posted through a form via the browser. Clever hackers didn't take long to write some ColdFusion code that downloaded and executed system-compromising utilities onto the server. All you had to do was find a site with the ColdFusion examples enabled, paste them in a prewritten script, and presto, instant hack! If the administrators of those machines had simply removed the examples from the production servers, none of this could have happened. If you don't need the examples in production, don't leave them in production.

DON'T GIVE THEM THE KEYS

We have previously stressed the importance of logging, and now we are going to step back a bit. Logging is critical for you, but it also provides a huge amount of information to a hacker. Keep this out of their hands at all costs. In practice, this is pretty simple.

Most high-level web-development languages go out of their way to provide detailed error messages when problems occur. These messages make it easy for the developer to find the problem and address it. However, they also give out far too much information. To see what I mean, look at the information on a default ASP.NET error page. In production, you should always use custom error pages and messages, and log the errors such that no end-user can see them. This will give you the critical information you need while keeping it from prying eyes.

Firewalls for Fun and Profit

Right now, you are probably reeling from this list of things to do, and trying to decide where to begin. Fortunately, there is a single tool that dramatically increases your server security across the board: the firewall. A properly configured firewall is critical to securing applications on the Internet.

While firewalls themselves are very sophisticated, the idea behind how to use one is quite simple. A firewall's job is to restrict access to the servers behind it. It provides a hardened front with only specific points of access, to limit the surface area of your application.

In practical terms, the firewall configuration for a virtual world would look something like the diagram below. As you can see, the firewall prevents all external access to the server or any of the software running on it (in this case, the database), and therefore, by its very nature, it is much more secure.

As you can also see from the diagram below, only specific ports are open inbound to the servers. This is all part of limiting access to the servers. For instance, the web servers can be called only on ports 80 (HTTP) and 443 (HTTPS). The game server is limited to 9899 (the default ElectroServer binary port).

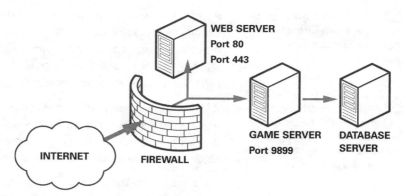

In a real-world scenario, there are likely other ports you'd want to open, such as SSH inbound and email outbound, but I've left them out of this diagram to keep it simple. The idea, though, is to minimize access in and out of the environment. This dramatically reduces the available options for a hacker.

Know Thy Enemy

It's important to know that the people most likely to exploit your system are looking to do it for fun. Sometimes they are power gamers and want that extra edge, or they want to just do something no one else can do for the ego stroking involved. In general, they are interested in taking advantage of your system rather than just crashing it.

Knowing this gives you an idea of the type of things they will try and the techniques they will use. Expect them to be exceedingly resourceful and clever. The advantage you have is that they have to work backwards from the final game and discover the details as they go, while you simply need to plan for security up front.

In the remainder of this section, we will explore the most common hacks against applications in general and against Flash content specifically. As part of this discussion, we will discuss how you can protect yourself from these attacks.

EXPLOITING GAME BEHAVIOR

This is almost certainly the first exploit you will see against your virtual world. Game exploitation is made possible by a design flaw or a poorly thought-out piece of functionality that a clever user will take advantage of for some gain in the game.

NOTE *"Clamp" is a programming term for keeping a value between a minimum and a maximum.*

A good example of this is a mini-game that can be slowed down with a CPU-slowing piece of software (like CPU Killer) and thus easily won. If the developer didn't clamp the maximum money for winning the game, this might make it possible to make lots of money by playing the game over and over, and getting very high scores, because the game is now so simple to win.

NOTE *As a way to identify exceptions, watch for users who are making too much money or advancing too quickly. Seeing how they do it will tell you a great deal.*

As always, the first step to preventing this is to clamp values and validate input in the first place. But one specific way to prevent the slowdown trick is to use time-based animation vs. frame-based. This will ensure that the objects on the screen move the same distance no matter the CPU speed.

The ultimate fix for this is testing. Make sure your game doesn't have easily exploitable loopholes.

SQL INJECTION

This is easily the most malicious of all possible hacks, from an application standpoint. It's also one of the most common. SQL injection is the process by which a hacker is able to inject an SQL statement and run it against the database, because a lazy developer didn't validate the input or bind the variables.

To really understand this, we need to get into a specific example. Let's say you have a high-score board in your system. The code to select a high score for a specific user looks like this:

```
select ScoreId, Score, Username, Date from Scores where
→ Username = '#name#'
```

Assume that #name# is coming from the client somehow. The clever hacker could simply pass a command like this:

```
'; drop table Scores; --
```

The final command as actually run would look like this:

```
select ScoreId, Score, Username, Date from Scores where
→ Username = ''; drop table Scores; --
```

This command would drop your entire scores table! This means that any code that attempts to access the table is now going to fail as well. This type of hack is both very dangerous and very common, so it's essential that you protect yourself from it at all times (and at all costs).

The good news is that actually preventing SQL injection attacks isn't terribly difficult. The first step is to validate inputs. This is something you should always do anyway, so it doesn't really add extra work. For example, if you are expecting an integer, make sure the value isn't a string.

The next thing to do is to escape (URL-encode) any data passed in. There are various commands to help you with this process, but the best solution is to use *parameterized queries*—queries where you tell the system what the query is, using placeholders for the dynamic parts. When you then populate those placeholders at runtime, the escaping will be handled for you. Not only do prepared statements give you better security, they also improve performance, since they can be cached by the database.

The final trick with SQL injection is simply to limit the harm. In the example above, the hacker was able to drop the database table. This can occur only if the database account used to run the queries can actually dump tables. That's not a good idea in general, of course—you need to keep the access restricted, allowing only the minimum level needed. Odds are that your virtual world doesn't need to support adding and removing database objects (tables, indexes, references) on the fly. Assuming that's the case, you should give the user as few privileges as possible. In highly secure systems, different accounts are used for different parts of the system, with table- and command-specific limits on what they can do.

CROSS-SITE SCRIPTING

Cross-site scripting is a very common hack for web applications. The basic idea is that input from the client is displayed without validation. This can be used to perform all sorts of dirty tricks in a web application. A common example that happens with cross-site scripting is that a forum that doesn't validate and doesn't strip special characters could be hijacked with some JavaScript code in a forum post to redirect users to a different site.

This is a bit less of an issue in Flash applications, as Flash doesn't allow for dynamic execution in most cases. The specific area where this can be a concern is in the use of HTML for field formatting. If you had a chat box, and the client sent HTML-formatted messages, it'd be possible to send a message with invalid HTML that ruined the display for the other users. For instance, the client could set the font to a tiny size and change the color to match the box background, but not close the font tag. This would result in all subsequent chat messages looking tiny with a bad color.

The solution in this case is simply validating the chat message and stripping unwanted characters. If all < and > signs were stripped, then HTML couldn't be injected.

Depending on the design of the system, this stripping could occur on the recipient client as well. If the text is sent plain, and any HTML required is added when received, any HTML that was received is obviously invalid, and would need to be stripped. This is a good example of where the receiving client can act as a last line of defense.

PACKET INJECTION

Packet injection is simply where the hacker injects a packet in the stream of data to the server with the command he wants to execute. Basically, this is letting him program the behavior he wants to occur automatically.

Let's say you have a real-time shooter game that's become popular. A clever hacker could write a program that intercepts all the messages between the client and server, and use that to build an in-memory representation of the game state. In this case, the program would behave like a proxy server; it intercepts everything and passes it along. This rogue program could then be used to automatically send a "shoot" message whenever someone is in range. This might seem far-fetched, but it really isn't—this attack has been successfully used against some popular first-person shooter games in the past.

There are various solutions for preventing successful packet injection. First and foremost, you need to validate the data from the client to ensure it's legit—make sure the client is not sending shoot messages too quickly, walking through walls, or otherwise breaking the rules of the game (or of physics). Important decisions should never be made on the client; they should always be made on the server. This will prevent a clever hacker from being able to send messages with too much power—death messages, hit detection, game state changes, etc.

Once you have ensured only valid data is being sent, you need to start hardening the protocol itself. One effective approach is to number packets automatically as they leave the game and server. This means if someone is going to inject a new packet, there will be a conflict with the numbers detected on the server, and it can be handled however makes sense for the game. For the examples in the book, this is done for us, because ElectroServer automatically numbers both inbound and outbound messages and tracks duplicates.

Another layer of security is controlling the format of the messages. If the hacker can't reverse-engineer the messages, they won't be able to duplicate them. As we said before, obscurity is not security, so don't rely on a complicated protocol alone—you need to use encryption of your protocol. It doesn't need to be strong; it just needs to be hard to break. Various forms of TEA (Tiny Encryption Algorithm) or XOR are both effective, though many other options exist as well. (ElectroServer has built-in protocol encryption that can be used to help with this.)

MESSAGE MODIFICATION

Message modification (the brother of packet injection) is when the hacker uses a tool like FireBug (a Firefox add-on) or a home-grown proxy server (as discussed previously) to modify the messages being sent from the client to the server. The hacker might modify an avatar movement message that would allow their avatar to teleport through walls. They might modify their attack message to do far too much damage or adjust the aim to be perfectly accurate. The possibilities are endless, and as this is easy to do, it's a very common attack.

The solution for preventing message modification is exactly the same as for preventing packet injection—encrypt your protocol, validate on the server, don't trust the client for important decisions, and so on.

IN-MEMORY VARIABLE HACKING

Editing variables in memory used to be the purview of skilled hackers, but with new tools, it's become easy to do. There are numerous articles that teach anyone how to do it, and, unfortunately, it's becoming a common hack.

The general process is to use a tool like Cheat Engine and tell it what process to hit (in this case, your browser). Then you search for a known value. Let's say you have 20 gold pieces in the game. You would search for an integer with the value of 20. This might return hundreds of results. Then you "lock" the results, and do something in the game that changes the amount of gold you have. Let's say it's down to 10 now. You then search in the original results for a value of 10. At this point, you should have only a couple of results, and you now know what memory addresses to change to impact the game. This technique can be used to increase your score, change the money, etc. As you can see, this gives a lot of power to the hacker.

NOTE *An ActionScript 3 utility that can make this process trivial to implement can be found in book_files/chapter3/MemoryCrypto.zip.*

Fortunately, the fix for this problem is basically the same as for the others: in a multiplayer game, you simply don't trust the client. Validate input from the client, and don't let the client make important decisions. Another highly effective solution that stops this technique dead in its tracks is to encrypt the variables in memory. By encrypting the important variables, the hacker isn't able to search for them, as they are not stored in memory in a "findable" state.

Final Notes on Security

In this chapter, we covered a lot of information to help you secure your virtual world. Most of the information is basic, but that's where good security starts—with the basics. Ensure that your world's code is well thought out and designed with proper validation (and just a touch of paranoia in the handling of client input), and you will be all set. Throw in encryption where appropriate, and a firewall, and you will have a virtual world that you can be confident is secure enough to let the users in.

CHAPTER 4

Introducing ElectroServer

IN CHAPTER 2, *Connecting Users*, we introduced socket servers— software that is usually running in a remote location, accessible over the Internet, that manages thousands of connections between client applications (in our case, games and virtual worlds). ElectroServer is one of the most-used socket servers for multiplayer Flash content.

In this chapter, you will be introduced to concepts and terminology specific to ElectroServer, as well as installing it and writing a simple hello-world application. We'll also look at how to configure the server using the web-based administration system.

ElectroServer is free and unrestricted for up to 25 connected users (at the same time). You can download and install it at www.electro-server.com/downloads.aspx.

Server Concepts

In this section, we look at ElectroServer concepts and some terminology. Most of these concepts are popular and are shared by other servers as well. Since they are generally found in most socket server choices, the concepts described here are useful to learn about beyond ElectroServer itself.

Users

NOTE *The term* user *is used throughout this book a little loosely. Depending on the context, it may refer to the representation of a connected client on the server, it may be used instead of the term* client, *or it may refer to the human being who is controlling the client.*

A *user* is a representation of a client connected to the server (and logged in). It is possible for a single client to establish more than one connection to the server and still be seen as a single user. Because of that, it should be noted that while a user usually has only one connection to the server, he can have more than one. For instance, to stream video from the server to a client using ElectroServer, a user establishes a second connection to handle the audio/video stream.

Clients are connected to the server. Notice that one client has more than one connection.

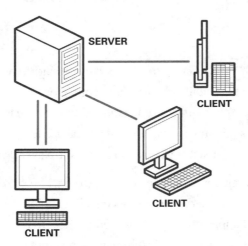

Rooms

A *room* is a common concept in the realm of socket servers that means a collection of users. In ElectroServer, a room is a way for one to many users to see each other and interact. If a user is in a room, then that user can send a chat message, which is then broadcast to all users in that room. That is a simple example of the use of a room. A user can be in multiple rooms at a time.

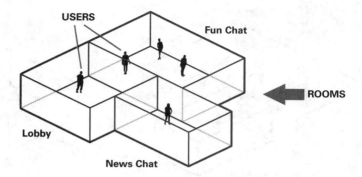

There are two types of rooms in ElectroServer:

- **Persistent**—A room that always exists, even if there are no users in it. A persistent room allows users to join and leave at any time.

- **Dynamic**—A room that is created for a single use. When the user list for that room drops to 0, meaning that all users have left, the room is destroyed. This is the most common type of room.

Rooms have many uses, the two most common of which are enabling chat and grouping users together to play a multiplayer game. Both of these common uses are explored in detail in later chapters.

Zones

A zone is collection of rooms. The concept of zones is mostly valuable as an organization tool for servers with large numbers of rooms. Rooms within a zone must be uniquely named. All users in a room within a zone have access to the room list for that zone. The user can subscribe to automatic list updates as the list of rooms changes.

NOTE *Having multiple zones allows for the same room names to be used again and again.*

If the room list is very large or very active (with many rooms being created and destroyed), you may find that connected users may receive too many updates per second to keep up with. Using more zones is one way to attempt to manage this.

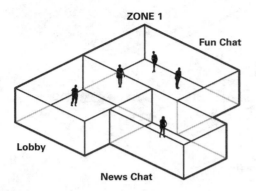

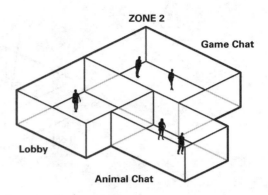

Chat

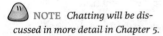 NOTE *Chatting will be discussed in more detail in Chapter 5.*

Chat is the primary method by which users interact with each other while connected to a socket server. A chat message is text sent from one user to other users. In ElectroServer, as in many other socket server solutions, there are public and private chat messages. A public chat message is sent from a user in a room to that room at large—that is, broadcast to all users in that room. Typically, a public chat message would end up being displayed on the client in a text field, such as the one seen below.

A private chat message is sent from one user directly to one, or to many, specific other users. Unlike with public messages, the target user does not need to be in the same room as the sender, or in any room at all, for that matter. Most typically, a private chat message is from just one user to one other user, for example, to hold a private conversation between users in a chat room or to allow for private communication between players on the same team in a game. Many times in multiplayer games and virtual worlds, private messaging happens only between users who are considered buddies.

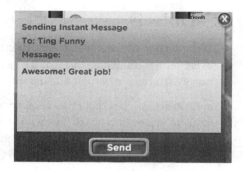

Buddies

Social networking is an enormous part of the typical multiplayer experience. In addition to playing games and competing, users like to form relationships that transcend a single play session. They like to flag each other as *buddies* to add to a list. When a user returns to the application on a future session, she sees her buddy list and can tell which of her buddies are currently online and which are not. A user can then message any of her buddies that are currently online and even challenge them to a game.

Some virtual worlds or social networks allow users to send messages to their buddies even when they aren't online. When the offline user returns, he sees the delayed message that was sent.

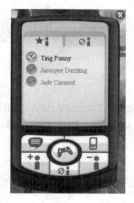

EsObjects

NOTE *The term* transaction layer *refers to the part of the client and server APIs that handles parsing and formatting data to be exchanged between the client and the server. It takes data, formats it to be sent over the socket, receives data over the socket, parses it into a usable object, and dispatches an event that can be captured by application-specific code.*

This is the first concept introduced that is truly ElectroServer-specific. An EsObject is something that may look a little odd at first, but is tremendously useful as you become familiar with it.

An EsObject is a class that exists in identical form on both the server and the client. A new instance of the class is created and data is then stored on this object. The object can then be exchanged between the client and the server easily, because the *transaction layer* knows how to serialize and deserialize the object.

Serialization and deserialization

When an object is *serialized,* that means that the data has been represented in another form that can be used for storage or transport. For instance, consider the following object:

```
var person:Object = new Object();
person.name = "Jobe";
person.age = 33;
```

That object could be represented as XML like this:

```
<person>
      <name>Jobe</name>
      <age>33</age>
</person>
```

The act of converting a data object to the string XML representation is *serialization*. It could have been converted to a byte array or a variety of other formats. When it is converted back to the data object, that is called *deserialization*.

EsObjects are used all through the API for client-server communication. Here is an example EsObject created using ActionScript:

```
var esob:EsObject = new EsObject();
esob.setString("name", "Jobe");
esob.setInteger("age", 33);
esob.setStringArray("petNames", ["elfie", "bosley", "clyde"]);
```

You can see in the example above that first you create a new instance of the EsObject class, and then you add the data. Each property that you add to an EsObject has a strict data type. In the example above, you can see that String, Integer, and String Array are represented.

NOTE The most commonly used data types are String, Integer, Boolean, Byte, and EsObject.

Here is the complete list of data types supported by EsObject:

- String / String Array

- Integer / Integer Array

- Number / Number Array

- Boolean / Boolean Array

- Byte / Byte Array

- Character / Character Array

- Double / Double Array

- EsObject / EsObject Array

- Float / Float Array

- Long / Long Array

- Short / Short Array

You may wonder at first why putting all data on an EsObject is a good idea. It seems like it takes a good bit of code, and having to identify the data types seems like overkill. Well, it comes down to saving time (and headaches) later. By using EsObjects and strict data types, you reduce ambiguity in your code and are forced to program in a way that ends up being more manageable down the road.

Another benefit—both more and less visible—of using EsObjects is bandwidth. The serialization process used for EsObjects (which is hidden from you) generates packet sizes that are miniscule and hence keeps bandwidth to a minimum.

Extensions

In addition to providing a highly scalable connection layer, the most useful socket servers primarily provide a basic level of functionality right out of the box, like rooms, chatting, buddies, and a few other things. But what about features and functionality that you need for your game or world that are not part of the core feature set of the server you are using? A good socket server provides a way for you to add these features yourself. By extending the functionality of the server with your own custom code, you can achieve anything that you want to do.

ElectroServer and many other servers provide support for what are called *extensions*. An extension is custom code run on the server to provide features and functionality not built into the server.

An extension can include one or many types of objects to extend certain functionality of ElectroServer. There are three types of objects supported to extend and enhance ElectroServer: *event handlers, plugins,* and *managed object factories.* Each object can include variables to define values that should be known to the object upon creation.

EVENT HANDLERS

Event handlers allow a developer to have some custom logic applied as a result of an event. These are typically written in Java, although they can be written in ActionScript 1 as well.

ElectroServer currently allows event handlers to be created for the following event types:

- Login—User is logging in to ElectroServer.

- Logout—User is logging out of ElectroServer.

- User Variable—User has updated the EsObject attached to the user object.

- Room Variable—User has updated the EsObject attached to the room.

- Buddy List—User has updated his buddy list (add / edit / delete).

- Private/Public Messaging—User has sent a message to another entity (room / user).

NOTE *Nearly all large applications created to use ElectroServer will end up using a custom-written login event handler to authenticate user credentials against a database.*

Let's take the Login event handler as an example. A client connects to ElectroServer and provides his login credentials. His name and password can then be authenticated against a database. The event handler then decides if it should accept or reject the user's connection.

PLUGINS

Plugins (often written in Java) provide extended functionality where the core features do not offer what is needed. Clients can talk to plugins and plugins can talk to each other. ElectroServer supports two types of plugins: *room* and *server.*

Room plugins are in charge of any functions that may need to be attached to any particular room. Most often, these are used to handle game logic and additional room functions. A good example of a room plugin would be a card game: the plugin would handle all of the logic for dealing cards, which players receive them, score calculation, and deciding the winner. A room-level plugin is created and scoped to a room; thus, it is instanced. Clients can talk to any room-level plugin that is scoped to a room that they are currently in.

Server plugins extend the abilities that ElectroServer can perform. These may range anywhere from globally enhancing room functions to exposing an external interface to other applications that wish to leverage certain aspects of your game. Server-level plugins are created once and always exist, as opposed to room-level plugins, which are created as needed. Clients can talk to any server-level plugin.

A good example of a server-level plugin is accessing a remote RSS feed. If your virtual world required news entries to be displayed in-world in some way, then the server would need to load that news. In this case, it would be smart to have a server-level plugin that loads and manages the latest news, so that any other plugin can access it as needed.

MANAGED OBJECT FACTORIES

Managed object factories allow you to create instances of objects that need to remain active over time. One common object created through this kind of factory is a database connection. This will allow you to define the properties and database type to connect to and retrieve data from within a plugin.

Here's an example of the creation of a MySQL-based managed object written for a Java-based plugin:

```
EsObject esDB = new EsObject();
esDB.setString("poolname","mysqlpool");
Connection c = (Connection)getApi().acquireManagedObject
    ("ManagedDBConnection", esDB);
```

Installation

TIP *The latest version of ElectroServer can always be found at www.electro-server.com/.*

TIP *For all of the installation methods, your Java VM must be up to date (the Java VM as of this writing is at version 6, update 13). Go to http://java.com/en/download/ to be sure you have the latest.*

One of ElectroServer's biggest strengths lies in the fact that it is multi-platform. In this section, we will show you how to install it on some of the supported platforms. For all installation explanations in this chapter, we will be using ElectroServer 4.0.6.

Windows

The following instructions pertain to Windows XP and Windows Vista.

1   Download and run the ElectroServer_4_0_6_Windows.exe installer from the ElectroServer website.

2   Follow the prompts until you reach the Select Components prompt. Leave everything checked, as these options will provide you with further reading materials and examples not within the scope of this book.

3   Continue with prompts, leaving everything at default until you reach the Select Server Mode prompt. Choose Professional mode.

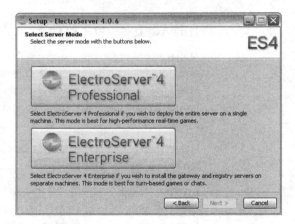

4   At the Web Server prompt, note the defaults for later reference, and click Next. The values here can be changed later if you so desire.

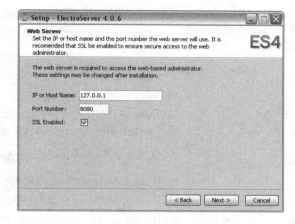

5   For the Administrator User prompt, leave it at the default values. The default administrator user is name is *administrator*, and the password is *password*. You will want to change this if you intend to share your server with the outside world. You can change the default user later, as well as add additional users. For now, click Next.

6   When asked to install as a Windows service, leave this unchecked, click Next, and grab yourself a cup of coffee as ElectroServer installs.

7   Once it has completed, click Finish, and you will be ready to use your freshly installed ElectroServer.

8   Go to the Windows Start menu, and navigate to Programs > ElectroServer 4.0.6. From this menu, choose Start ElectroServer.

ElectroServer will launch into a console window. This will provide an output for any messages that ElectroServer may need to display to you.

Linux / UNIX Variants

The following instructions pertain to CentOs, Fedora, and other distributions that support RPM.

1   For CentOS, Fedora, or any other RPM-supporting distribution, select the **ElectroServer_4_0_6_linux.rpm** package. For any other distribution, select the **ElectroServer_4_0_6_unix.tar.gz** tarball package.

   • To install for CentOS, Fedora, or any other RPM-supporting distribution, either use the package manager provided in your OS, or install it from the command line as follows:

```
rpm -i ElectroServer_4_0_6_linux.rpm
```

- To install for any other distribution, either extract it with your unpacker of choice, or do so from the command line using this command:

```
tar -xvzf ElectroServer_4_0_6_unix.tar.gz
```

2   After the package has been unpacked, you are ready to run ElectroServer. All of the defaults from the Windows installation apply here, so there is minimal configuration to do.

3   Navigate to the directory of your new installation:

- If you have unpacked using the tarball package, navigate to the **ElectroServer_4_0_6** directory.

- If you have installed an RPM distribution, navigate to the **/opt/ElectroServer_4_0_6** directory.

Within the appropriate directory, you will find three shell scripts: *ElectroServer, GatewayServer,* and *RegistryServer*.

4   Run the *ElectroServer* script using the following command:

```
./ElectroServer
```

ElectroServer should now be up and running from within a console window. This will give you a display for any messages that ElectroServer may need to tell you about.

Mac OS X

For the Mac OS X installation, follow the directions used for the non-RPM Linux installation. Please note that if your version of Mac OS X is earlier than 10.5, you will need to update in order to take advantage of Java VM version 6 update 7 or later.

Hello World

What better first application to write than *hello world*? It's about time we write a little code!

In this section, we will introduce you to the ElectroServer API, and then use that to connect to ElectroServer, log in, and send a private chat message.

The ElectroServer API

The ElectroServer API is an ActionScript 3 API used by a multiplayer application to connect to and communicate with ElectroServer. The API is provided as a SWC file, which you will find it in the 'lib' directory of all examples in this book that communicate with ElectroServer.

NOTE *Chapter 5, Chat, will show by example most of the data that is automatically managed by the API.*

The ElectroServer API allows the client to establish a connection with the server and then communicate with the server. It also does some amount of automatic management of data. For example, the API keeps track of which rooms you are currently in as well as the user list in each of those rooms.

There are three main types of messages that can travel in either direction between the client and the server:

SWC files

A SWC file is precompiled code used during development time. It can contain code or binary assets such as user interface elements. A SWC file can be used by an application as long as it is placed within the application classpath.

- **Requests**—Objects created by the client and then sent to the server. For instance, when you want to log in, you create a login request, and send that to the server. For all intents and purposes, anything that the client sends to the server is a request.

- **Responses**—Objects created by the server as a result of a request and then sent to the client. For instance, once the server receives a login request from a client, it processes the request and generates a login response. This response would contain information such as whether or not the login was successful.

- **Events**—Messages (sent from the server to a client) that did not necessarily originate from a request. For example, receiving a chat message in a chat room is an event. That chat message may have been generated by that same user, another user, or even by the server itself.

NOTE *We'll discuss API calls as we get to them throughout the book. You'll find comprehensive documentation on the ElectroServer website (www.electro-server.com/documentation.aspx).*

Most of what you can do with the API is request-driven. The client creates a request object of some type, populates it with information, and then sends it to the server.

Writing Your First Chat

In this section, we look at the example you'll find in book_files/chapter4/hello_world.

Open the project file. Using the project tab, browse and open the Main.as class file. This is the only class file used in this project. There are no visual assets needed to compile this project. The only thing that you can see is a text field, created using ActionScript.

Flash Develop

Like all examples in this book, this Hello World. as3proj file is a Flash Develop ActionScript 3 project. You can download Flash Develop (a free ActionScript code-editing program) at www.flashdevelop.org.

Compile the application to see what it looks like. Make sure ElectroServer is running. You should see something that looks like the screen below.

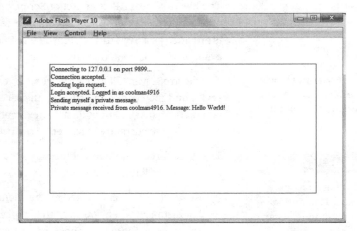

The compiled application will run through the following steps:

- Prepares an ElectroServer instance to be used

- Connects to ElectroServer on 127.0.0.1 and port 9899

- Logs in with a random username

- Sends a private chat message to itself, and captures that message

Each step of the way, the application logs what is going on to a text field on the screen.

PREPARE AN ELECTROSERVER INSTANCE

The first thing you need to do before connecting to ElectroServer is create a new instance of the ElectroServer class. The ElectroServer class is the gateway to the entire API.

On line 36 of the Main class, you can see the creation of the new ElectroServer instance :

```
_es = new ElectroServer();
```

Since we will be using this class instance from other functions later, it is a class-level property.

Now that the ElectroServer instance exists, we add event listeners, so that we can capture the responses and events that come back from the server:

```
_es.addEventListener(MessageType.ConnectionEvent,
➛ "onConnectionEvent", this);
_es.addEventListener(MessageType.LoginResponse,
➛ "onLoginResponse", this);
_es.addEventListener(MessageType.PrivateMessageEvent,
➛ "onPrivateMessageEvent", this);
```

The first line establishes an event listener for the connection event. When a connection occurs or times out, the `onConnectionEvent` function is executed. Likewise, the next two lines establish event listeners for logging in and for private chat messages. They will be discussed further below.

Each of the `addEventListener` function parameters is worth discussing. First is the `MessageType` class. That class is used to store references to every request, response, and event type that is possible with the API. When adding an event listener, you use the `MessageType` class to point to the response or event that you want to capture.

The second parameter is a string that contains the name of the function you want to be called when the event occurs. This one item is something that is not ideal about the ElectroServer API; the code base for the API is maintained in ActionScript 2 to support older clients, and ActionScript 3 up-conversion code is used to generate the ActionScript 3 version of the API. Having to use a string function name when adding an event listener is an unfortunate side effect of that process. However, it doesn't slow down code or present any problems other than the lack of compile-time checking of the function names used.

The third parameter describes the scope in which the function exists.

CONNECT

Now that the ElectroServer class instance exists and has the proper event listeners added, we can actually do something—connect! ElectroServer supports several different protocols (text, binary, HTTP, and RTMP). We'll use binary throughout the entire book; it's the best choice for our purposes because it is lightweight and fast.

So first, we tell the API which protocol we want to use on line 44:

```
_es.setProtocol(Protocol.BINARY);
```

Next, we make the connection attempt to ElectroServer, on line 47:

```
_es.createConnection("127.0.0.1", 9899);
```

Assuming all of the default ElectroServer settings are being used, and it is running, then this makes ElectroServer listen for socket connections at the local IP address of 127.0.0.1 on port 9899.

When the connection succeeds or fails, the onConnectionEvent function is called:

```
public function onConnectionEvent(e:ConnectionEvent):void {
  if (e.getAccepted()) {
      log("Connection accepted.");

      //build the request
      var lr:LoginRequest = new LoginRequest();
      lr.setUserName("coolman" + Math.round(10000 *
      ➥Math.random()));

      //send it
      _es.send(lr);

      log("Sending login request.");
  } else {
      log("Connection failed. Reason: " + e.getEsError().
      ➥getDescription());
  }
}
```

Notice the ConnectionEvent parameter passed into this function. All events and responses have typed objects passed in that contain information about what happened.

In the if statement, you can see that this event object contains a Boolean value indicating whether the connection was successful or not. If the connection was not a success, then we log that, and then log the error that describes why the connection failed.

If the connection was successful, we log that it was a success, and then attempt to log in to the server.

LOGIN

By default, ElectroServer will allow a user to log in with any username—provided that it is unique (no one else already has that name) and that it passes the default vulgarity test included as part of the application. (Try replacing the username with profanity, and you will see an error logged.)

To log in to ElectroServer, first a LoginRequest object is created, a username is populated onto that object (a random name, in this case), and then this request object is sent to the server. All requests are handled in this way: create the request, populate it with information, and send to the server.

The server processes this request and sends back a login response. This response is captured in the onLoginResponse function:

```
public function onLoginResponse(e:LoginResponse):void {
  if (e.getAccepted()) {
        log("Login accepted. Logged in as " + e.getUserName());

        //create the request
        var pmr:PrivateMessageRequest =
        new PrivateMessageRequest();
        pmr.setUserNames([e.getUserName()]);
        pmr.setMessage("Hello World!");

        //send it
        _es.send(pmr);

        log("Sending myself a private message.");
  } else {
        log("Login failed. Reason: " + e.getEsError().
        getDescription());
  }
}
```

If the login was accepted, then the getAccepted() method of the LoginResponse object returns true. If it was not accepted, then we log that information, and then log the error description about why it failed.

If the login is successful, then we send a private message to our own user.

SEND A PRIVATE MESSAGE

To send a private message with ElectroServer, you first create a SendPrivateMessageRequest object. This object is then populated with information such as the list of usernames it should go to, and the message payload. In this example, you'll see that the list of usernames is an array of just one name, our own.

The server processes this request and ends up sending private message events to all users in the list. A private message event in this example is captured by the onPrivateMessageEvent function:

```
public function onPrivateMessageEvent(e:PrivateMessageEvent):
  void {
  log("Private message received from " + e.getUserName() +
  ". Message: " + e.getMessage());
}
```

In this function, we simply log that a private message was received, who it was from, and the message itself.

Administration Panel

Now that you've successfully written your first client application, you should be ready to connect it to ElectroServer. However, before you can do that, you must ensure that ElectroServer's settings are configured to your needs. To that end, let us introduce the administration panel, which exists to allow configuration of ElectroServer's many options.

NOTE *In case this point isn't obvious, ElectroServer needs to be running in order for you to use the administration panel.*

Within the administration panel, you'll be able to define the IPs and ports on which ElectroServer listens for socket connections. Also, it will allow you to manage extensions, configure the number of users the server will allow, and even create language filters to protect users from obscene language in chat messages.

Once you are running ElectroServer, open a browser, and point to the default address for the administration panel (*https://localhost:8080/ admin/*). You will then see a screen that looks similar to this:

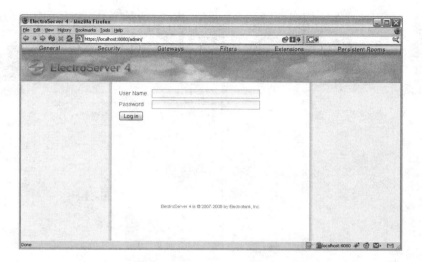

Enter the login credentials that you provided during the installation process. (Refer back to the "Installation" section if you need the default values.) Upon logging into the administration panel, you will be provided with several menu options. We'll look here at the three that are most commonly used:

Gateways Menu. The Gateways menu provides the configuration for adding addresses and ports to enable socket communications between ElectroServer and any connecting clients.

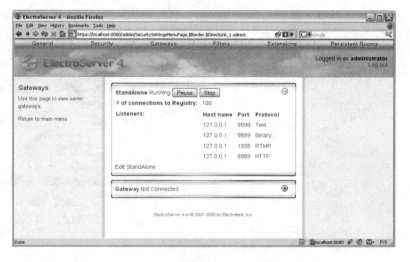

If you need to edit any of these addresses, click on Edit StandAlone, which will bring up the configuration for these listeners.

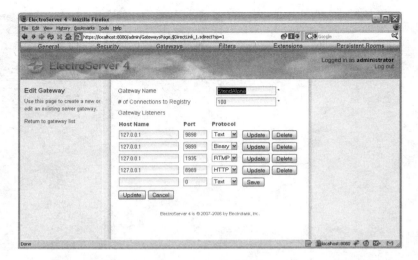

TIP *You may create listeners only for IP addresses and ports that are available to the server running ElectroServer. If an address is unavailable on the server, or the port is in use, ElectroServer will give an error the next time it is rebooted.*

For any address and port combination required, add a new line to the bottom of the list. The default values should be sufficient for the scope of this book.

Extensions Menu. In the Extensions menu, you can install and configure any server extensions to be used with ElectroServer. The front screen of the Extensions menu provides a list of currently installed extensions as well as the option of installing new ones. We'll cover the installation of extensions thoroughly in the Appendix.

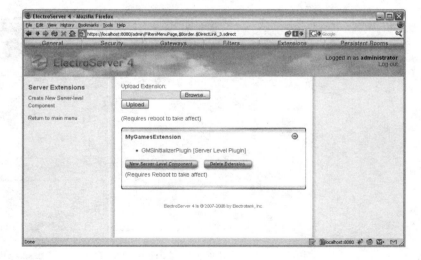

Persistent Rooms Menu. This menu provides a means of creating rooms and zones that will persist while (and whenever) ElectroServer is running. For example, it's good to use these for rooms that you want to have remain constant, such as lobbies or commonly played public games.

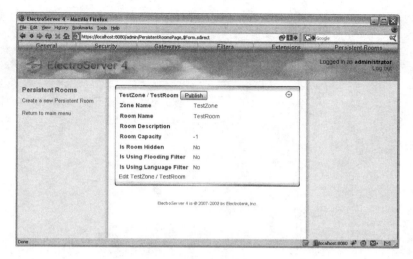

Persistent rooms share the same configuration options as those found when creating a room using the client API. They are a great asset when implementing chat functionality into any client application, as well as remaining available for any connecting clients to automatically join upon login.

CHAPTER 5

Chat

CHATTING IS PRESENT in all multiplayer games and virtual worlds. It allows users to send messages for others to read immediately. In this way, users have conversations to get to know each other, trash-talk, or coordinate strategies in team-based games.

In this chapter, we look at the various ways users chat, and how those ways work with ElectroServer. We'll discuss some new room concepts, and then look at the code used to build a simple chat room.

Overview

When it comes to programming a chat, there are several concepts that you should become familiar with. These concepts govern where you chat, who can see your chat messages, and how those messages are created in the first place. In this section, we'll present those basic concepts, as well as language filtering.

Chat Visibility

When a chat message is sent from a user to the server, who will see it? The answer depends on the visibility of the chat message. In most chat applications, a chat message is designated as either public or private.

A public chat message is one that a user sends to the server with the understanding that other users in some context will see it. Under simple conditions, public chatting occurs in ElectroServer between users in a room. Any user that is in a room can send a public chat message directly to the room. That chat message will then be broadcast to all users in that room.

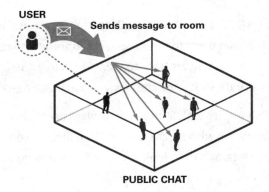

A private chat message (also sometimes called a *whisper*) is one that a user sends directly to one or more other users. With ElectroServer, a private message can be sent to a single user or to many users by populating an array, and the user does not have to be in a room to send a private message.

PRIVATE CHAT

In general, public and private chatting as described above are what you will find in most multiplayer applications. However, with custom programming, chatting can occur with visibility determined in other ways. For example, you could program a *shout* chat message—one that is sent to everyone connected to the server, or one that goes only to thieves at level 30 or higher.

In some of the stricter virtual worlds for kids, the ability to see any chat messages is disabled unless granted by a parent. In that scenario, the child would not see chat messages even if they exist. The parent could grant permission for the child to see chat messages from their friends only, from everyone, or governed by any other set of custom rules you can imagine.

Chat Type

The two primary chat types that you'll find in most multiplayer games and virtual worlds are *free-entry chat* and *list-based chat*. Most kids' virtual worlds have a combination of these two chat types, enabled or disabled based on parental controls.

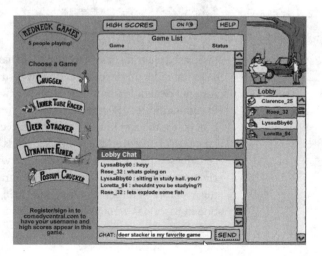

Free-entry chat is the standard type of chatting that you would expect. Users are free to use the keyboard to enter anything they want to say. Some filtering may occur on the input, but it is mostly unrestricted.

List-based chat, which is sometimes called *safe chat*, allows users to choose chat phrases only from a hierarchical list. While this method is commonly used and has a few benefits (discussed below), it can also be frustrating. Much more chatting and user interaction occurs, of course, when users can create their own chat messages.

List-based chatting has a couple of benefits. For one, it is considered much safer for children, since there is heavy restriction on what can be said. Another benefit is that it can allow users who speak different languages to communicate "directly." In code, each phrase has a unique ID. When a user enters the application, the list-based chat data is loaded based on their language preference. When the user sends a chat phrase, what they are actually sending is just the ID associated with that phrase. The receiving clients use this ID to determine which phrase to show. So a user viewing the application in Alabama can send Hello, and a user viewing the application in Barcelona would see Hola, while another in Paris might see Bonjour, and so on.

While these are the two primary chat types, they are not the only ones. Voice and video chat are less common, but do exist. Also, I have seen more than one multiplayer application that allows users to form sentences by dragging-and-dropping words from an approved list.

Room Concepts

We briefly discussed rooms in Chapter 4, but in this section we will look at rooms as they work in ElectroServer in a more comprehensive way.

QUICK REVIEW

Simply put, a room is a collection of users, and a zone is a collection of rooms. The concept of a room exists to provide some organization, so that groups of users have a way to congregate and interact. In any server solution, it is typical for users to join one or more rooms simultaneously, and then interact with users in that room (or those rooms) through chat.

With ElectroServer, any user in a room can send a chat message directly to that room. This chat message is a *public chat message,* broadcast to all users in that room. Private chat messages can be sent from any user to any other user, regardless of what room they are in.

As was discussed in Chapter 4, there are two types of rooms: dynamic and persistent. A dynamic room is created on the fly as needed. A user can use the API to create a room and join it. Other users can also join this room. Eventually, when all users leave the room, the room will automatically be removed from the server. A persistent room is one that always exists. Using the ElectroServer administration panel, you can configure persistent rooms. These are identical to dynamic rooms in every way except that they do not get removed when empty.

ROOM BEHAVIOR

There are two methods by which a user can join a room by using the client API:

- JoinRoomRequest—This request object is used to join a room that already exists. The user would have to specify the ID of the room and of the zone.

- CreateRoomRequest—This one is used to create *or* join a room. In a dynamic room setup, it is common to use this request when trying to join a room, because it will create the room if it doesn't already exist.

We'll use these request objects in the chat example file we look at later in the chapter.

The user can create user-specific settings through the request object when joining a room, and the room creator can establish room-specific settings at create time. There are too many of these settings to be looked at here, so we will just look at those that are most commonly used. The rest of the settings have default values.

Here are a few settings that you can specify when joining a room:

- Receive user list updates—Defaults to true. If `true`, the user will be told by the server whenever a user joins or leaves the room. In rooms that don't need to show a user list or which happen to have a very aggressive rate of users joining and leaving, it makes sense to set this value to `false`.

- Receive room list updates—Defaults to true. If true, the user will be told about other rooms in the zone that contains the room they are joining. The user will be told when new rooms are added, removed, or when any of their public properties are changed (such as room description). In a very active zone, it is common to turn this setting off, so the client is not inundated with messages.

And here are a few settings that you can specify when *creating* a room:

- Capacity—This is a quantity specifying the maximum number of users allowed in this room. A user trying to join a room that is at capacity will receive an error event indicating that the room is full. The default value is -1, which indicates there is no limit.

- Hidden—Defaults to false. If true, the room does not show up in the room list for a zone.

- Plugins—As discussed in Chapter 4, plugins are custom code written on the server that can be instanced and scoped to the server or to a room. They are the way that most games and virtual worlds achieve custom behavior. When creating a room, you can specify one or more plugins to be created and scoped to the room.

Chat Filtering

When you give users the ability to chat, you will quickly learn that those who participate in chat fall into two main categories: *socializers* and *griefers*. A socializer is a person who chats to socialize—to talk about any topic, such as the game or current events, or to get to know the person on the other end. A griefer, on the other hand, is a person whose sole purpose is to aggravate other users. Griefers can achieve their goals through profanity and insults in a chat room, or through their actions in a game.

Sadly, there is no way to completely keep users from abusing a chat, short of switching it to list-based. What you *can* do is take steps to minimize the ways a user can abuse the system. Chat filtering is one major thing that you can do.

Chat filtering, sometimes referred to as *language filtering*, is the act of analyzing a chat message and taking some action based on that analysis. Usually chat filtering is used to detect profanity and then kill the chat message. (An alternative action used in some chat filters is to find vulgar words and replace them with something non-offensive.)

TYPES OF FILTERING

Most chat systems rely on two distinct classes of filtering, *blacklist* and *whitelist*. In a blacklist scenario, you've got a list of words that are not supposed to be in a chat message—typically, vulgarity or short offensive phrases. If a word or phrase from the list is found in the chat message, then some action is taken. A whitelist filter is quite the opposite. In this scenario, there exists a list that includes every word that *is* allowed to exist in a chat message. If a word is found in the chat message that isn't in the whitelist, then some predetermined action is taken.

ElectroServer has filtering built in, and uses a small blacklist as a default. Through the administration tool, you can add lists of words, defining them as whitelists or blacklists. Then you can choose which filter to use per room.

The key to developing an effective chat-filtering strategy is to use a combination of filters that can be run in a chain. Imagine a chain of two filters where one is a whitelist and the other is a blacklist. The goal is to allow good words to pass, and bad words to fail, respectively. You could whitelist the entire dictionary, and then blacklist words that you want to omit.

NOTE *Some companies allow users to say whatever they want, but a human has to approve every message. Another client of ours wanted such a system. In this scenario, a user types a message and sends it. This message ends up on the screen of a moderator. The moderator will manually approve or deny this (and every) chat message. What a job!*

Some advanced filtering systems do more than allow or block specific words. At Electrotank, we worked on a system, for a client, that would see certain words or phrases as indicative of pedophile grooming behavior. Often, these are words or phrases that in most contexts are perfectly innocuous, so we didn't want to block them outright. So when this type of wording was detected, we created a log of that user's chat transcript, saving everything the user said in the previous few minutes and for the following few minutes. This chat transcript was then raised to a human moderator where it could be inspected, and then action taken to ignore the message or, potentially, to report the user to the authorities.

PERFORMANCE CONCERNS

In practice, the task of filtering chat can end up consuming a considerable and sometimes surprising amount of resources—both in terms of development and raw computing power. There are well-known virtual worlds that spend more than 50% of their computing resources on chat filtering alone.

A typical whitelist or blacklist filter can contain hundreds or even thousands of words to match. Switching from brute force to a Trie-based matching scheme can save an enormous amount of execution time. ElectroServer uses a Trie algorithm for its built-in filtering. You can learn more about Trie at Wikipedia (http://en.wikipedia.org/wiki/Trie).

Building a scalable filter system

Despite your best efforts at optimization, your filtering system may still require a great deal of computing muscle. One solution is to build chat filtering to be both stateless and distributable from the ground up, so it would be handled on multiple servers instead of just one. In this context, stateless means you can pass all the needed information to your filters at runtime, so they require little or no access to state information in your virtual world. This gives you the ability to distribute your filtering across relatively inexpensive and independent computing nodes to attain flexible scalability, and doesn't increase the load on your core virtual world.

Simple Chat Room

Now that we have covered the general concepts of a chat room and how they apply to ElectroServer, let's look at a simple example that we've created for this chapter. Below we'll describe the feature found in this example and then follow it up with a walkthrough of the relevant portions of code.

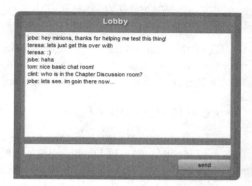

Features

NOTE While these are the only features programmed into this example, you should be able to easily add others if you want a more feature-rich experience. Try adding more options to the create-room screen or adding audio/video chat.

This simple example allows a user to perform actions found in a typical chat room. They include:

- Logging in
- Sending a chat message to the room
- Sending private messages
- Viewing the list of users in the room
- Viewing the list of rooms in the zone
- Joining any room in the room list
- Creating a new room

Walkthrough

NOTE Find the source code for this example in book_files/chapter5/ chat_room.

The Flash Develop project file used in this project is called **Chat Room. as3proj**. If you want to browse the source code while reading this section, open that project file and start ElectroServer.

Here is the general application flow. When the chat is launched, it loads an XML file that tells it which IP and port to connect to. The chat then attempts to connect to ElectroServer using those settings, and shows the user a screen indicating this. If the connection is successful, then the chat removes the connection screen and shows the user login screen. Here, of course, the user can enter and submit a username. The login screen is then immediately removed, and the login request sent to the server. A login response is then sent from the server to client. If the login is successful, then the user sees a chat room user interface, and is joined to a default room.

From this chat room screen, a user can view the user list, the room list, and the chat messages. They can also send public and private chat messages as well as create a new room or join any room in the room list.

CONFIGURATION FILE

Like all examples in this book, the source code compiles to the bin directory. If you look in the bin directory, you'll see that there is a file called **server.xml**. This is an XML file that contains the server connection settings (IP and port). The chat application loads this file, extracts the connection settings, and uses them to connect to ElectroServer:

```
<server>
  <connection ip="127.0.0.1" port="9899" />
</server>
```

Keeping the connection settings external like this allows you to change which IP and port the chat application uses without having to recompile it.

THE CHATFLOW CLASS

This class handles loading the XML file, connecting to ElectroServer, and administering the user login. In Chapter 4, we looked at what it takes to create a new instance of the ElectroServer class, create a connection, and log in, so we won't cover those things again here. However, there is something new to talk about that is used here: the ConnectionClosedEvent.

As you know by now, the client establishes a socket connection with the server. The ConnectionClosedEvent is fired if that connection is severed for any reason. The connection may have been lost due to some issue between your location and the server, the server being turned off, the server forcing a disconnect, or the client disconnecting on purpose. Whatever the reason, it is good to be able to capture an event telling you that the connection has been closed, so that you can inform the user or establish a new connection.

In the `initialize` function, we add an event listener for this event:

```
_es.addEventListener(MessageType.ConnectionClosedEvent,
→ "onConnectionClosed", this);
```

Further down in the class, you can find the `onConnectionClosed` function:

```
public function onConnectionClosed(e:ConnectionClosedEvent):
→ void {
  showError("Connection was closed");
}
```

In this example, we just inform the user if the connection is lost. You can test it by connecting and then turning off ElectroServer. The `showError` function simply gives the user an alert display containing a message. This function is also used if the initial connection attempt fails or if the login attempt fails.

THE CHATROOM CLASS

After the user successfully logs in, an instance of this class is created, and an instance of the ElectroServer API instance is passed in. This class handles all client-server communication as well as the chat room user interface.

After the class instance is created and the ElectroServer API instance is set on it, the `initialize` method is invoked:

```
public function initialize():void {
  //add ElectroServer listeners
  _es.addEventListener(MessageType.JoinRoomEvent,
    → "onJoinRoomEvent", this);
  _es.addEventListener(MessageType.PublicMessageEvent,
    → "onPublicMessageEvent", this);
  _es.addEventListener(MessageType.PrivateMessageEvent,
    → "onPrivateMessageEvent", this);
  _es.addEventListener(MessageType.UserListUpdateEvent,
    → "onUserListUpdatedEvent", this);
```

```
_es.addEventListener(MessageType.ZoneUpdateEvent,
➤ "onZoneUpdateEvent", this);

//build UI elements
buildUIElements();

//join a default room
joinRoom("Lobby");
}
```

This function registers several event listeners for server events, calls a function to build the user interface, and then joins a default chat room. The event listeners have been added to handle receiving chat messages, updating user lists and room lists, and knowing when you've successfully joined a room. For the remainder of this section, we will look at the event handlers for each of those as well as a few new request objects.

CREATEROOMREQUEST AND LEAVEROOMREQUEST

The joinRoom function is used to join a user to any room that he specifies. It introduces two new request objects: CreateRoomRequest and LeaveRoomRequest.

The default server behavior of the CreateRoomRequest object is to create the room that the user specifies or join the user to that room if it already exists. The object can be configured to return a failure if the room already exists. There are too many extra and advanced settings available on the CreateRoomRequest object to be covered here. The default settings are fine for most uses:

```
//create the request
var crr:CreateRoomRequest = new CreateRoomRequest();
crr.setRoomName(roomName);
crr.setZoneName("chat");

//send it
_es.send(crr);
```

The code you just saw is found in the joinRoom function. First, the request object is created. The target room name is then set on the object, based on the roomName function parameter. The target zone for the room to be created is also specified. (Any name will be fine for the zone.) Once the object has been configured, it is sent to ElectroServer. If the user successfully joins that room, then the onJoinRoomEvent function is called. We'll look at that in a bit.

This conditional is also found in the joinRoom function:

```
if (_room != null) {
  //create the request
  var lrr:LeaveRoomRequest = new LeaveRoomRequest();
  lrr.setRoomId(_room.getRoomId());
  lrr.setZoneId(_room.getZoneId());

  //send it
  _es.send(lrr);
}
```

Later on, when we look at the onJoinRoomEvent function, you will see that we store a reference to the Room object that you belong to in a class-level property called _room. In the code above, if _room is not null, then that means you are in a room, and we send a LeaveRoomRequest to remove you from that room. ElectroServer allows you to join multiple rooms at a time, but since the user interface allows you to interact with only one, we make sure that you are in only one at a time. In the code above, we create a new LeaveRoomRequest object, and set the room ID and zone ID on it. It is then sent to ElectroServer.

USERMANAGER AND ZONEMANAGER

In addition to providing a framework for client and server communication, the ElectroServer API keeps track of the rooms for all zones that you are in as well as the users for all rooms that you are in. This is very convenient, since you don't have to manage a list yourself by watching for all additions and removals. But if you want to do that anyway, you do have access to that level of detail.

There are three class types that should be introduced here:

- **User**—Instances of this class are used to represent actual users on the server. The UserManager class maintains a master list of all users that are currently visible to you (the client).

- **Room**—This class is used to represent rooms found in a zone. The room object for a room that you are in contains a list of users for that room.

- **Zone**—This represents a zone that you are in, and contains the list of rooms that you can see in that zone. The ZoneManager class maintains a master list of all zones that you are currently in.

You will see these in use shortly.

JOINROOMEVENT

The onJoinRoomEvent function is called (not surprisingly) when a user has joined a room. In this example code, we use this event to tell us we are in a new room, and then we update the user interface as a result:

```
public function onJoinRoomEvent(e:JoinRoomEvent):void {
  //the room you joined
  _room = e.room;

  //update the display to say the name of the room
  _chatRoomLabel.label_txt.text = e.room.getRoomName();

  //refresh the lists
  refreshUserList();
  refreshRoomList();
}
```

The JoinRoomEvent object contains a reference to the room you just joined. We store a reference to it in the class-level _room property. Next, we update the user interface to show the name of the chat room above the history field.

The last thing that occurs in this function is to refresh the user list and room list. We'll look at how that is done next.

REFRESHING THE USER LIST AND ROOM LIST

Both the user list and the room list use the standard Flash List component. (We use this so that we don't have to write our own from scratch!) This component is populated with content by providing it a DataProvider class instance. In the functions used to populate the user and room lists, we create a new DataProvider instance, add data to it, and then set that on the component.

Here is the function used to refresh the user list:

```
private function refreshUserList():void {
  //get the user list
  var users:Array = _room.getUsers();

  //create a new data provider for the list component
  var dp:DataProvider = new DataProvider();

  //loop through the user list and add each user to the data
  provider
  for (var i:int = 0; i < users.length;++i) {
      var user:User = users[i];
      dp.addItem( { label:user.getUserName(), data:user} );
  }

  //tell the component to use this data
  _userList.dataProvider = dp;
}
```

First we grab the user list array from the room object. This is an array of User class instances, each of which represents a user in this room. Then a new DataProvider object is created. After that, we loop through the user list array, and add to the data provider a formatted object for each user. It takes a label property (a string), which is what is displayed in the list, and a data property, which is the data associated with the list item. Lastly, the data provider is set on the component to tell it to display the data.

Now let's look at the function used to refresh the room list:

```
private function refreshRoomList():void {
  //get the zone
  var zone:Zone = _es.getZoneManager().getZoneById
  (_room.getZoneId());

  //get the room list
  var rooms:Array = zone.getRooms();

  //create a new data provider for the list component
  var dp:DataProvider = new DataProvider();
```

```
//loop through the room list and add each room to the data
→ provider
for (var i:int = 0; i < rooms.length;++i) {
    var room:Room = rooms[i];
    dp.addItem( { label:room.getRoomName(), data:room} );
}

//tell the component to use this data
_roomList.dataProvider = dp;
}
```

This function follows a similar pattern to the refreshUserList function. It builds a data provider and sets that on the room list component to display it. What you haven't seen before is how to access the zone manager, grab a zone off of it, and then get the room list from the zone. The first thing done in this function is to create a local reference to the zone that you are in. The zone object contains a list of all rooms in it that can be accessed by the zone.getRooms() array. Each element in the array is a room object. These are used with the data provider to render a list.

SENDING A CHAT MESSAGE

When the Send button is clicked, the onSendClick function is executed. This function contains logic that checks to make sure the message field isn't blank, and when it isn't, analyzes what is in the field to determine if a public or private message should be sent.

One feature of this chat is that you can send public or private messages. If you type normally into the message field and click Send, then a public message will be sent. If you type a forward slash (/) followed by a username and then a colon (:), then the rest of the message is sent to that user as a private message. For instance, this message field content would send "dude, omg!" to Fezik:

```
/Fezik: dude, omg!
```

Look at this line of code in the onSendClick function:

```
if (msg.charAt(0) == "/" && msg.indexOf(":") != -1) {
```

NOTE *We looked at the* PrivateMessageRequest *request in Chapter 4, so we won't look at the code again here. It is handled the same way—a message is sent to an array of usernames. In this case, the array contains just a single name.*

The `msg` variable is a string that contains the contents of the message field. If the first character is a slash, and then a colon occurs anywhere later in the string, then you would assume this is supposed to be sent as a private message, and would enter the leg of the if statement that you just saw at the bottom of the previous page.

If the message is determined to be public, then we use the `PublicMessageRequest` request. Here is the code that creates and sends that request:

```
//create the request object
var pmr:PublicMessageRequest = new PublicMessageRequest();
pmr.setMessage(_message.text);
pmr.setRoomId(_room.getRoomId());
pmr.setZoneId(_room.getZoneId());

//send it
_es.send(pmr);
```

First a new `PublicMessageRequest` object is created. Then we set the chat message text onto it. Since you can belong to many rooms at a time, you need to specify which room you want this message to go to, so the room ID and zone ID are set on the object as well. The request is then sent to the server.

Both private and public chat requests result in events. We look at those next.

RECEIVING A CHAT MESSAGE

This is the easy part! When a chat message is received, then either the onPublicMessageEvent or the onPrivateMessageEvent is fired. In both cases, we use the data on the event object to add a chat entry in the history field:

```
public function onPublicMessageEvent(e:PublicMessageEvent):
    void {
  //add a chat message to the history field
  _history.appendText(e.getUserName() + ": " + e.getMessage() +
    "\n");
}
```

In this function, we grab the name of the user who sent the message to the room, and their message, and we add that to the chat history field.

Now for the private messages:

```
public function onPrivateMessageEvent(e:PrivateMessageEvent):
→ void {
  //add a chat message to the history field
  _history.appendText("[private] "+e.getUserName() + ": " +
  → e.getMessage() + "\n");
}
```

We handle private messages the same way as public messages, except that we add a string of [private] to the front of the chat message. Easy.

CHAPTER 6

Where Decisions Are Made

IN MULTIPLAYER GAMES and virtual worlds, logic can be found on both the client and on the server. But if game logic can exist in both places, which has the authority to make important decisions? And why? We answer these questions in this chapter. By making the best development choices of where to maintain game state and place game logic, you will save time when tracking down bugs later, and end up with a more secure game.

We'll start this chapter discussing the concept of authority (who's in charge). The rest of the chapter will be spent introducing the first server-side plugin used in this book, some new ElectroServer API information, and then walking through a simple ActionScript example game.

New Concepts

If you are used to coding single-player games, then you are also used to all game logic existing within the Flash client, where there is no need to think about where decisions will get made. In multiplayer games, it matters where decisions are made. Games that have most important decisions being made on the client are called *authoritative client*, and those that have most important decisions being made on the server are called *authoritative server*.

Authoritative Client

Let's look at a couple of authoritative client game examples. In these examples, the server is used simply to route messages between the clients. We'll see one example of when decision-making on the client works and one where it doesn't.

Consider a two-player, turn-based game of pool.

Authoritative client: good choice for a simple game of pool.

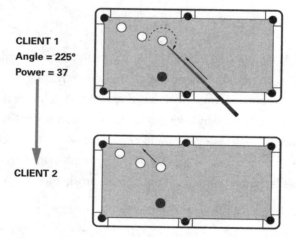

CLIENT 1
Angle = 225°
Power = 37

CLIENT 2

In this game, all of the logic is contained within the Flash client. When the game starts, both clients see the exact same layout. When it is a player's turn, he is able to use the cue stick to choose at which angle, and how hard, to hit the cue ball (angle and power as shown in the figure above). As soon as the player clicks to strike the ball, a message is sent from Player A to Player B, containing the angle and power values. Given the same input (angle and power), both clients are able to have the game play out identically. Both players will always be able to tell when a ball is supposed to go in a pocket, when a turn ends, and who won the game. Authoritative client works well in this case.

Now consider a two-player, real-time tank-shooter game. In this game, a user can control his tank quickly through keyboard input. The tank will shoot when the mouse is clicked in whichever direction the turret is facing. A projectile is fired from the turret and travels in a straight line.

Authoritative client: not such a good choice for a real-time tank-shooter game.

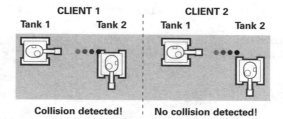

Let's look at the situation in this game. Imagine that Tank 1 is facing Tank 2, and neither tank is moving. Client 1 (who controls Tank 1) clicks to fire on Tank 2. The projectile leaves the turret and moves toward Tank 2. Client 2 is watching the bullet come toward his tank, and so at the last moment he starts to move his tank to avoid destruction. We are left with a situation where Client 1 will detect a collision and Client 2 will not. This is an example of where an authoritative client approach will not work.

Don't be too clever

If you are a clever programmer and are trying to avoid writing custom server code, then you can probably think of some options to resolve the disparity seen in the tank-shooter game shown above. For instance, players can message each other whenever they detect a collision. Then the client will react to the collision only if both players agree. This is just one possibility.

But I want to suggest that you avoid this type of solution. Not only will it result in reaction delays as the clients sync with each other, but it can be extremely difficult to debug, and become super complex to keep track of in code. Not to mention that one of the two clients can employ a hack in which he never agrees that his own tank was hit, making it invincible!

Authoritative Server

We've just seen an example of an authoritative client that leads to a disagreement between the clients. The solution to this problem is to move that important decision-making to the server. In an authoritative server setup, the server is the single decision maker, so there is never any confusion about what is going on.

When applied to the tank example discussed above, the server keeps track of the state of the entire game. Since the server knows the locations of all of the tanks and all of the bullets, it can then determine when a collision has been made and inform the clients.

The same real-time tank-shooter game, now controlled on the server.

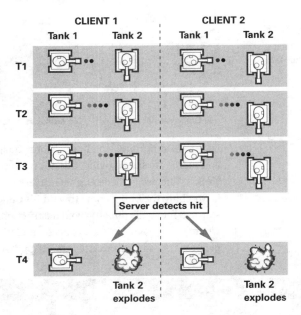

Here you see what the clients would look like over four slices in time in the shooter-game situation we discussed above. You can see that over the first three time slices, the projectile ends up looking like it collided on Client 1, and having a near miss on Client 2. But in the end, both clients register it as a hit, because the server says so. Obviously Client 1 is a superior player!

When to Use Which Model

How do you know when you should take one approach over the other? There is no single answer to this that can apply to all cases, but there are some trends in certain types of games and questions you can ask yourself that can give you guidance as to the right choice.

A turn-based game where all of the information is known will most likely fit into an authoritative client model. When I say "all of the information is known," I mean that there is nothing left up to chance and nothing left to be revealed. Some games that fit these criteria are chess, checkers, Connect Four, and pool. You could easily create any of these games and have the game logic run on the client.

Most real-time games (games where there are no turns) will automatically need to be authoritative server. Also, turn-based games where some things are left up to chance or haven't yet been revealed would be best handled as authoritative server. Here are some examples of games, along with my reasoning as to whether they should be authoritative client or authoritative server:

- Texas Holdem Poker—This game requires a deck of shuffled cards and opponent cards to be hidden. If a game like this is maintained on a client, then a clever person could use a memory reader tool to inspect the card deck or to create a hacked version of the client to reveal their opponent's cards. If real money is on the line, then having decisions controlled on the server is a must.

- Monopoly—This is a good template for most modern board games. You have the element of chance with a roll of the dice, and two decks of cards that are hidden from view. And of course there is the banker!

- Car racing game—In a race, the winner is the first one to cross the finish line. Especially when they are going at a fast pace, you can't trust all of the clients to agree precisely where all cars are. Because of this, the server needs to keep track of car placement and be the final decision-maker.

TIP *When in doubt, put the logic on the server.*

Now, just to confuse you, it is possible (and common) to have games that have both authoritative server pieces and authoritative client pieces. In this hybrid approach, the authoritative client pieces are usually unimportant. Take Texas Holdem, for example. You may program the ability to taunt your opponents—mumble insults, shake the table, or jingle your keys. These are unimportant things that don't directly affect the outcome of the game. So they can be driven completely by the client.

ElectroServer Plugin Concepts

We touched on the idea of server extensions in Chapter 4, *Introducing ElectroServer*. Extensions are used to extend the functionality of the server. There are three types of extensions: managed objects, event handlers, and plugins. In this section, we review what plugins are and then learn how to invoke them from the client.

NOTE *Plugins can be written in Java or in ActionScript; all of the plugin examples used in this book are written in Java.*

Plugins

A plugin is custom code run on the server. If you are going to write an authoritative server game, you need to write a plugin.

A plugin can be conceptualized as a class. New instances of the plugin can be created by the server and scoped to the server or to a room.

Since games take place between users in a room together, the plugins that are most useful for our purposes are room-level plugins (as opposed to server-level). To use a plugin with ElectroServer, it needs to be installed (see "Installing the Extension" for information on that). This installed plugin is specified by knowing the *extension name* and the *plugin handle*. When creating a new room using the ActionScript API, you can specify one or more plugins that you want created and scoped to the room. You do this by specifying the extension name and plugin handle.

Talking to Plugins

TIP *EsObjects were introduced in Chapter 4. We will use them extensively throughout the rest of the book, so you may want to look over that section again.*

Once the room is created, the client can communicate with the plugin through the API. Custom information is passed from the client to the plugin or from the plugin to the client through the use of EsObjects. You can format the EsObjects with any data that you want.

By default, an EsObject contains no data. So for anything useful to be exchanged between the client and plugin, custom data will need to be added to it. We will look at the code that goes into complete plugin-client communication later in the chapter.

Message order is guaranteed

The client and server communicate over a socket using the Socket class available in Flash. The Socket class uses the TCP protocol, which guarantees that every message sent will arrive at its destination. If something happens to the message along the way, it will be resent automatically. One important thing to note is that the order in which the server and the client handle messages is the same order in which they are sent. So you can trust that if you send several messages in rapid succession to the server, they'll be received and processed in that order.

EsObject Formatting Approach

There is a basic EsObject formatting approach that I have found very useful for every multiplayer game that I've programmed over the last few years. This approach is used for all examples in this book, and we'll go over it here.

Every message sent between a client and a plugin during a game can be thought of as an action. So I always make sure that every EsObject used for communication between client and plugin has a variable used to represent an action. The remainder of the object formatting would, of course, depend on what the action is.

For example, let's look at a turn-based pool game. There is only one action that clients can ever perform—they can shoot. The EsObject going from the client to the plugin would contain these variables:

- Action = shoot
- Angle = the angle of the shot
- Power = the power of the shot

Tracing an EsObject

EsObjects play a large role in game development. The client and the server developers need to agree on EsObject formatting so that the two sides can communicate effectively and accurately. But as you would expect when developing applications, in the process of making sure they agree, there will be bugs. An easy way to debug parts of your code is to check what's on an EsObject before it is sent. You can do that by tracing it.

For example:

```
var esob:EsObject = new EsObject();
esob.setString("name", "Magilicuddy");
esob.setInteger("age", 25);
trace(esob);
```

The trace output for the above looks like this:

```
{EsObject:
        name:string = Magilicuddy
        age:integer = 25
        }
```

No matter how complex the EsObject data structure is, you can view the entire contents just by tracing it. This can be done on the server as well as the client. You and your server developer will find this useful when inspecting what is sent or received.

The plugin can send one of several actions to the client in a pool game, such as change turns, shoot, scratch, and game over. The EsObject for game over would contain these variables:

- Action = game over

- Winner = name of the winner

This is a very simple concept, but it still took me several games to realize that it's ubiquitous—it works for every action in every game.

Installing the Extension

The custom server code for a game (and for all of the examples in this book) exists within an extension. In order for ElectroServer to use an extension, that extension has to be in a specific location. You can simply copy an extension into the server/extensions folder of your ElectroServer installation.

NOTE *Find an example of just such an extension in book_files/ examples_extension/extension/ GameBook. For more information on installing extensions, please see the Appendix.*

For instance, with the example file that you download here, if ElectroServer was installed to C:\Program Files\ElectroServer4_0_6, then after you copy the GameBook folder, you will be able to find Extension.xml in C:\Program Files\ElectroServer4_0_6\server\extensions\GameBook. After pasting a copy of the GameBook folder into the proper location, restart ElectroServer.

Server-level Components

If the extension has any server-level components, you will need to use the administration panel to mark these as server-level the first time they are added. This only needs to be done once for each server-level component. For this chapter we don't need this step; however, the TimeStampPlugin that is provided within the GameBook extension will be needed in later chapters as a server-level plugin, so we'll do that now.

After restarting ElectroServer, open the administration panel. If you are running ElectroServer locally, you usually do this by opening a web browser to https://localhost:8080/admin. After logging on as administrator, go to the Extensions tab. You should see every extension that is installed on ElectroServer. Click the plus button (+) for GameBook, and then click the New Server-Level Component button. The next screen should show

GameBook in the Extension Name field. Choose TimeStampPlugin from the Plugin Handle drop-down menu, and then type **TimeStampPlugin** into the Plugin Name field.

After adding any needed server-level components, restart ElectroServer again. Please note that you will also see other plugins listed. You don't need to do anything with those at this point.

Building an Extension

If you are creating an extension from scratch, the necessary components are:

- An appropriately named folder placed within server/extensions

- An extension.xml file, with XML nodes specifying each managed object, event handler, and plugin that will be used in this extension

- A lib folder, with any jar files needed for Java code, including a jar for your own custom code

Dig Game

So far in this chapter, we've looked at the concepts of authoritative client and authoritative server, and discussed some new ElectroServer concepts relating to plugins. Now, with the Dig game, we'll look at a real example of these concepts.

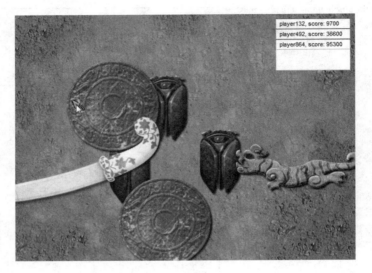

Features

NOTE *This simple game has no end. You can join the game simply by launching the SWF file. More users can join and leave at any time.*

In this game, the user's mouse is replaced with a trowel, and the background image is of dusty ground. Users can click anywhere with their trowel to dig in that location. The trowel plays a digging animation for two seconds and then reveals a found item or nothing. Once a spot has been dug, it can't be dug again. If you find an item, then you are awarded points for it, and your score is updated in the user list.

The Dig game is an authoritative server game. The client chooses where they want to dig and sends that request to the plugin. The server then checks to see if that spot has been dug before, and if so, tells the client that they can't dig there. If the spot hasn't yet been dug, then the server waits for two seconds, and then tells the user if they dug up an item (or not). There are four types of items that can be found, of varying rarity and value.

Walkthrough

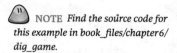 NOTE *Find the source code for this example in book_files/chapter6/ dig_game.*

The Flash Develop project file used here is called Dig Game.as3proj. To browse the source code while reading this section, open that project file. To test the application, you'll need to start ElectroServer and make sure the plugin is installed.

Since there is only one screen, the application flow is simple. When the game is launched, it loads an XML file that tells it which IP and port to connect to. The game then attempts to connect to ElectroServer using those settings. If there is a successful connection, then it logs the user in with a random username. After a successful login, an instance of the DigGame class is created.

Minimizing Data Exchanged

When the client and plugin communicate, they do so using an EsObject with custom formatting. EsObjects can be formatted in any way that you want. But if you expect a high volume of message transfer—due to game popularity or because of the needs of that game—then it makes sense to minimize the size of the data exchanged. That is where the PluginConstants class comes in handy.

The PluginConstants class simply stores public static variables with useful names and tiny values. Here are all of the variables used in this example:

```
// actions
public static const ACTION:String = "a";
public static const DIG_HERE:String = "d";
public static const DONE_DIGGING:String = "dd";
public static const INIT_ME:String = "i";
public static const PLAYER_LIST:String = "ul";
public static const ADD_PLAYER:String = "au";
public static const REMOVE_PLAYER:String = "ru";
public static const ERROR:String = "err";


// parameters
public static const ITEM_FOUND:String = "f";
public static const ITEM_ID:String = "id";
public static const NAME:String = "n";
public static const SCORE:String = "s";
```

```
public static const X:String = "x";
public static const Y:String = "y";

//errors
public static const SPOT_ALREADY_DUG:String = "SpotAlreadyDug";
```

The server plugin has a similar class that matches all of these values. We would format an EsObject in another class like this:

```
var esob:EsObject = new EsObject();
esob.setString(PluginConstants.ACTION, PluginConstants.
➤DIG_HERE);
esob.setInteger(PluginConstants.X, mouseX);
esob.setInteger(PluginConstants.Y, mouseY);
```

The above is equivalent to this:

```
var esob:EsObject = new EsObject();
esob.setString("a", "d");
esob.setInteger("X", mouseX);
esob.setInteger("Y", mouseY);
```

NOTE *The advantage to using* PluginConstants.ACTION *versus* "a" *is that you get compile-time checking and code hinting while programming. If you mistype* PluginConstants.ACTION, *then you are told during compilation. If you mistype a string, you won't find out until a run-time error occurs.*

Maintaining a List of Users

Since we are joining a room in this example, you would assume that we'd use ElectroServer's built-in user list and user list updates for the client to maintain the user list. That is certainly possible. However, my personal preference is that if we are going to use a plugin for anything in a room, then we use a plugin for *everything* in that room. When a user joins the room, they will get an initial user list from the plugin, and then add or remove events as needed.

There are a few reasons for bypassing the normal user-list behavior:

• In a game, when you first learn about a player, there might be custom information that you need to know, such as what color should be used to represent them or what their current rating is in that game. If we rely on the room's natural user list, then we don't have those custom properties associated with the users.

• It is clean to be able to have all important things get routed through the same bit of code. I like having one area that handles every type of action that can occur.

- Depending on the game you are creating, there may be multiple types of users. Unlike the more rigid built-in user list, the plugin could potentially allow some users to just watch and not be added to the list of active players.

The DigGame Class

This class—where most of the functionality exists—handles creating a new room, communicating with the plugin, and what little bit of logic exists on the client. We'll focus on the code used to interact with the server that hasn't been introduced before.

ELECTROSERVER LISTENERS

There are only two listeners needed in this class:

```
_es.addEventListener(MessageType.JoinRoomEvent,
→ "onJoinRoomEvent", this);
_es.addEventListener(MessageType.PluginMessageEvent,
→ "onPluginMessageEvent", this);
```

The JoinRoomEvent listener was covered in Chapter 5, *Chat*. The PluginMessageEvent is new. This event is fired when a new message goes from a plugin to the client. We will look at both of these event handlers a little later.

CREATING A ROOM WITH A PLUGIN

The code used to create a room was first introduced in Chapter 5. As we mentioned then, there are a lot of options to configure a room during creation. For this game, and for many of the examples in the book, a plugin will be specified when creating a room.

When the DigGame class is created, the joinRoom function is called to create or join the user to a room. That function contains this code:

```
//create the request
var crr:CreateRoomRequest = new CreateRoomRequest();
crr.setRoomName("Dig Game Room");
crr.setZoneName("Dig Game Zone");

//create the plugin
var pl:Plugin = new Plugin();
```

```
pl.setExtensionName("GameBook");
pl.setPluginHandle("DiggingPlugin");
pl.setPluginName("DiggingPlugin");

//add to the list of plugins to create
crr.setPlugins([pl]);

//send it
_es.send(crr);
```

The portion of the CreateRoomRequest configuration that is new is highlighted above. First, a new Plugin instance is created. We then set some variables on the plugin object to tell it which plugin we want to have created. We do that by specifying the extension name and plugin handle. The plugin name is the name that you are giving the new instance of the plugin in the room. You will use that name later when sending a message to the plugin. I usually keep the plugin handle and plugin name the same, since I've never needed to create two of the same plugin in the same room. If for some reason you wanted to created multiple instances of the same plugin in the same room, then you would want to name the plugin instances uniquely.

After the plugin object has been created and configured, it is added to the CreateRoomRequest instance via the setPlugins method. This method takes an array of plugins. Since we are creating only a single plugin in this case, the array contains only a single element.

Once the CreateRoomRequest instance is completely configured, it is sent to the server. After the room is created (or you are joined to the existing room), the onJoinRoomEvent function is fired. From that moment forward, you are able to communicate with the plugin.

onJoinRoomEvent

The onJoinRoomEvent function is called after you have successfully joined the room. Here are the contents of that function:

```
//store a reference to your room
_room = e.room;

//tell the plugin that you're ready
var esob:EsObject = new EsObject();
```

```
esob.setString(PluginConstants.ACTION, PluginConstants.
➤ INIT_ME);

//send to the plugin
sendToPlugin(esob);
```

We store a reference to the object representing the room we just joined as a class-level property.

Next, we communicate with a plugin—for the first time in this book! We tell the plugin that we are here, and ready to play the game. To do that, we create a new EsObject, and set an action of INIT_ME on it. No extra properties are needed for this action. After the EsObject is created and formatted with the needed properties, the sendToPlugin function is called, passing in the EsObject. We'll look at that function next.

sendToPlugin

Whenever the client needs to send something to the plugin, it creates an EsObject, formats it, and then sets it on a PluginRequest object, which is sent to the server. For most examples and games in this book, the client will be talking only to a single plugin. Since that is the case, we can wrap the bulk of the code used to send a message to a plugin in a single function:

```
private function sendToPlugin(esob:EsObject):void {
  //build the request
  var pr:PluginRequest = new PluginRequest();
  pr.setEsObject(esob);
  pr.setRoomId(_room.getRoomId());
  pr.setZoneId(_room.getZoneId());
  pr.setPluginName("DiggingPlugin");

  //send it
  _es.send(pr);
}
```

A new instance of the PluginRequest class is created. The EsObject that was passed into the function (containing the custom data) is set onto it. We then have to specify which plugin this message goes to and what room contains that plugin. Once the PluginRequest instance is completely configured, it is sent.

DIG_HERE

Now let's look at what goes into telling the server where we want to dig. When a mouse click is detected, the mouseDown event handler is invoked, which contains this code:

```
if (!_trowel.digging && _room != null) {
  //tell the plugin you want to dig here
  var esob:EsObject = new EsObject();
  esob.setString(PluginConstants.ACTION, PluginConstants.
  ➞ DIG_HERE);
  esob.setInteger(PluginConstants.X, mouseX);
  esob.setInteger(PluginConstants.Y, mouseY);

  //send
  sendToPlugin(esob);

  //animate
  _trowel.dig();
  playSound(new DIG_SOUND());
}
```

As you can see, the main code is wrapped in a conditional statement. Before telling the server that we want to dig in a spot, we check to make sure the digging animation isn't already playing, and that we've joined a room. The _trowel property references the cursor icon. If the digging animation is playing, then _trowel.digging returns true.

If you are not already digging and you are in a room, then an EsObject is created, formatted, and sent to the plugin. It is given a DIG_HERE action, and specifies the x and y coordinates of the spot where the client wants to dig.

After the EsObject is sent to the server, the client tells the trowel icon to play the digging animation, and then to play a short digging sound.

onPluginMessageEvent

The onPluginMessageEvent function is called—you guessed it—when the client receives a message from the plugin. The way we handle it here is how we will handle it for the rest of this book: we use a switch statement with the action variable found on the EsObject. Then, for each case, we pass the EsObject on to a custom handler for that action.

Here is the function:

```
public function onPluginMessageEvent(e:PluginMessageEvent):
→ void {
  var esob:EsObject = e.getEsObject();

  //get the action which determines what we do next
  var action:String = esob.getString(PluginConstants.ACTION);
  switch (action) {
        case PluginConstants.DONE_DIGGING:
              handleDoneDigging(esob);
              break;
        case PluginConstants.PLAYER_LIST:
              handlePlayerList(esob);
              break;
        case PluginConstants.ADD_PLAYER:
              handleAddPlayer(esob);
              break;
        case PluginConstants.REMOVE_PLAYER:
              handleRemovePlayer(esob);
              break;
        case PluginConstants.ERROR:
              handleError(esob);
              break;
        default:
              trace("Action not handled: " + action);
  }
}
```

The `PluginMessageEvent` object contains an EsObject sent from the plugin, the room ID and zone ID of the room that sent it, and the name of the plugin that it came from. In an application where you have multiple plugins or where you are joined to multiple rooms, you would likely use the room ID, zone ID, and the plugin name to determine what to do with the EsObject.

A variable called `action` is created with a value of `esob.getString` `(PluginConstants.ACTION)`. It is used in a switch statement to marshal the EsObject off to a custom handler for each action. The `DONE_DIGGING` action is the only action that will be unique to this game. The other actions handle user-list updates and errors that can occur, and will be repeated in most future examples exactly as they are seen here.

handleDoneDigging

This function is executed when the DONE_DIGGING action is processed in the onPluginMessageEvent function. The DONE_DIGGING message is sent from the server to all players in the room whenever any player has completed a digging action. It broadcasts that player's new score to everyone in the game. If you were the one doing the digging, and an item was found, then we create the item and add it to the screen.

Here is the code that gets the player name and score value off of the EsObject (all players are managed in a class created called PlayerManager):

```
//grab some initial information off of the EsObject
var name:String = esob.getString(PluginConstants.NAME);
var score:int = esob.getInteger(PluginConstants.SCORE);

//find the player and update the score property
var player:Player = _playerManager.playerByName(name);
player.score = score;
```

NOTE *Extra actions are taken if the player for whom the event occurs also happens to be "you." You'll see this kind of treatment recurring throughout the book.*

Next, let's look at the code that runs if the player happens to be the same player that the client is managing:

```
var found:Boolean = esob.getBoolean(PluginConstants.
ITEM_FOUND);
if (found) {
  //get the id that says which of the 4 item types was found
  var itemId:int = esob.getInteger(PluginConstants.ITEM_ID);

  //create item, set its type, position it, and add to screen
  var item:Item = new Item();
  item.itemType = itemId;
  item.x = _trowel.x;
  item.y = _trowel.y;
  _itemsHolder.addChild(item);

  //play a positive sound since you found an item
  playSound(new FOUND_SOUND());
} else {
  //play a negative sound since you found nothing
  playSound(new NOTHING_SOUND());
}
```

A Boolean value is pulled off the EsObject to see if an item was found or not. If this returns `true`, then that means an item was found and there will be an ID for that item also in the EsObject. Since there are four types of items in this game, there are four possible item ID values, 0–3. A new `Item` instance is created, the ID is set on it (so the item knows which image to show for itself), and is then added to the screen.

If an item was found, then we play a positive sound; if not, we play a negative sound.

Player list actions

Earlier in this chapter, I mentioned that we made the choice not to use the room's built-in user-list abilities—that since we are using a plugin, we'll use it for everything. The plugin knows all, so it can tell the clients the full user list when they join and send them updates to the user list as it changes.

To avoid confusion between the `User` class that is part of the ElectroServer API and the user-list abilities that are built in, we are going to manage connected clients using the `Player` class, and we'll refer to the list of players as the *player list*. Each entry in the player list is a `Player` class instance. The players are managed in a class called `PlayerManager`. The `PlayerManager` class lets you get the full player list, add and remove players from it, and look up a player by name.

When a player first joins this room, the client sends the `INIT_ME` message to the plugin. The plugin responds with a `PLAYER_LIST` action providing the full list of players in the room. From that point forward, the player will receive `ADD_PLAYER` and `REMOVE_PLAYER` messages to keep the list up to date.

Let's look at the contents of the `handlePlayerList` function:

```
var players:Array = esob.getEsObjectArray(PluginConstants.
 ➤ PLAYER_LIST);
for (var i:int = 0; i < players.length;++i) {
  var player_esob:EsObject = players[i];

  var p:Player = new Player();
  p.name = player_esob.getString(PluginConstants.NAME);
  p.score = player_esob.getInteger(PluginConstants.SCORE);
  p.isMe = p.name == _myUsername;

  _playerManager.addPlayer(p);
}
refreshPlayerList();
```

The first line grabs an array of EsObjects off of the EsObject passed into this function. Each EsObject in the array is formatted to contain information about each player in the room, containing the player's name and current score. So, we loop through this array and process each EsObject to create the player list. When that's complete, the `refreshPlayerList` function is called. That function takes the player list and displays it in a `List` component on the screen.

Server Code

NOTE *Find the full source code in book_files/examples_extension/server/src/com/gamebook/digging.*

The server plugin for the Dig game maintains the full game state, which includes information on each of the players and the locations that have already been dug. There are five Java classes:

- **DiggingPlugin** handles the logic and the communications with the client.
- **PluginConstants** is used in the same way as the client `PluginConstants` class.
- **PlayerInfo** is an object class used to store information about any single player of the game.
- **ItemType** is a Java enum class that specifies the different types of items that can be found from digging.
- **Grid** is a data structure that keeps track of each location that's been dug.

Now let's look at seven important methods found in the `DiggingPlugin` class.

INIT

This event handler is called each time the DiggingPlugin is created. It is the best place to add any code that needs to be executed before clients start entering the room, such as initializing data structures and variables.

USERENTER

The userEnter event handler is invoked each time a user attempts to enter the room. Complicated games may have logic here that determines whether the user is allowed to enter at all. For DiggingPlugin, we simply log the fact that the user has entered, and assume that the client will send a request to be initialized shortly.

USEREXIT

NOTE   *The first five methods in this list are actually event handlers that capture room or server-based events.*

This event handler is invoked each time a user leaves a the room. For DiggingPlugin, we remove the user from the data structure that keeps track of the players (playerInfoMap), and then broadcast a message to the remaining players. In other games, we may need to then determine if the game should end at this point due to too few players remaining. Turn-based games in particular require some cleanup code in the userExit event handler, to prevent the game stalling if a player leaves.

DESTROY

The destroy event handler is called when the plugin is destroyed, which happens right after the last user leaves the room. This method should cancel any scheduled callbacks. DiggingPlugin uses scheduled callbacks for the two-second wait between the "dig here" client request and sending the results of the dig.

REQUEST

This event handler is the heart of most plugins. It is the server analog to the client-side `PluginMessageEvent` event. The request method handles each plugin request sent by clients. For the Dig game, there are only three actions that users can request:

- **INIT_ME** informs the server that the client has received and processed the `JoinRoomEvent`. The server invokes `handlePlayerInitRequest`, which announces the new player, adds the player to the `playerInfoMap` data structure, and then sends the new player a list of all the players in the room.

- **POSITION_UPDATE** is relayed to all the players, with the name of the player added to the message but no additional processing by the server.

- **DIG_HERE** informs the server that the client wants to dig in a given location. The server invokes `handleDigHereRequest`, which checks that the location is allowed and that the player is not already digging. If it is an allowed location, then a timer is set using a scheduled callback, which then sends a message to all players after the two-second wait elapses.

SENDANDLOG

The sendAndLog method is used to send a message to all initialized players in the room, and to log the message that was sent. For instance, whenever a user has completed digging, this method is used to send a message to the clients about it.

SENDERRORMESSAGE

This method sends (and logs) an error message to the specified player. This method is useful in keeping the client informed about problems it may cause and by logging the event for later analysis.

CHAPTER 7

Real-time Movement

YOU CAN CREATE a broad spectrum of multiplayer game types in Flash—card games, trivia games, and some games that show real-time movement of player-controlled game objects (such as racing games, shooters, or virtual worlds), to name a few. I conducted a casual poll of my colleagues, asking what kind of multiplayer games they would like to build if given the chance. They mostly said shooters, fighting games, racing games, RPGs (role playing games), and even real-time strategy games. To pull off any of these well, and provide a fun experience, all of these game types require real-time movement of one or more game objects.

I scoured Google for 90 minutes and was able to find only a small number of multiplayer Flash games that filled that requirement. With so much interest in games that call for real-time movement, you may wonder why there are so few examples out there. I see two reasons for this. First, while it may be the game *you* want to build, it isn't what clients are asking for (i.e., no one wants to pay you to make it).

Second is the lack of educational resources. There isn't much information available on real-time movement techniques, latency hiding, and predictive movement. So game developers are forced to figure it out for themselves.·

The concepts outlined in this chapter are among the most important in the book. With them, you'll be able to do a good job at achieving smooth game play while keeping movement synchronized across screens. Code and concepts introduced here will be used at certain times throughout the rest of the book (largely in Chapters 9 and 10).

In this chapter, we'll look at the types of paths that exist for directing a game object and how they are conveyed to the server and clients; what it means to move an object based on frame intervals versus time intervals; and latency. Finally, using time-based movement, we'll look at various predictive movement concepts used in latency hiding, and see one of them through in two examples.

Responsive Controls

Most multiplayer games are authoritative server. A client can't *really* move its character/car/ship/etc. without the server allowing it and validating this movement. One mistake that I made when programming my first real-time character movement game (a side-view platformer) was that I waited for server feedback before moving my own character. I captured keyboard input and sent that to the server, truly making the client a dummy terminal. The server analyzed the keyboard state and sent updated movement information to the clients. This resulted in a synchronized system, but frustrating game play. The key control responses were delayed due the client relying on the server. When played over a local network the delay was not noticeable, but over the Internet, it certainly was.

If the game is time-synchronized and the client has a reasonable sense of what it should be able to get away with for movement and collisions, then the best user experience is to have the client immediately respond to user input, with the assumption that the server will agree. If the server agrees (which should almost always be the case), then the client and server are in sync. In the rare case that the server rejects this movement, it needs to be handled, which can result in a blip as the object corrects itself. This rare blip is OK, because the overall experience is satisfactorily responsive.

Path Types

Think about the following common game objects that move along a path in real time:

- A missile moving in a straight line

- An avatar in a virtual world walking around items

- A character in a first-person shooter

- A car in a racing game

While each of these needs to move on the screen in a real-time fashion, they can all have different techniques for determining their paths in the first place. Here we look at a few ways to determine which way a game object should go. We then discuss line of sight, and how that can be used to restrict a path.

Waypoints

A waypoint is simply a target position for a game object. The game object travels from its current position to the waypoint. Multiple waypoints can be established ahead of time. In a real-time strategy battle game, for example, you might establish several waypoints that direct a vehicle along a specific path. The vehicle then travels from its current position to the final way-point, hitting all waypoints along the way.

In a tile-based virtual world, a pathfinding algorithm such as A* would return a list of tiles contained in the resultant path. Each tile in the path can be thought of as a waypoint.

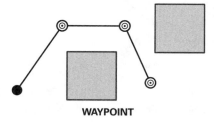

WAYPOINT

Vector / Heading

We have all played first-person shooters (FPS). In an FPS, you can usually control your character by running, walking, and jumping. You start, stop, and change directions very quickly, giving this the type of responsive control the name *twitch*.

In an FPS or a car-racing game, you can imagine that a user would be able to control their car (or character) so quickly that it would be difficult for other players to properly and smoothly infer where they are and where they are going. The first thing that may come to mind to inform other players of where you are is to simply transmit your position. While something that simple could work for much slower-paced games (and is demonstrated in an example below), in a faster game, players will not have enough information to render all game objects smoothly and with reasonable precision.

This is where vectors can help us out. A vector is a mathematical concept that groups a value with a direction. For example, *30 mph wind blowing east* constitutes a vector. With that in mind, think about a car in a racing game. At any given time, it is traveling along some vector (speed and direction). In a fast-paced twitch game, you can see where it could be useful to know vectors for all moving objects, rather than just where they are at any given moment in time.

I find it useful to group a vector with the position of the game object at some point in time. I put the vector information, position, and some extra information (discussed later in this chapter) into a *heading*. The heading is the complete and most up-to-date information about a moving game object.

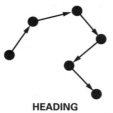

HEADING

Knowing the heading of all moving game objects allows you to perform *predictive movement,* which allows you to continue to move an object in what is most likely the correct direction until more up-to-date information is received.

Line of Sight

The concept of line of sight is simple. Imagine that there is some origin point, such as the position of a vehicle or a gun. Line of sight traces a path from this origin in whatever outward direction is chosen (say, the angle the gun is facing), and then eventually stops when it hits something.

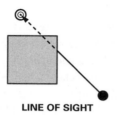

LINE OF SIGHT

Artificial intelligence (AI) uses line of sight in games to determine what it (the AI) can see, as if it were another game player. For example, it can be used for targeting a gun in a game, or in games where a vehicle or character moves based on a mouse click, where the intention is to establish a straight-line path. In a game like that, line of sight may help determine whether a desired or attempted path is valid or invalid. Or, while a user is establishing waypoints, line of sight can help them determine whether each leg of the path is allowed. (If any leg of the path intersects an object that it cannot move through, then the path is not allowed.) You'll see all of this used in Chapter 9.

Frame-based Movement

There are two ways to update the position of a moving game object: based on frame interval or based on time interval. When updating based on a frame interval, time is completely ignored, and the position of the object is updated based on the fact that a frame has passed. For example, you could update the position of a flying missile by 3 pixels in the +x direction and by 6 in the +y direction for every frame.

Time-based movement updates the position of a game object based on how much time has passed. With time-based movement, you are still updating objects visually on the screen for every frame, but those positions are based on the elapsed *time*, not the elapsed number of frames. We'll discuss time-based movement in detail later in this chapter.

When to Use Frame-based Movement

Frame-based movement works fine for nearly any single-player game you would ever create. When it comes to multiplayer games, though, frame-based movement isn't always the best choice. But it would work all right for rendering moving objects in turn-based games such as pool, and in most social virtual worlds.

In both of these examples, the precise time when a moving object is at any specific location isn't important; it's just important that the paths are adhered to and the objects end up in the correct final locations. Due to frame-rate variance across clients, frame-based movement could result in the same animation taking much longer on one client than on another. But the end result of the animation will be identical on all clients.

Now let's look at a situation where this approach doesn't work so well. Consider a two-player shooter game that uses frame-based movement. A bullet is fired horizontally, traveling at 8 pixels per frame. Due to hardware differences and this being an intense game, Player 1 achieves a frame rate of 30fps, while Player 2 achieves only 25fps. Over the course of one second, the bullet travels 240 pixels for Player 1 and only 200 pixels for Player 2. The longer the game play goes, the further out of sync the players will get. If the server sends events to the client indicating when collisions occur, then some of the out-of-sync state will be reconciled, but it is still likely to be a poor experience for the player with the slightly slower computer (in this case, Player 2).

To summarize, frame-based movement is usually OK for games where time synchronization between multiple players isn't very important.

Current Position: Here I Am

NOTE *Find the "Here I am" example files in book_files/chapter7/ hereiam.*

In this section, we look at an example of frame-based multiplayer movement where only the game object's position is transmitted. I refer to this method as a "here I am" approach—each object frequently says "here I am, here I am, here I am." It doesn't say where it is going, just where it is.

The Flash Develop project file is called Here I Am.as3proj. To test the example, start ElectroServer, open the project, and compile it. Like all of our examples, it loads an XML file that specifies the connection settings.

The ups and downs of the Here I Am approach

The benefit of this approach is that it is very easy to program. It can work well in situations where time synchronization isn't very important. One simple example is showing the mouse position of other connected users. If you wanted to interact with an application and see a representation of all other connected users' cursors moving across the screen, this approach would work fine, because it isn't important how precise the movement and positions are.

The main downside to this approach is that a moving game object will never be rendered at the spot that it is supposed to be in *right now*. The object is always seen at some position it was in the past. This is because it takes time for the message to arrive at the client.

In this example, you control a walking alien with your arrow keys. You can see other users who may also happen to be in the room (you can launch multiple copies of the SWF to test this). When your alien moves, you'll see a faded-out copy following it, which I call the *mirror*. You control your alien locally, but the mirror is rendered based on information that comes back from the server. The mirror allows you to see the position(s) in which other users will see your alien.

Since the mirror is moved at a constant speed, it will never be able to catch up as long as it is moving. In fact, as minor latency spikes or frame-rate dips occur, the mirror will get further and further behind. When the alien stops walking, the mirror will finally be able to catch up and stop.

This example performs only a few basic multiplayer actions: it detects when to add or remove a user, and it allows EsObjects to be broadcast to everyone in the room. Because it does such basic things, we don't need a plugin; we can achieve everything with default room events. The EsObjects are attached to a `PublicMessageRequest` instead of a plugin. If you were to take this example and try to make a game with it, you'd want to get a plugin involved so that the game state can be managed and validated on the server. The EsObject formatting and the client handling of position updates are managed the same way whether we're dealing with a plugin or with default room events.

When the application is launched, a connection is established, and the user is logged in with a random name and then joins a room. Event listeners are set up to listen for the `JoinRoomEvent`, `PublicMessageEvent`, and `UserListUpdateEvent`.

Let's look at how your alien is added, how position updates about your alien are sent, and then how you would handle position updates that are received.

Here is the onJoinRoomEvent event handler:

```
public function onJoinRoomEvent(e:JoinRoomEvent):void {
  _room = e.room;

  var guy:Guy = new Guy();
  guy.x = 200;
  guy.y = 200;
  guy.playerName = _es.getUserManager().getMe().getUserName();
  _myGuy = guy;
  addGuy(guy);
}
```

First, a reference to the room just joined is stored as a class-level property. Then a new Guy class instance is created to represent you. The Guy class contains the alien graphics and positional information. It is placed at a starting position of 200, 200; given your name; stored as the class-level property _myGuy; and then sent into the addGuy function. The addGuy function stores all Guy references for later lookup.

This example has an event fired every frame to handle movement, key capturing, and sending updates:

```
private function enterFrame(e:Event):void {
  if (_myGuy != null) {
      checkKeys();
      moveGuys();

      //send a position update every 500ms
      if (getTimer() - _lastTimeSent > 500) {
          sendUpdate();
      }
  }
}
```

A condition is in place to make sure that your guy exists. If it exists, then you would call the checkKeys function, which inspects the state of the arrow keys and moves your guy a step in one of eight directions (or not at all, if no keys are pressed). The moveGuys function loops through all guys on screen and walks them one step from where they currently are toward their target position. Then, if 500ms has passed since the last time a position update was sent to everyone else about your guy, you would send another one. Note that this send frequency could be made smarter by sending the update only if the position has changed and 500ms has passed.

Now let's look at the sendUpdate function:

```
private function sendUpdate():void {
  //format the EsObject to send
  var esob:EsObject = new EsObject();
  esob.setString(PluginConstants.ACTION, PluginConstants.
  → UPDATE_POSITION);
  esob.setInteger(PluginConstants.X, _myGuy.x);
  esob.setInteger(PluginConstants.Y, _myGuy.y);
  esob.setString(PluginConstants.NAME, _myGuy.playerName);

  //send the EsObject via the PublicMessageRequest
  var pmr:PublicMessageRequest = new PublicMessageRequest();
  pmr.setRoomId(_room.getRoomId());
  pmr.setZoneId(_room.getZoneId());
  pmr.setMessage("");
  pmr.setEsObject(esob);

  _es.send(pmr);
}
```

This function handles sending an update to everyone in the room about the position of your guy. An EsObject is created to store the custom information, and then an action variable of UPDATE_POSITION is set on it—the only action type in this example. Then the x and y position of the guy as well as its name are added to the object. As mentioned earlier, we use the PublicMessageRequest in this example for sending EsObjects to all users in the room, so a PublicMessageRequest instance is created and populated with the needed information.

When the message is received by a client, the onPublicMessageEvent is called, which immediately plucks off the EsObject and sends it to the handleUpdatePosition function to be processed. This function pulls the player's name and x and y position off of the EsObject. It locates the Guy instance based on the player's name (or creates a new one if it doesn't exist), and then updates the target position like this:

```
if (!guy.isMe) {
  guy.walkTo(x, y);
}
```

You would call the walkTo function on the guy instance only if it refers to a guy other than your own. The walkTo function sets a new target for the guy to move toward. The guy will continually move toward that position every frame until it reaches it, or receives a new target position.

You'll notice that your own guy is updated immediately in response to your arrow keys—you don't rely on a server response to move your own guy around. Later you'll see more examples that also work this way. When you bring a plugin into the picture, it can be used to validate that the movement and position updates that you send are within ranges that a properly behaving client would allow.

Server update: how often?

Why did we choose to send the update to the server every 500ms in our alien example? Why not every 5ms, or every 5,000ms? For objects that change frequently in real-time multiplayer Flash games, you don't want the updates to go out *too* fast. How fast is too fast? In my experience, too fast is more than 2–3 times per second—more frequently than that, the added information doesn't make the end result look better, and so is of no benefit. In this example, 500ms works well to allow others to see your alien respond to user input.

Latency and Clock Synchronization

The ultimate goal of this chapter is show how to achieve smooth, well synchronized time-based movement across multiple screens. One thing that's critical to achieving this goal is that all clients have to agree on what time it is. This is a more challenging task than you might think! In this section, we'll discuss the terms *ping* and *latency*, delve into how to narrow in on your true latency, and then show how to use the Clock class to find out the true server time.

Ping and Latency

NOTE *According to Wikipedia, the definition that we give* ping *is incorrect. But in the context of gaming, it is acceptable usage.*

Most of us understand the word *ping* to mean either the time it takes a small message to go from a client to a remote location and back, or just the act of sending a small message anywhere. In this book, we use the word to refer to the total round-trip time for a small message.

Ping is the total round-trip time for a message—in this case, $t_1 - t_0$.

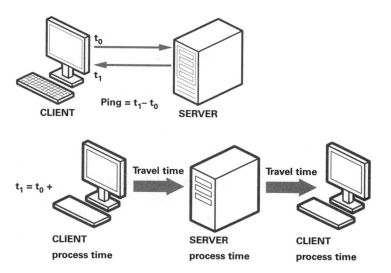

The figure above shows the major things that happen during this round trip that take up time. If you want to measure the ping time, you would look at the time when the request is sent, and then look at the time when the response comes back, and take the difference. Most of that time is spent traveling over the Internet, but some is spent by the application trying to send the message, the server processing the inbound message and then sending another one out, and then the client processing the final inbound message. The total time processing this message on the client and the server is likely to be under a millisecond, whereas the time spent traveling over the Internet is likely to be in the range of 70–200ms. Since the processing time is negligible compared to the travel time, we think of the ping time as being time spent traveling.

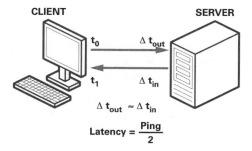

Latency, as I use the term, means the time it takes for a message to get from the server to the client. When measuring ping, there is no way to know if the message spends 90% of its travel time getting to the server and only

10% getting back, or 50/50, or whatever. All you know is what time you sent the message and what time it returned. In order to proceed with our time synchronization effort, we have to make an assumption: that the ping round trip spends half of its time going to the server and half of its time returning to the client. With this assumption, latency is one half of the ping value.

In order to synchronize movement on all screens, the clients have to agree on the time. But instead of synchronizing with each other, they all just synchronize with the server. In the technique we use for this book, the client sends a ping request, and the server sends a response that contains a time stamp in milliseconds. The client is then able to determine what time it is on the server using this simple calculation:

```
server time = client time + offset
```

where offset is:

```
offset = server time - client time + latency
```

Note that "server time" above is the time stamp on the ping response, "client time" is the time at which the response was received, and "latency" is half the round-trip time.

NOTE *An incorrect latency measurement could be due to a minor, temporary issue that made the message take a little too long to get to the server, or to get back to the client, which would result in a higher latency measurement (because we are assuming both legs of travel take the same time).*

Looking at the calculation above, you should notice how important it is to have the latency value correct. The server-time value is taken straight from the ping response, and the client-time value is taken from the client's system clock. The latency value is measured as precisely as possible, but this measurement sometimes contains assumptions. If the latency measurement is wrong, then your clock is wrong. The further off it is, the worse your playing experience will be.

So how can we increase our confidence level in that latency measurement? The approach I take was inspired by an article called "Minimizing Latency in Real-time Strategy Games," by Jim Greer and Zachary Booth Simpson, from a book called *Game Programming Gems 3*, published by Charles River Media. Instead of just measuring the latency a single time, we measure it several times. In the code written for this book, I default this to 10 measurements. Your first instinct would probably be to then just take the average of these values. We will—but not just yet. During your multiple measurements, it is possible that a packet died and was automatically retransmitted (out of your control, this is handled low level), or something else happened such that the time out isn't close to the time in. We do our best to detect these abnormal data points by comparing each measurement to the median value of the entire group.

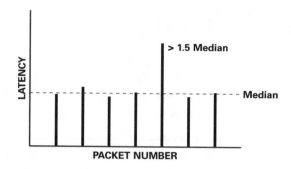

This figure shows an example data set of seven measurements. You can easily pick out one that seems out of place. When we see a measurement that is greater than 1.5 times the median value, we assume something went wrong with it, and we discard it. What is left is a data set with no bad data. This is averaged to arrive at a latency determination in which we can have confidence.

Using the Clock Class

The Clock class exists in the com.gamebook.utils.network package and will be used many times throughout the rest of the book. To use the Clock class, you simply create a new instance of it, pass it a reference to the ElectroServer API, tell it which plugin name to use, and then tell it to start:

```
_clock = new Clock(_es, "TimeStampPlugin");
_clock.start();
_clock.addEventListener(Clock.CLOCK_READY, onClockReady);
```

The default settings (used in the example above), will send requests to ElectroServer ten times and then run the logic discussed above to arrive at a precise latency value. When this is done (which should take no more than about a second), the Clock.CLOCK_READY event is fired. After that, you can get what time it is on the server like this:

```
_clock.time
```

Then you can use _clock.time in your code wherever you'd normally use the Date class or getTimer function.

NOTE *See an example of this in book_files/chapter7/clocksync.*

Time-based Movement

Now that we've covered time synchronization, we're ready to jump into time-based movement. You'll recall that this is an important concept in games where movement needs to be synchronized across multiple clients and the server, such as racing games, shooters, and RPGs.

In this section, we'll look at the equations that drive movement based on time (predictive movement), latency hiding concepts, the `Converger` and `Heading` classes, and then two time-based movement examples.

Equations of Motion / Predictive Movement

When it comes to moving things based on time, we turn to physics and the classical equations of motion. These equations are used to determine where an object will be at some point in the future based on where it is now, its current speed, and constant acceleration (which could be 0). This isn't a physics book, so we won't spend much time on this.

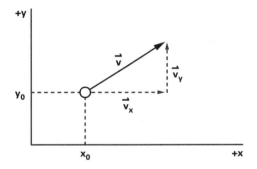

```
x = x0 + vx*t + (1/2)*ax*t^2
y = y0 + vy*t + (1/2)*ay*t^2
```

> **NOTE** *In physics, the term* accelerate *refers to any time the velocity changes. Velocity is a vector, so it includes angle and speed. So whenever the speed or angle changes, it has accelerated (even deceleration is acceleration).*

As you can see from these basic equations, if you know where something is, its speed, and its acceleration, you can calculate where it will be at any time in the future, as long as nothing else changes. So once you receive information about an object describing where it is and where it is going, you can continue to move that object as time goes on. The act of moving an object along a path based on previous information, as we've mentioned a few times before, is called *predictive movement*.

Latency Hiding

Time-based movement can do great things for your game. You are able to handle many objects moving at once and show them in the same spot for all clients that have up-to-date information. But using time-based movement in your game brings with it some challenges. We'll discuss one here and one in the next section, "Acceleration."

If you are showing something *exactly* where it is supposed to be based on the equations of motion, then you will also show a gap in position due to latency the moment a heading update is received. Let's say you have Client A and Client B, and Client A fires a bullet horizontally at a speed of 100 pixels/second. Let's say it takes 150ms for the "shoot bullet" message to arrive at Client B. The bullet traveled 15 pixels during the time it took Client B to even get the message, so it is added to the screen based on the equations of motion in the correct spot, which is 20 pixels to the right of the gun muzzle.

	t = 0 ms	t = 75 ms	t = 150 ms
CLIENT A	☐●→	☐ ●→	☐ ●→
CLIENT B	☐	☐	☐ ●→
			⊢ **15 pixels** ⊣

In the example described above, both clients show the bullet precisely where it should be. This may not be really noticeable with a bullet. But imagine you were driving a car or running around in an FPS. The more the object accelerates, the more it will hop around on other clients' screens (aka "blipping"). Again, it is important to note that a car or character blipping on a screen in this manner is actually expected. As updated information is received, the screen has to update based on the time that elapsed during message transfer. If latency were 0, there would be no blipping.

This is where *latency hiding* comes in. Latency hiding refers to techniques used to provide a smoother game experience by minimizing the effects of latency. In this chapter, we discuss latency hiding only as it relates to movement (also referred to in the industry as *dead reckoning*). What we want to achieve is predictive movement combined with smooth course correction, to converge on the true heading of the object.

The solution to this problem is to come up with a way to move an object smoothly from the last known heading to the updated heading that you just received. If you do this too slowly, then the screen won't be up-to-date enough to be considered synchronized, but it will result in the smoothest movement. If you do this too quickly, then the screen will show objects closer to where they really should be, but will result in jerky movement as updates come in. Based on your game, you'll configure your smoothing algorithm to converge on the real heading as quickly as possible without being noticeably jerky.

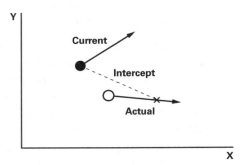

The black dot in the figure above shows the heading that a client currently sees for an object. The dot with the black outline shows the (actual) new heading that the client just received. The dashed line shows a projected interception path to smooth the transition from the previous heading to the new heading.

Let's look at four ways that this can be done.

FOUR METHODS FOR SMOOTHING PATHS

The following four procedures each make an assumption that the object will move from its current heading to match up with a position on the true heading at some point in the near future (typically within a few hundred milliseconds). Each diagram shows a vertical dashed line that represents the time when the true heading is completely converged on.

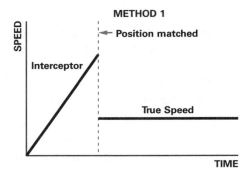

Here you see the object changing its speed at a constant rate to catch up with the true heading until positions are matched. This doesn't appear to be a good solution, because the speed of the object when the paths converge can be much greater than the speed it will adopt after it converges. Visually, this could result in an object rapidly increasing speed and then immediately dropping to a much lower speed.

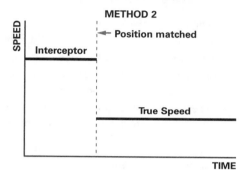

The second method shows the object just picking a constant velocity that will allow the headings to converge. This looks like it could have a similar quick speed change issue as described for Method 1. However, if the game object isn't going to accelerate dramatically, this approach can work very well—meaning that the movement is smoothed without causing noticeable jerkiness. Since this works well and is easy to implement, we'll use it for the examples shown later.

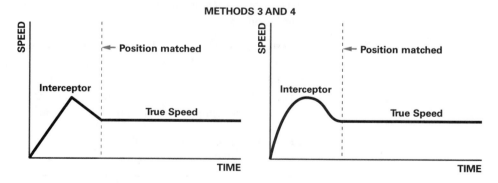

These two methods are very similar. They attempt to solve the dramatic speed change seen in the previous two strategies. They both attempt to modulate the current heading to converge on the true heading by smoothly changing the speed so that when the convergence is complete, the speeds are already matched. The approach in Method 3 can be achieved using the equations of motion, whereas the approach seen in Method 4 is likely to be achieved using Bezier-curve math. The Bezier-curve approach will probably result in the best looking and smoothest path for latency hiding, but is also likely to be the most computationally intensive.

Acceleration

When using time-synchronized movement, there's another issue you have to account for as well. Imagine Client A and Client B are controlling cars in a game. Client A is driving to the right at a speed of 100 pixels per second. Client B shows Client A's car perfectly. Then Client A stops short—no skidding, just completely stops in place. Assume it takes 150ms for the message to get to Client B. By the time Client B receives this information, Client A's car has been (predictably) moved forward another 15 pixels.

You may think, "well, so this is where the smoothing we just talked about comes in handy." You'd be partially right. The smoothing will make sure the car ends up at the right spot, but it has to drive backwards to make that happen.

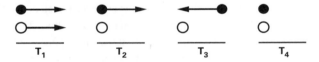

The figure above illustrates the problem. The black dot is how Client B renders Client A's car at moments in time. The black outline dot represents the true heading of Client A's car.

The solution to this problem is acceleration (remember that deceleration is also acceleration). If, when Client A decided to stop the car, it actually slowed to a stop over 500ms instead of stopping instantly, then that would give all other clients plenty of time to receive the information, and also to slow the car to a stop at the right time.

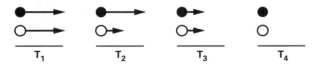

Here you see how this would play out with acceleration. Due to the latency, the acceleration is adjusted on each client, so that the final speed (in this case 0) is met at the right time. Two examples coming up soon both use acceleration.

Heading and Converger Classes

These two useful classes (created by me) handle the motion smoothing. They exist in the com.gamebook.utils.network.movement package included with all examples in this book. The Heading class keeps track of where an object is going. That would be a starting position, the time it started moving in this direction, its angle of movement, and its speed. If the object is accelerating, then it contains that information as well.

The Converger class is what handles the smoothing algorithm. It keeps track of three headings:

- course—The most up-to-date true heading of an object. As soon as new information is known about an object, this heading is updated to reflect that.

- interceptor—This heading sends the object in a direction and at a speed such that it will smoothly converge on the true heading a short time in the future. Every time the course heading is updated, the interceptor heading is recalculated.

- view—This heading is updated every frame to use values from the interceptor or the course to represent where an object should be shown on the screen. When it comes time to move the visual representation of the object on the screen, the application uses the view heading, not the interceptor or the course.

We use an instance of the Converger class to control the positioning of an object, such as a car or a bullet. This is done by giving the moving object the Converger class instance. In the upcoming examples, the Converger instance (hereafter just called "the converger") is exposed so that it can be updated by the game as new data comes in. Every frame, the run method on the converger is called, which updates the view heading and where we are on the actual convergence.

Now let's look at two examples! Each has very different user input controls, but is able to use the same smoothing code.

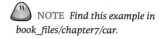

NOTE *Find this example in book_files/chapter7/car.*

NOTE *This example does not take into account the turning radius of a normal car in a game.*

DRIVE THE CAR

In this example, you control a car by moving your mouse; the car rotates to drive toward your current mouse position. When the car gets within 50 pixels of your mouse position, it slows to a stop. When your mouse moves away from the stopped car, it accelerates to a maximum speed and then follows the mouse again.

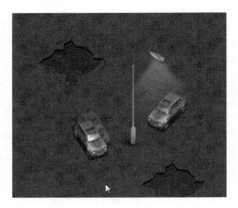

Your own car's true heading is updated every frame. A snapshot of its current heading is sent to the server every 250ms if it has changed, or if the car is going to accelerate or decelerate. You can see a faded-out version of your car in addition to your regular car. This faded-out version we call its *mirror*. As with the alien in the frame-based movement example earlier, the mirror represents how other clients probably see your current car position.

Now let's look at how to work with the Converger class and headings. The following code is found within the constructor of the Car class:

```
_converger = new Converger();
_converger.interceptTimeMultiplier = 7;
```

TIP *Try altering the value to see how it affects the movement.*

A new Converger class instance is created and stored to control updating the car's position and smoothing the path. The second line controls how quickly the interceptor will converge on the true heading (the course). The higher the number, the further in the future the convergence will take place. A higher number means smoother movement but less up-to-date positioning. A lower number means jerkier movement but more up-to-date positioning. In the testing I've done with the examples in this chapter, I've found values between 5 and 10 to give a good mix of smoothness and precision.

The Converger instance needs to have access to the Clock class instance used in your application. This is set directly onto the converger after the car is created in the CarExample class.

Also in the Car class, you'll find a function called run, marked as public. This function is called every frame by the CarExample class. Here is the content of the run function:

```
_converger.run();

x = _converger.view.x;
y = _converger.view.y;

var rotationIndex:int = NumberUtil.findAngleIndex(_converger.
➤ view.angle, 10);
gotoAndStop(rotationIndex + 1);
```

NOTE *The* NumberUtil. findAngleIndex *method is useful in determining which frame is best to show, based on the angle and the number of degrees per frame.*

The first line updates the view heading in the Converger class. Then the position of the car is updated based on the position found in the view heading. The final two lines determine which frame of the car to show. The car is made up of 36 images (one for every ten degrees of rotation).

The CarExample handles joining you to a room, adding and removing cars based on who is there, and sending and receiving heading updates. On every frame, the heading of your own car will be updated by calling the updateHeading function. That function first checks to see if it is OK to update your heading. If it is, then it runs the following code:

```
checkMousePosition();

var ang_rad:Number = Math.atan2(mouseY - _myCar.y, mouseX -
➤ _myCar.x);
var ang:Number = ang_rad * 180 / Math.PI;

_myCar.run();
var course:Heading = _myCar.converger.course;

if (course.speed > 0) {
  course.angle = ang;
  course.x = _myCar.x;
  course.y = _myCar.y;
  course.time = _clock.time;
}
```

The checkMousePosition function checks to see if your mouse is close enough to have the car decelerate or far enough away to have it accelerate. The next two lines determine the angle the car should now be heading.

Then your car's `run` method is called to make sure that everything in the converger is current before it is modified. We then proceed to directly update the position and angle of the course heading if the car is moving. It is important that the time be updated whenever the course is updated.

When you want your car to accelerate or decelerate, you update the course heading by changing some other properties on it. You do this in the `accel` and `decel` functions. When configuring a heading to accelerate, you must update the following properties:

- `time`—The time the acceleration started

- `accelTime`—The amount of time it should spend accelerating

- `endSpeed`—The speed that should be achieved by the time it is done accelerating

- `accel`—The acceleration value, which is `(speed-endSpeed)/accelTime`

In the `accel` and `decel` functions, we have the car speed up or slow down over the course of 500ms, and then we immediately send an update to the server.

The update that is sent to the server is treated the same way that you've seen in several examples now. So we'll just look specifically at what properties are set on the EsObject. In the `formatHeading` function, the following code populates the EsObject with properties representing your car's current course heading:

```
esob.setNumber(PluginConstants.X, heading.x);
esob.setNumber(PluginConstants.Y, heading.y);
esob.setNumber(PluginConstants.SPEED, heading.speed);
esob.setNumber(PluginConstants.ANGLE, heading.angle);
esob.setNumber(PluginConstants.TIME, heading.time);
esob.setNumber(PluginConstants.ACCEL_TIME, heading.accelTime);
esob.setNumber(PluginConstants.END_SPEED, heading.endSpeed);
esob.setString(PluginConstants.NAME, _myCar.playerName);
```

If the car is not accelerating, then ACCEL_TIME and END_SPEED are both 0. Taken together, these properties completely describe your car's current heading.

When an update is received by a client, it ends up being processed by the `handleUpdateHeading` function. This function grabs all of the heading information off of the EsObject and then uses it to update the converger for the car it refers to (as long as it is not your own car). Here is the code that updates the converger for a car (all of the values came from the EsObject):

```
var path:Heading = new Heading();
path.x = x;
path.y = y;
path.speed = speed;
path.time = time;
path.angle = angle;
path.accelTime = accelTime;
path.endSpeed = endSpeed;

car.converger.intercept(path);
```

You can see that we create a new Heading instance, populate it with data, and then call the intercept method on the converger passing this new heading in. The intercept method will take the new heading, set it as the new course, and then establish a new interceptor heading that converges on the course in the near future. As the game plays out, the updated car will move smoothly from the heading it was moving on to the updated course. Refer back to the figure on page 106 to refresh yourself on the intercept heading.

MOVE THE ALIEN

NOTE *Find this example in book_files/chapter7/arrowkey_ timesync.*

In this example, you control a walking alien using your arrow keys—the same character we used in the Here I Am example. It can walk in a total of eight directions, depending on which arrow keys are held down. As the character starts and stops, we use a little acceleration to hide the latency.

This example introduces nothing new from a multiplayer standpoint; it just shows a second usage of the converger. The Guy class is what represents each walking character. Just like in the previous example, it creates a Converger class instance in the constructor used to control its movement:

```
_converger = new Converger();
_converger.interceptTimeMultiplier = 5;
```

Notice that we use a slightly lower value for the interceptTimeMultiplier than we did in the car example. Since the speed of the character is fairly low, we can converge quickly, because the character is never very far off of where it should be.

The code found in the `ArrowKeyExample` class is surprisingly similar to the code found in the `CarExample` class. The primary difference is in capturing user input and mapping that to a course change for your own character. In the car example, we used the angle between the car and the mouse and the distance between the car and the mouse to govern everything. In this example, we check every frame to see what combination of the four arrow keys are pressed, and update the course angle to one of eight angles based on that. This is done in the `moveGuy` function.

An update is sent to the server every 250ms if the course has changed. Updates can be sent immediately if there is acceleration. The code that processes a received update is the same as it was in the car example. The character will follow a smooth path to converge with its true heading. The smoothed character will not necessarily stick to just eight angles; it will take a direction that best brings it in line with the true heading quickly.

A better Converger

The `Converger` class does a pretty good job of synchronizing position based on time while smoothing between a predicted path and a new updated path. However, there are a few things that I think can be improved upon.

Currently the view heading updates its angle property by using an easing equation to have its angle quickly match that of the interceptor or course headings. While this achieves a smooth rotation, it doesn't quite match up to the direction the object is moving; it can result in an object that stops and then rotates just a little bit more. Also, I think that it may be smart to completely decouple art rotation from the converger. The converger is meant to be reusable for many different situations. But you can imagine that the rotation of the moving object may depend on circumstances other than just the path it is on. Yes, a walking character should probably have its rotation match the rotation found in the view heading. But what about a car driving on ice? Or a boat in the water? Or a ship in an Asteroids clone? In these cases, the rotation is really based on environmental conditions other than just the path it is on.

Another improvement would be to have better acceleration handling. Right now the object is locked in the direction it is moving until it is finished accelerating. In the examples here, that works fine, because we are just using it to hide latency over a very short amount of time. But what if acceleration was part of the game? If you had a real driving game, with acceleration applied over longer periods of time, and angle changes while this is happening, then you'd want better handling of it in the converger.

Finally, I think the converger could benefit from one of the other smoothing techniques discussed earlier in this chapter (method 4 on page 107). It would take some time and experimentation to implement well, but it could result in something that looks great.

CHAPTER 8

Lobby System

ONCE YOU HAVE a multiplayer game, you're going to have to figure out a way to allow players to play it. This is where a lobby system can help. A lobby system, sometimes just called a game lobby or just a lobby, is used to help players get into a multiplayer game. Lobbies can be set up to function and to display information in many different ways.

In this chapter, we'll look at common lobby-system features and see visual examples from a well-made multiplayer Flash game lobby system. We'll show a common workflow for people getting into and back out of a game, and we'll break down the steps of that workflow into four flow states. Finally, we'll look at a simple lobby system created for this chapter.

Common Features

As stated above, at its core, a lobby system helps players getting into a multiplayer game. Let's look first at features that are common to most lobby systems, and then at a few less common features.

Chat—This is a very common, though not mandatory, lobby feature. While chatting isn't integral to getting a player into a game, it allows players to talk about the game. This may lead to them playing each other or becoming buddies through a buddy feature. I guess what's surprising, given how common and "expected" it is, that it isn't found in 100% of lobby systems.

Game list—Many lobby systems allow you to see a list of games that exist on that server. Some of the games may be full and currently in play, some may be partially full and waiting for more players, some may be password protected. The game list feature can be set up in many ways on the client. Extra game-specific information can be displayed if appropriate, such as which map is being used in a shooter game or the names of the current players.

Quick Join—It is common for a lobby to have a Quick Join button, which is meant to be the easiest way to get into a game. If you click this button, the server-side portion of the lobby system will search for an open game to add you to. If none exists, it will create a new one for you and add you to it.

Create Game—A Create Game button allows a player to create a new instance of an existing game rather than joining an already existing game. If a player creates a new game, it would likely be configured with properties such as the game name, whether it's password protected, and maybe game-specific settings like how long the game will last. The ability to create a new game can be as simple or as complicated as you need it to be.

Now let's look at some other features that may be a little less common:

Challenge system—The ability to challenge another player to a game is most likely to be found in turn-based games like chess, but is not limited to them. Challenge systems sound simple, but can actually be very tedious to implement properly (see the sidebar).

Invite system—Unlike a challenge system, an invite system assumes that the inviter is already in a game waiting state (see the sidebar) and that you—the inviter—would like some specific players to come join you. Any player can send one or more other players an invitation to join the game.

Reusability—This is an important developer-facing feature. A lobby can look and act uniquely per game that you need it to manage. But most implementations need the same fundamental features. Since a lobby system can be a substantial multi-week development effort, you should consider spending the time up front to make it generic and reusable so that you can save time on future projects by reusing as much of a single system as possible.

The challenge challenge

Programming a challenge feature into a lobby system or virtual world can be a real pain. There are a lot of scenarios that need to be considered and managed for the challenge feature to work well. Describing some of the many situations that need to be handled will hopefully prepare you for what you'll need to resolve.

First I'll describe a happy path. Player A challenges Player B. Player B shows a challenge dialog box, and clicks to accept. Player A receives the acceptance, and both players are whisked into a game. Not too bad—that was easy.

Now we'll look at some of things that can—and will—happen to break you out of the happy path. Player A challenges Player B. Player B shows a dialog box, but decides to never respond. This creates two issues to be resolved. First, Player A sees an animation on his screen indicating that he has challenged someone. This needs to somehow expire or be cancelable. Second, Player B continues to see the dialog box because he hasn't responded to it yet. If a feature is added to allow Player A to cancel the challenge, then Player B has to be informed that the challenge was cancelled, in order to remove the dialog box that he hasn't responded to. If the challenge is cancelable, and Player A cancels at the same time that Player B finally accepts, then Player A has to handle receiving an accept response for a challenge that is no longer valid. If all of those things are done, then this situation is handled.

Here is another situation. Player A challenges Player B, and Player B sees a dialog box showing this challenge. Then Player C challenges Player A, and of course Player A sees a dialog box showing the challenge. If Player A accepts Player C's challenge, then Player B needs to be informed so the dialog box from A to B will go away. But what if Player A accepts Player C and Player B accepts Player A at the same time? Without proper handling, that would lead to very buggy situations. So perhaps Player A should auto-decline Player C's request if he already has an outstanding challenge.

There are a few more tricky situations that can arise with a challenge system, such as challenging a player who then leaves the server. I am not trying to scare you away from building a challenge system—just preparing you for some of the conditions you'll need to handle. The best way to tackle this is to write the logic on the server. It will help resolve these situations.

Lobby

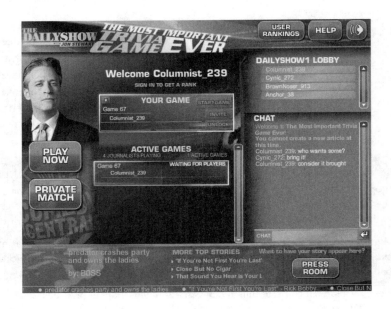

Game Flow

Think for a moment about the user experience you would expect from a player getting into a game from a lobby system. You might rattle off something like this:

- Clicking on a game in the list to play it
- Seeing a loading screen as the game loads
- Starting the game
- Playing the game
- Finishing the game
- Going back to the lobby

These are the steps a player takes to complete the full experience, with the main lobby screen serving as both the starting and ending point. There are some fundamental state changes that occur throughout this process, which I call the game flow.

That's all true and sensible, but here's another, more developer-centric view of the same generic game flow, that works very well for all types of games. Each bullet point below is a state that the player will exist in for some amount of time:

- Waiting
- Initializing
- Playing game
- Game over

Each of the above states has a little more going on internally than you'd think. We'll look at each of these states in greater detail right now.

Waiting

A player decides he wants to play a game by creating a new game, choosing to join an existing one, or by doing a quick join. The server receives this request and, assuming that the game he wants to join isn't full and hasn't yet started, he is joined. The moment this happens, the player is in the waiting state.

The waiting state is where one or more players are waiting for more players to join and final game configuration can happen. Visually, this state is often a brand new screen that shows numbers of available slots for new players to fill. As players join, the slots are filled. If the game allows for further customization, then players can do things like vote on which map to use in the next race.

In some implementations, players need to indicate that they are ready to play. The player is joined and waiting, but needs to flag that he is ready. The reason for this is that if the game were, say, a robot battling game, then each player might be allowed to customize their robot before saying that they are ready.

Most games have a range of players that's acceptable (for example, 2 to 4 players for a game of cards). When the minimum number of players is reached, waiting, and marked as ready, a countdown starts. This countdown is intended to give anyone else not yet marked as ready a chance to mark themselves as ready. Also, more players can join during the countdown.

If the number of players in the game drops below the minimum needed during the countdown, then the countdown stops until the condition is met again. If it succeeds, then players marked as ready are moved on to the initializing state. The players not marked as ready are sent back to the lobby.

NOTE *This flow is valid for a typical multiplayer game that has a distinct start and end. If the game is party style—meaning that players can join and leave at any time and the game lives on—then a different flow makes sense.*

NOTE *For simple games, all of this can be quickly automated. A client can automatically flag itself as ready the moment it hits this waiting state, which could bypass all of the UI that might otherwise have to go into making this work well.*

NOTE *Some games integrate the waiting screen with the main lobby screen.*

Waiting during countdown

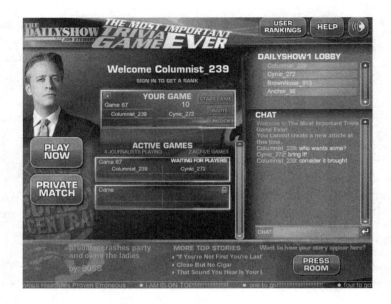

Initializing

This state is used to give each client the time needed to set up for the game that is about to be played. Imagine that in the waiting state each player customizes a robot to use, and chooses a map for the battle site. Each client has to then load all of this data and set it up on screen.

Many games won't have to do anything here except tell the server that initialization is done. Think about a game of chess: nothing to load or initialize (assuming the primary game file was preloaded).

If the game does requires loading, this could be shown visually by displaying a loader bar for each player in the game. This way, all players can see the load progress of their opponents.

Once all the players have told the server that they are done initializing and ready to play, the game is started, and they are moved into the playing game state.

Game loading

Playing Game

When this state is reached, you know that all players are in place, and have loaded and set up everything they need to use. Now the game can be played!

This state is reserved for custom game logic. Anything can happen here until a game-specific end-game condition is reached. When the game has ended, players are taken to the game over state.

Game in progress

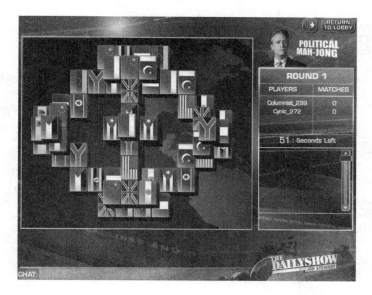

Game Over

In this state, players are still grouped together, but the game play is over. Typically, the results of the game are displayed for everyone to see. Players often chat at this stage about what happened in the game.

You can program your system so that players can go from this state back to the waiting room or back to the lobby.

End of game

Dig Game 2

To illustrate the most basic things found in a lobby system, we took the Dig game found in Chapter 6, enhanced it a bit (discussed later), and built a lobby system to help players find and join games. We'll look at what built-in features ElectroServer has to help with lobby systems.

New ElectroServer Concepts

NOTE *A game on the server is nothing more than a room with one or more plugins associated with it.*

ElectroServer provides some features that are very useful in lobby system development. A plugin can be registered with ElectroServer as a game, called a *server game*. Every server game has a unique string ID called the *game type*. Clients use this game type along with some new API calls to do the following:

- Load a list of all games of a type

- Quick-join a game of a type

- Join a specific existing game of a type

- Create a new game of a type

On the client, there is a `ServerGame` class that is used only when a list of games has been requested. This class contains information about the game, such as:

Game type—The string name that indicates what type of game this is.

Game ID—A unique ID per game type that is used to join a specific game.

Locked—The plugin that controls the game has the ability to lock itself. A locked game will not allow new players to join. Usually a game starts out not locked, and then locks when full or when the game starts.

Game details—This property contains an EsObject, and is optionally populated by the game. This property is intended to be publicly-viewable custom information about the game. Let's say that players are in a waiting room and waiting for more players. They choose a new map to play in the next game. The game details can be updated to contain this information, and then ultimately displayed in the lobby in any way that the developer wants—icons, numbers, a video, and so forth.

We'll look at the following API calls in use when discussing the example. But for starters, here are the handful of requests and one response used when working with server games:

FindGamesRequest / FindGamesResponse—Used by a client to load a list of games by type. If the list needs to be kept current, you'd reload this every 10 or 20 seconds. The response contains the list.

CreateGameRequest—Used to create a game of a specific type. Custom game details can be passed to the game plugin during the request.

QuickJoinGameRequest—Used when a player just wants to join any game. A game type is specified as a filter, and then the list of available games is scanned. The player will be joined to the first available game, or a new one will be created.

JoinGameRequest—Used when a player wants to join a specific game (probably one seen in a game list); the game ID is added to it.

CreateOrJoinGameResponse—Players can get into a game in the three ways just mentioned—creating a game, joining one directly, or sending a quick join request. Ultimately, the response to any of these requests will be CreateOrJoinGameResponse. The response says if the join was successful or not. If not a success, then it contains an error. If a success, then it contains the room information.

Lobby System Example

 NOTE *Find these files in book_files/chapter8/lobby_system.*

A few of the modifications we made to the Chapter 6 Dig game are that you can now see the mouse cursor for all other players as they move around and dig; there is a countdown at the beginning of the game where more players can join; and the game ends when a player reaches 10,000 points.

Another modification we made was, of course, a lobby system to give players a way to get into games. This lobby system is pretty basic and has the following features:

- Chat

- Game list

- Join a game in the list

- Quick join

The modified Dig game lobby

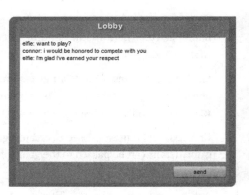

Coming up, we'll look at the newly introduced ElectroServer requests and response and how they are used. And then we'll look at how the game handles the four game flow states of waiting, initializing, game play, and game over.

REQUESTS AND RESPONSE

Here we'll look at how our simple lobby system uses all of the new requests we've introduced (except for CreateGameRequest). To show the game list on screen and to keep it up to date, we request the list from the server every two seconds. This is scheduled using a timer. When the timer executes, the onGameListRefreshTimer function is called in the Lobby class:

```
//create request
var fgr:FindGamesRequest = new FindGamesRequest();

//create search criteria that filters the game list
var criteria:SearchCriteria = new SearchCriteria();
criteria.setGameType(PluginConstants.GAME_NAME);

//add the search criteria to the request
fgr.setSearchCriteria(criteria);

//send it
_es.send(fgr);
```

The request is created and populated with a SearchCriteria class instance (which can be used for advanced filtering, a topic beyond the scope of this book). For our purposes, we just give it a game type, which is used to return a list of all games of that game type. When finished loading, the onFindGamesResponse function is called. The event object passed into this function contains an array of ServerGame objects, which we pass on to the refreshGameList function so that it can be displayed. A list box component displays the list of games. The game list is looped through, and each game object is used to format an element for display in the list. Here is a snippet of that code from the loop:

```
var game:ServerGame = games[i];
var label:String = "Game " + game.getGameId();
label += " [" + (game.getLocked() ? "full" : "open") + "]";
dp.addItem( { label:label, data:game } );
```

We reference the ServerGame element for this iteration, and then use it to format an item in the data provided for the list. The label property is what is displayed in the list and the data property is content that the list stores for that list item. The label displayed for this element in the game list is "Game" plus the ID for that game, followed by "[open]" or "[full]". We determine if a game is open or full by the value of the locked property.

When a player clicks on a game in the list, the Join Game button is enabled. By clicking Join Game, a JoinGameRequest is generated and sent to the server. That is done by calling the joinGame function and passing it a ServerGame instance. Here is that function:

```
private function joinGame(serverGame:ServerGame):void {
  var jgr:JoinGameRequest = new JoinGameRequest();
  jgr.setGameId(serverGame.getGameId());
  jgr.setGameType(PluginConstants.GAME_NAME);

  _es.send(jgr);
}
```

First a JoinGameRequest instance is created; then it's populated with the game ID for that specific game, and with the game type. The request is then sent to the server. We'll look at the quick join feature and then move on to the response that the client will receive as a result of either of these requests.

There is a Quick Join button under the game list. The quick join feature joins a player to an open game, or creates a new game if no open game is found. When the Quick Join button is clicked, the following function is executed:

```
private function quickJoin():void {
  _quickJoinGame.enabled = false;

  var qjr:QuickJoinGameRequest = new QuickJoinGameRequest();
  qjr.setGameType(PluginConstants.GAME_NAME);
  qjr.setZoneName("GameZone");
  _es.send(qjr);
}
```

First you see that the Quick Join button is disabled. Sending a quick join request guarantees that the player will end up in a game, even if it's a newly created one, so the button is disabled because it won't need to be clicked again. The request is created, and the game type is set on it. We also set the zone name in which we want the game room to be created. The request is then sent, which eventually results in a CreateOrJoinGameResponse.

The CreateOrJoinGameResponse event will be handled by the onCreateOrJoinGameResponse function. The event object contains a success property. If the player successfully joined a game, then the success property is true, otherwise it is false. If the player failed to join a game, then a descriptive error is contained on the event object. When it is a successful join, the event object contains the room ID and zone ID for the room they are now in. This needs to be kept track of so that the client knows where to send messages to the game.

After the lobby has detected that the player has joined a game and stored the room ID and zone ID, it dispatches a JOINED_GAME event, captured by the LobbyFlow class. The LobbyFlow class then removes the lobby and instantiates a DigGame class instance, passing it an API reference and room information.

GAME FLOW STATES

In our lobby system example, we use all four states, but only visually show three of them. The initialize state is handled silently. The moment the player receives a successful CreateOrJoinGameResponse event, that player is in the waiting state. On the client, we remove the lobby screen and create the game screen, which is an instance of the DigGame class.

The DigGame class is passed a reference to the ElectroServer API and the room information. This class immediately sends a plugin message of the action type INIT_ME. The server takes this to mean that the client is initialized and ready for game play. In this case, the player is initialized, but the game is still in the waiting state.

The waiting state displays the text "Waiting for players..." if there is only one player in the game. As soon as the second player joins, a ten-second countdown starts and is displayed. Other players can join during this countdown. If the player list drops back down to one during the countdown, then the countdown stops and "Waiting for players..." is displayed again. Other players who join during the countdown stage will see the countdown starting from the proper value.

When the countdown is complete, the game bypasses the initialize state, since all players have already flagged themselves as initialized, and goes into the game play state. It is the same game play as you saw in Chapter 6, with the exception that the game ends when the score reaches 10,000.

When a player reaches 10,000, the game moves into the game over state. During this state, a list of player names is displayed, in the order of their scores. A button allows each player to click to go back to the lobby whenever ready.

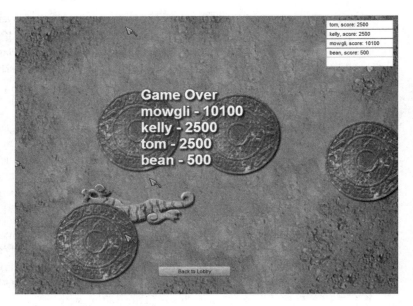

This lobby system could be enhanced by allowing the players who just completed their game to play again—by sending them back to the waiting state instead of the lobby.

Registering a Game Type with ElectroServer

NOTE *For our extension, find this plugin at www.electrotank.com/ gamebook/server/src/com/ gamebook/gamemanager/ GMSInitializer.java.*

Each game type needs to be registered with the Game Manager when ElectroServer starts up. Normally this is done by having a single server-level plugin that registers all the games at once.

The `initOneGame` method, which is part of the GMSInitializer plugin, is an easy way to register a game that has no default game details and uses the same game name as the plugin name. A game can have multiple plugins associated with it, but most games have only one. If you have additional games in the extension that will use the Game Manager, invoke `initOneGame` for each of these games, in the init method of `GMSInitializer`. You may also write a custom method for one or more of your games, and invoke that instead.

Next, open ElectroServer's administration panel, and go to the Extensions tab. Click the plus sign (+) next to GameBook. If you do not see GMSInitializer listed as a server level component, click the button to add it as a new server-level component. You may use any unique string as the plugin name, since this plugin runs only when ElectroServer starts up. Restart ElectroServer, and then check the console or ElectroServer4.log file. You should see a WARN level logging line saying "DiggingPlugin2 game registered with GameManager."

CHAPTER 9

Real-time Tank Game

WE'VE COME A long way in this book. We've learned the basics of communicating over a socket using the ElectroServer API, explored client-server authority in games, and looked at real-time movement concepts in detail. This is the chapter where it all comes together in the form of a real-time multiplayer tank game!

This chapter is partly devoted to discussing how things learned up to this point have been applied in this game. After that, we look at line of sight in detail as it is used for path validation and predicting some bullet collisions. In addition, we will briefly discuss the level editor as well as introduce the concept of spatial audio.

Game Overview

NOTE *Find the files for this game in book_files/chapter9/ tank_game.*

In this game, you control a tank using your mouse and the keyboard. The view is top-down. As you move your mouse, the tank's turret rotates to face toward your mouse cursor. When you click, the tank fires a bullet. If you Shift-click, a new target destination for the tank is established, and the tank moves toward it.

The map contains objects, some of which allow your tank to move through them and some that don't. Some objects stop bullets and some don't. Here are all of the objects in the game and their properties:

- Tree—Tank can drive under it without being stopped. Does not stop bullets. Used for hiding.

- House—Tank cannot drive through this and bullets cannot pass through.

- Water—Tank cannot drive through water but bullets can pass over it.

- Bridge—Tank can drive over bridge and it does not stop bullets.

- Wall—Does not allow a tank to pass through and stops bullets.

- Powerup—Special icon in the game picked up by driving over it.

The goal of the game is to destroy other opponent's tanks. You do this by shooting them. There is no end to the game. When a tank is destroyed, it respawns in another location after a few seconds.

This game also supports the concept of powerups. A powerup is something that gives your tank a benefit for collecting it. The only powerup in this game is a health boost. A health boost powerup is collected by moving your tank over it. When it's collected, your tank health is increased.

This game is 1600x1600 but is played in a 800x600 Flash window. Since the map is four times the size of the window, it scrolls as your tank moves. We use a mini-map that shows a small-scale version of the entire map with dot representations of all tanks on it. As the tanks move, the dots move. This allows all players to see where all other players are with real-time updates.

The game is not limited to a single map layout. The map layout is stored in an XML file which is created using a level editor. The level editor allows you to be creative and come up with your own tank game levels. This is discussed later in this chapter.

Authority and Prediction

Chapter 6 introduced the idea of client versus server authority. Chapter 7 was devoted to exploring real-time movement and latency hiding for objects in a multiplayer game. Those concepts drive the core game play in this game. In this section, we'll talk about where decisions are made, point out where the Converger class is used, and mention some other predictive aspects to the game.

Tank Paths

There are two things about the path a tank takes in this game that are worth discussing: how it determines the path in the first place, and how it moves along that path once it is known.

A path is determined by drawing a straight line between where the tank currently is and where the mouse is when clicked. In this game, we use line of sight to make sure that a path is valid. If you draw a line between where the tank currently is and its intended destination, and that line intersects an object that won't let the tank move through it, then we have to disallow that path. We do two levels of checks to determine a valid path. On click, the client does a line-of-sight check to make sure the path doesn't cross any static map objects. If it is deemed a valid path, then the path information is sent to the server, which validates it.

If the server is going to validate the path anyway, why do we bother validating it on the client? It comes down to giving the client instantaneous feedback on their user input with the assumption that the client validation is correct. The moment the user clicks and has client-side validation, that user's tank starts to move along the path (before receiving a server response). If the path is rejected by the server, then the client needs to correct its own movement. The goal is to minimize the chance of the client sending a bad path. (The line-of-sight code used in this game is discussed further later in the chapter.)

The second item worth discussing is how the tank moves along a path. The tank makes use of the `Converger` class that was discussed and used in Chapter 7. Due to the fairly slow speed of the tank and the fact that its final destination is known well before it is supposed to stop, we don't need to use acceleration in this game to smooth the end points. The only new thing here is that we use the `targetX` and `targetY` properties on the `Heading` class. Those properties specify the final destination of the tank.

Shooting

As the player moves the mouse cursor, the tank's turret rotates to point toward it. The turret rotates independently of the motion path of the tank. When the player clicks, the tank fires a bullet in the direction its turret is facing.

When the player clicks to shoot the tank, the client sends a message to the server. The client does not fire the tank until the server says it's OK. My testing on this showed the slight server delay was not noticeable and so the user experience was good. However, if we wanted it to be even more reactive, then we'd fire the bullet on the client just as the server is informed. This is possible, but creates an issue to be handled. The main issue to be resolved here is that each bullet has a unique ID so that the server can refer to it later to tell the clients to remove it or that it hit something. If a bullet is fired on the client before getting a server response, then it has no ID to be referred to later. You'd have to keep track of the bullet with no ID, and give it one when the server confirmation came in. Also, you would need to handle the situation where the server says it was an invalid shot (the bullet would have to be removed).

The bullet movement is controlled using the Converger class. The bullet moves at a constant speed in a specific direction. The gap in position from where the bullet leaves the muzzle of the tank that shot it and where it is by the time the clients receive the message is smoothly handled by the latency-hiding algorithm in the Converger class.

Collision Detection

Collision detection is the act of determining if an object is colliding with another object. In the context of this game, bullets are checked against tanks and against static objects. The ultimate decision on what collisions have occurred is made on the server. However, due to the speed of the bullets, some client-side prediction about what the bullet will probably collide with helps make it a better user experience. Why is that? Let's start by understanding the problem. It is similar to a problem that was outlined in Chapter 7 about a car stopping suddenly with no deceleration and the rendering glitch that will occur if no smoothing or predictive steps are taken. In this game, the bullets travel 240 pixels per second. Consider a bullet headed toward a tank. When a collision is detected on the server, an event is sent to all clients, telling them of the collision. If the latency of a client receiving this message is 50ms (which is low), then the bullet has overshot by 12 pixels. That is best case. If the latency is a little higher or there happens to be a small latency spike, then this gap will only be bigger. This results in a visual discrepancy during game play that is always there. With something so common in the game, it makes sense to find ways to address it.

Bullet fired

Server sends collision event

Client receives collision event

Now that the problem is clear, let's look at the steps taken in this game to minimize the effects of latency of collision events. There are three ways a bullet can "die" in the game. It can reach its range limit; hit static obstacles such as a wall; or hit a tank. We'll consider them in that order.

The range for bullets in this game is about 600 pixels. At a speed of .24 pixels per millisecond, a bullet will live at most for about 2500 milliseconds. When a bullet is fired, we store the time value at which it should be removed due to reaching the range limit. The position of the bullets is updated every frame based on the total time elapsed since the bullet was fired. If the clock time of the current frame is greater than or equal to that of the bullet's natural "death date," then we remove the bullet. If no collisions have taken place by the time the life of the bullet is up, then it makes sense to remove it. You must keep open the possibility that the server will tell you differently. For example, the bullet may have clipped a tank at the last moment. But we know that no matter what, it is time to die.

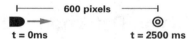

Predicting a collision with a static obstacle is a straightforward task once you think about it. The bullet is moving in a specific direction at a constant speed. The obstacles aren't moving. The moment a bullet is fired, we look at its position leaving the tank muzzle and what its position would be at the time it reaches the range limit. A line is drawn between these two points showing the path the bullet would take. If that line intersects any obstacles, then the bullet will collide with one of those before the range limit is reached. We detect all collisions along the path and then take the one that occurs closest to the bullet starting point. The time that collision should occur is stored. If the game time reaches this predicted collision time and the bullet is still alive, then remove it. (More on line-of-sight collision detection coming up in the next section.)

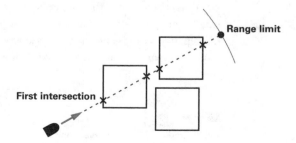

So far we've looked at how to predict when a bullet should die in two of the three cases. The final situation is that of predicting bullet–tank collisions. There are two ways to do this: frame-based collision checks or predictive collision detection. For this chapter, we chose the simpler but less precise way. The simplest way to predict bullet–tank collisions is to check every frame to see if a collision is visually happening right now. Since we are using time synchronization, there is a very good chance that if it looks like there is a collision on the client, then there really is one, but you just haven't gotten the message yet from the server. So if the client detects a collision that is currently happening, stop the bullet. We don't play the bullet explosion animation, or any sound, or decrement the health of the tank until the server tells us that we can.

NOTE *It is OK for us to use a client-side collision detection approach that isn't perfect. The server detects all collisions. So the worst-case scenario is that a bullet moves a little bit past the target before the client learns that a collision occurred.*

The problem with this approach is that it just looks at snapshots in time. It is possible—even likely—that a bullet did collide with a tank, but we don't detect it with this technique, since we just look at where it is at a given instant.

There is another predictive collision approach—the most precise one possible on the client. At any given moment in time, we know the trajectory of all tanks and all bullets. Assuming no more input from the server, we can predict with 100% accuracy all collisions that will occur, and we can run a frame-independent collision-detection check between two moving objects. It is fed the path of any two objects and will determine if they ever collide, and if so, when. This is run for every tank against every bullet to generate a list of collisions. The list is then sorted based on time to determine which happened first. It's possible that you may predict a collision based on information (about a tank) that is no longer accurate. So in a game like this, you can never have complete confidence in collision predictions with objects whose movements can't be completely predicted. You are forced to do the best you can with the information at hand. Note that there is no sample code provided for covering this particular approach.

Line of Sight

A line-of-sight check is one that extends out from a position in a straight line in any one direction until it hits something. Line of sight is used in games in many ways. Here are a few:

- It can be used by an AI creature to determine what it can see. That way, the creature won't react to things it shouldn't know about.

- It can be used in shooting games to show where a bullet would hit if shot—or just to know where a moving bullet will hit.

- It can be used to determine the validity of a path choice.

In this game, we use line of sight to validate a path attempt by a tank and to predict what static object a bullet will hit if not first intercepted by a tank. Let's look at how we calculate line of sight and then how it is used for path validation and collision prediction.

Line Segment Intersections

In this game, a bullet starts at a certain position, and if it hits nothing, it will die at a predictable position. A line drawn between the starting and ending position is a line segment. When a new path is created for a tank, it has a start and end point that also make a line segment. All static objects (such as walls) are rectangular. As such, the boundaries of static object are made up of four line segments. Looking at the game from this perspective, you can see that if we have a way to detect line segment intersections, then we can figure out if a tank path is valid or if a bullet will collide with an object.

We use some classes found in the com.gamebook.utils.geom package to represent line segments and detect intersections between them. Before showing how to use those classes, let's briefly look at the math behind that.

Any straight line is represented by the equation $y = m*x + b$.

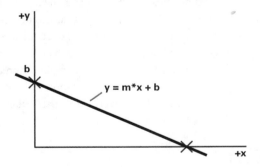

SYMBOL	REPRESENTS
m	The slope of the line. The larger the slope, the steeper the line.
b	The y value of the line when it intercepts the y-axis (if it intersects the y-axis).
x	Any x position.
y	The y value based on the x value input.

Applying this to our situation, if you had two lines, they would be represented like this:

y1 = m1*x1 + b1

y2 = m2*x2 + b2

If the two lines ever intersect, then at that point they share the same x and y position. So the two equations above become the following at that intersection point:

m1*x + b1 = m2*x + b2

When you solve the above for x, you get:

x = (b2-b1)/(m1-m2)

That is the x position of two intersecting lines. Feed that x position back into either of the line equations, and you'll find the y position of this intersection.

Just because two lines are intersecting doesn't mean that two *segments* of those lines are intersecting. There is one more step that we have to perform after finding the intersection of two lines. We need to check to see if that point of intersection is found on each of the two segments. If it is, then the line segments are intersecting.

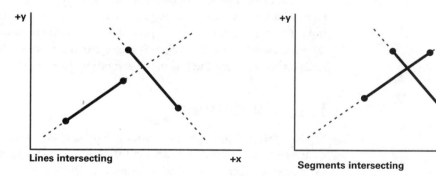

Lines intersecting   Segments intersecting

Now let's look at the classes used to handle all of this. The LineSegment class is used to represent a single line segment. It is created and populated like this:

```
var seg:LineSegment = new LineSegment(new Point(10, 20),
  → new Point(15, 30);
```

The Point class is part of the ActionScript library. It just stores an x and y value. The LineSegmentCollection class stores an array of LineSegment instances. This is useful for storing the segments that form a shape. It is created like this:

```
var seg1:LineSegment = new LineSegment(new Point(10, 20),
    new Point(15, 25));
var seg2:LineSegment = new LineSegment(new Point(5, 15),
    new Point(20, 30));
var collection:LineSegmentCollection =
    new LineSegmentCollection();
collection.addLineSegment(seg1);
collection.addLineSegment(seg2);
```

These can be used with a class called IntersectionDetector to detect—you guessed it—line intersections. This class exposes two static methods of detection. One tests for an intersection between any two line segments using segmentSegmentTest, and the other tests for an intersection between a line segment and a collection of line segments using segmentCollection-Test. These methods return an instance of the IntersectionTestResult class. This instance contains a property indicating that an intersection was found, and a point object representing the point of intersection.

The segmentCollectionTest method can find many intersections. If you're testing to see if a path is valid, then that is all the information you need. But if you want to test for when a bullet hits an object, then you would want to know which intersection point found is closest to where the bullet came from. This method allows for an optional point object to be passed in for distance checks. If the point object is supplied to this method, then any collision point returned will be the closest one to the point passed in.

Path Validation

The Map class interprets the map layout data to build the level. It also stores all line segments needed for the various static objects in the map. The TankGame class contains most of the game logic. When the player Shift-clicks, the TankGame class tries to create a new path for the tank. Here is part of the function executed:

```
private function sendNewWayPoint():void {
  var course:Heading = _tankManager.myTank.converger.course;
  var view:Heading = _tankManager.myTank.converger.view;

  //where the tank is now
```

```
var sx:int = view.x;
var sy:int = view.y;

//where the tank wants to go
var tx:int = _map.mouseX;
var ty:int = _map.mouseY;

//check for path validity
if (_map.validatePath(new Point(sx, sy), new Point(tx, ty))) {
```

The first two lines of code just create references to the client's course and view headings for its tank. The next four lines store the x and y coordinates of the tank where it is now and at its desired destination. These coordinates are then passed into the validatePath method of the Map class. If this method returns true, then the path is valid and the code sends a message to the server (where the server also validates). Here are the first few lines of the validatePath method in the Map class:

```
//create a line segment that connects the two points
var seg:LineSegment = new LineSegment(point1, point2);

//check for a collision between the segment and all obstacles
var res:IntersectionTestResult = IntersectionDetector.
    segmentCollectionTest(seg, _pathItemsCollection, point1);
```

First a new line segment is created, using the start and end points passed in. Then the IntersectionDetector class is used to check that line segment against a collection of line segments that make up all static obstacles on the map. Each object in the map has a Boolean obstacle property. If true, then that object cannot be driven through. Each object also has a Boolean hittable property. If true, a bullet cannot pass through. In the code above, we validate the path against all obstacle objects, not the hittable objects. Notice that point1 is passed in as the third parameter of the segmentCollectionTest method. That means that if line intersections are detected, we want to know which one is closest to point1.

If the path validation fails, then we inform the user by playing a sound and drawing a line from their tank to the point where the path collides with an obstacle. This line fades out very quickly.

Collision Prediction

As discussed earlier in the chapter, predicting where a bullet will collide with a static object is a straightforward process. The moment the client receives a shoot event, it runs a check to see where a collision will take place, if at all. We store the collision point and the time it happens. If the moment in time is reached when the bullet should have collided with the obstacle, it is then removed from the screen.

Here is a snippet of code from the `parseAndApplyBulletHeading` method in the `TankGame` class:

```
var life:Number = 2500;
var endx:Number = course.x + course.xspeed * life;
var endy:Number = course.y + course.yspeed * life;

var point:Point = _map.getCollisionPoint(new Point(course.x,
➤ course.y), new Point(endx, endy));
```

You find the position that the bullet would be at if it reached its limit by advancing it along its path. The start and end positions are then passed into the `getCollisionPoint` method of the `Map` class. This method checks a line segment against all hittable objects and returns the intersection point that occurs first. Here is all of the of code from that method:

```
var seg:LineSegment = new LineSegment(point1, point2);
var res:IntersectionTestResult = IntersectionDetector.
➤ segmentCollectionTest(seg, _bulletItemsCollection, point1);
var point:Point = res.point;
return point;
```

It creates a line segment using the bullet start and end points. This segment is then used to detect intersections against all hittable objects. The point found that is closest to `point1` is returned. If no collision is found, then `null` is returned.

Game Messaging

As you've seen throughout this book, client and server communicate by sending formatted EsObjects to each other with an ACTION variable. The value of that variable indicates what the message is for and what other data is on the object. We won't fully define the format of all message objects here, but we'll name the actions and describe their purposes.

EsObject actions and their purposes

ACTION	WHERE IT IS SENT	DESCRIPTION
INIT_ME	Client to server	Sent to server when client has joined the room successfully and is ready to receive game data. Server responds with board state.
BOARD_STATE	Server to client	Contains everything a newly joined player needs to know to render the board—map data, which powerups are on screen, location and destination of all tanks and bullets.
ADD_TANK	Server to client	Sent to all clients when a new tank joins.
REMOVE_TANK	Server to client	Sent to all clients when a tank leaves.
UPDATE_TURRET_ ROTATION	Client to server / Server to client	Contains client's turret rotation information; client sends this to server frequently. Server does nothing with this except aggregate it with other turret updates and send back to clients. See the "Message Aggregation" section for details.
HEADING_UPDATE	Client to server / Server to client	When player Shift-clicks to establish a new waypoint, it is validated client-side and sent to server. Server then validates it and sends to all clients if valid. If not valid, client receives an error containing the latest valid heading that the server has for that tank. Client uses this to correct its path.
SHOOT	Client to server / Server to client	Sent to server when player clicks to shoot. Server validates to make sure client isn't shooting too quickly, and then sends a shoot message to all clients.
SHOT_HIT	Server to client	Server keeps track of all tank and bullet positions and checks for collisions. If a shot collision with a tank is detected, server tells all clients.
HEALTH_UPDATE	Server to client	Sent to all clients informing them of change in health of a tank. (When a tank is shot, its health changes. When the health reaches 0, the tank is killed.) Rather than being contained in the SHOT_HIT message, this message is a separate update, in case new ways to get damaged are introduced.
TANK_KILLED	Server to client	Sent to all clients when a tank's health reaches 0 (and dies). Tank is immediately respawned to another location, which is the SPAWN_ TANK message.
SPAWN_TANK	Server to client	Sent to all clients when a tank dies and is resurrected and placed in a new location.
COLLECT_POWERUP	Client to server / Server to client	Sent to server when a client detects when the tank should collect a powerup. Server validates that tank is close enough to pick up the powerup, and then tells all clients that it happened.
SPAWN_POWERUP	Server to client	Tells all clients to add new powerup to the screen. (Remember, a collected powerup will respawn in the same location after a ten-second delay.)
ERROR	Server to client	Sent to client if something goes wrong, like the client shoots too fast or tries to go along an invalid path.

Mini-map

In games whose geographical area comprises multiple screens, it's common to have a miniature representation of the full area on screen—a mini-map. The purpose of the mini-map is primarily to give the player a sense of where they are in the world and, in many cases, where others are in the world as well.

Mini-maps are usually stylized in some way rather than literally being a shrunken version of the actual map. Major landmarks may be represented by icons, and dynamically moving objects (such as other players) as colored dots or other small icons appropriate to the game. The mini-map can be rich and colorful, or a simple span of flat color showing only walls and players.

In the tank game, we took an approach that is simple to program. The moment the map is built but before any tanks are added to it, we create a BitmapData instance and draw the map onto it using the draw method. We then create a MiniMap class instance and pass the BitmapData instance into it. The BitmapData is added to a Bitmap object, shrunk to 1/16 its current size, and added to the stage. A drop shadow is applied.

At this point, we have a miniature representation of the larger map. Because of the art style, the map is still very recognizable at 1/16 actual size. We don't have to come up with creative ways to show map information. As players join the game, the addTank method on the MiniMap class is called. This creates a dot to represent the tank, and adds it to the screen. The position of all dots are updated every frame by positioning them at 1/16 the x and y positions of the corresponding tank.

The end result is a mini-map that shows the positions of all tanks and is updated in real time. A client's own tank is seen as a white dot with a green halo, while opponent's tanks are seen as white dots with blue halos.

Message Aggregation

Using a socket server to handle game messaging is great. It allows multi-player games to be programmed in an event-based way. If a collision occurs, the server will let the clients know. If the client does something, like update its heading, it lets the server know. Having a separate message for every event that occurs can start to cause problems if the message frequency gets too high. One thing I have observed in Flash Player is that as the message frequency increases, the client can experience a perceived greater latency. The messages arrive on time, but it takes a little extra time for Flash Player to process them and make them available to ActionScript.

It's hard to see exactly how many client-bound messages per second is too many, but I try to keep it to five or fewer client-bound messages per second. There will be times when you get message-frequency spikes, such as if a few collisions just occurred, or a few new players just joined the game. That is OK, but you want to do your best to keep the message frequency low over the course of the game.

NOTE *The nice thing for you as a client developer is that you don't even have to know messages were aggregated. The ElectroServer API receives the combined message and then rips it back into the constituent smaller events. These events are then individually fired as separate* PluginMessageEvent *events. If you received an aggregate of five messages, then five* PluginMessageEvent *events will be fired.*

In the tank game, tanks shoot relatively infrequently (maybe on average once per second) and they move infrequently (probably setting a new path once every ten seconds). But what they do a lot is rotate their turrets. The tank turret moves to face the mouse constantly. The clients send their turret rotation updates to the server two times per second so that other clients can see the turrets updating. If there are ten tanks in this game and we just let the message events go to the clients, then that works out to 20 client-bound messages per second just for turret updates. Kind of a problem!

The solution is *message aggregation*—the act of collecting multiple messages together and sending them out in one larger message, as opposed to individually. ElectroServer plugins have the ability to use message aggregation for some messages and not for others. (For example, we don't want to wait another 50ms before receiving a shot or collision event.) In the tank game, we aggregate all turret update events and send them out twice per second. No matter how many tanks are in the game, you won't receive more than two turret update events per second. This allows Flash to quickly process the messages and make them available to your code.

Level Editor

NOTE   *The Flash Develop project for this game is Tank Game Editor.as3proj.*

Level editor, map builder—whatever you call it, you need one for most games and virtual worlds. A level editor is used to create levels (aka maps) for your game in a highly visual way. It is a welcome alternative to building levels by writing XML directly into Notepad. During development, having a level editor helps you create layouts that can help you find and fix map-related bugs quickly. After development, it allows you to create an endless number of levels for your game. In this section, we discuss the features of the level editor and talk a little bit about how the level data is stored.

The level editor uses much of the same code as the game. When the compiled editor application is launched, you will immediately see two buttons: Open and New Map. By clicking Open, you get a dialog box that allows you to browse your hard drive for existing map files (these would have an XML extension). If you select such a valid map file, it will be loaded, and the map displayed. If you click the New Map button, a new map is created, but no file is saved for it yet.

When you create a new map, you should see a screen that contains only the ground; a Save button and a spot where you can type the filename; and many small images representing objects that can be dragged into the world.

If you click Save, you see a dialog box that lets you browse to where you want to save the file. When the application tries to save the file, it takes the map information and formats it onto an EsObject. The EsObject has a toXML method on it that is used to get the XML-formatted string to store in the XML file. When the file is loaded in the future, a new EsObject is created and the XML is passed into it to populate the EsObject using the fromXML method. The application then uses the properties on the EsObject to build the map layout.

Building a map is very easy. New objects are created by simply dragging and dropping an object from the top of the screen into the map. You can drag any object that is in the map at any time. Just click and drag to a new position, and then release. To remove an object, just double-click it. The screen size cannot be edited, nor can the ground texture. You can add to the ground by placing water objects.

The screen scrolls when the mouse is placed within 10 pixels of the top, bottom, right, or left edge of the application.

You can add tank spawn points and powerup spawn points as if they were normal game objects. These allow you to specify valid locations for powerups, and for spawning tanks after they die.

The tank game editor allows you to easily get the job done. But there's still a lot of room for improvement if it were to be adopted for a larger project. Some quick ideas are:

- Allow for changing what the ground looks like.

- Let the user configure the size of the map.

- Put in a more intuitive way to scroll the map.

- Add the game objects to a scrolling list so that more can be added to the editor.

Spatial Audio

Audio is often the most overlooked piece of a small production game. I've witnessed countless smaller game projects that have lasted 4–8 weeks, only to have the sound effects located (or created) within the final few days of the project. Well-executed audio can lend a lot to a game and to the overall user experience. When done right, the audio is usually not noticed—it just helps the user stay immersed in the game play and can enhance the connection the user has with the game.

Other than choosing appropriate music and creating appropriate sound effects, you may wonder what you can do to use audio to enhance the experience. You might want to consider spatial audio.

Spatial audio is the act of modifying the sound settings of effects based on where the sound originates as it relates to the player. In Flash, we can control the volume and pan settings of the sound. When applied to the tank game, this feature allows us to hear bullet explosions of varying volumes based on how far away they are, and with varied pan levels out of the left and right speakers based on the horizontal positioning of the sound event.

In the tank game, we vary the volume of all spatial events as it relates to the position of the center of the viewing area on the screen. If the event occurs within 200 pixels, then we keep the volume at its maximum. After that, we taper it over 400 pixels to a volume of 0. The pan settings are varied between -1 and 1 over a distance of 400 pixels.

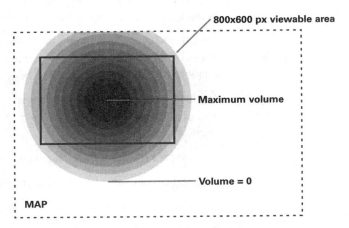

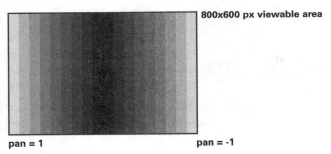

Let's look at the code used to do this for the tank shooting sound. The following code snippet is found within the parseAndApplyBulletHeading method in the TankGame class:

```
var snd:Sound = new ShootSound() as Sound;
var transform:SoundTransform = getSpatialSoundTransform(.35,
 ➤ new Point(course.x, course.y));
if (transform.volume > 0) {
  snd.play(0, 0, transform);
}
```

With that, a new Sound instance to play is created. We then call the getSpatialSoundTransform method, which accepts the maximum volume you want for this sound and the location of the sound event.

What is returned is a SoundTransform object that is already prepared with the correct volume and pan settings. If the volume is still greater than 0, then we play the sound.

The getSpatialSoundTransform method is where the volume and pan calculations are handled. We'll look at this function in four chunks, moving from the top down. Here is the first bit:

```
private function getSpatialSoundTransform(maxVolume:Number,
   point2:Point):SoundTransform {
  //center of screen
  var point1:Point = new Point( -_map.x + _viewWidth /
     2, -_map.y + _viewHeight / 2);
```

The maximum volume setting that we want to use is passed in. The volume will be varied between 0 and that maximum setting. The point where this sound event is taking place is passed in as point2. A variable called point1 is created to store the position of the center of the viewable area of the map.

Moving on:

```
var volDis:Number = Math.sqrt(Math.pow(point1.y - point2.y, 2)
   + Math.pow(point1.x - point2.x, 2));
var maxVolDis:Number = 400;
var volumeMultiplier:Number = 1 - Math.min(Math.max(volDis -
   200, 0) / maxVolDis, 1);
```

The volDis variable contains the distance between the sound event and the center of the viewable portion of the map. The maxVolDis variable stores the number of pixels over which we want to have the volume taper off, after the 200-pixel max volume region. The final line above creates a normalized value—a value between 0 and 1. 1 is maximum volume, 0 is minimum. Usually it will be somewhere in between.

Here is the code that handles finding the pan setting:

```
var maxPanDis:Number = 400;
var panMultiplier:Number = (point2.x - point1.x) / maxPanDis;
panMultiplier = Math.max( -1, panMultiplier);
panMultiplier = Math.min(1, panMultiplier);
```

The maxPanDis variable stores the maximum horizontal distance that we use to vary the pan setting between -1 and 1. The normalized factor panMultiplier is created and then clamped to stay between -1 and 1. If the sound event occurs 400 pixels or more to the left of the center of the viewable map area, then the sound will play completely out of the left speaker; if greater than 400 pixels to the right, it will play out of the right speaker. Anywhere in between, it will vary in balance between the speakers.

The final line in this function is this:

```
return new SoundTransform(maxVolume * volumeMultiplier,
    panMultiplier);
```

A new SoundTransform object is created and returned. The volume and pan settings are set based on the normalized values calculated. The volume is the product of the max volume passed in and the volumeMultiplier.

Spatial audio—or even just varying volume dynamically in a game— can really help make the experience more immersive. You can try using dynamic volume in simpler games like pool. Not all collisions should sound the same. In a game like that, it would be good to vary the volume based on momentum transfer. In a virtual world, you can use the same technique discussed for this tank game. There is no need to have sounds that are barely offscreen play the same way as sounds closer to your area of focus.

CHAPTER 10

Tile-based Games

TILES HAVE BEEN used in video games since the beginning. We've all played tile-based games. Some old favorites are Donkey Kong, Pac-Man, and many of the Legend of Zelda games. Tiles are visual chunks that are positioned and reused throughout a game to make up the entire map. Using tiles has many benefits for game programmers and content developers.

You get a little multiplayer break in this chapter. The concepts discussed here are used in the game in Chapter 11 and in the virtual world discussed over the remainder of the book. We'll focus on outlining tile-based game concepts and the performance and game logic benefits they bring. We also cover A* pathfinding in detail, as this is used in many virtual worlds (including the one in this book).

Tile-based vs. Art-based Levels

Today most large-scale commercial games are 3D. They make heavy use of 3D models for the environment and for characters, which are rendered real-time. When dealing with a platform such as Flash, or many handheld devices that don't have the horsepower to render everything from 3D models, you need to find another way to build large game levels or areas of a world. We'll just call these things *levels*. There are two primary ways to build levels when not using 3D models: art-based and tile-based.

An art-based level is one that is just drawn by an artist or has objects laid out by hand (the tank game in Chapter 9 is an example of this). The developer must then figure out a custom way to program the game play so that it works with the art that was delivered. This approach can be time-consuming if it takes a lot of custom code to make the environment work the way it's supposed to. In the case of the tank game, we made some assumptions that simplified the necessary code.

NOTE *Some games choose to use hexagonal tiles. This is rare, but it happens.*

Tile-based levels are much more structured than art-based. A tile-based level is made up of individual tiles that are packed together in an ordered way to achieve the entire look of the level. In games that have a side view or top-down view, the arrangement is usually in a grid that lines up the screen's x and y axes—like Zelda games. In most tile-based virtual worlds, the tiles are diamond-shaped (discussed in Chapter 12).

You could take a hybrid approach between art-based and tile-based levels as well, using a large unique image as a background, but then choosing to use tiles for logical storage of data, character positioning, and collision detection. The virtual world worked on later in this book has a hybrid approach, though it still makes use of repeatable objects such as trees, rocks, and fences.

Some games allow for layers of tiles. You might have a grass layer and then lay many flower tiles on top of that. Tiles that are layered may make use of an alpha channel so that a layer blends well with the one beneath it. Look at the Precious Girls Club interface below. It has grass tiles with flower tiles layered on top.

Levels are one of the many benefits to using a tile-based approach in a game. Creating a level editor for a tile-based game is usually straightforward. It may take a lot of time to add fancy features like being able to copy and paste groups of tiles or being able to "paint" tiles onto the grid, but the basic level-editing code is shared with the game itself.

Other Tile-based Benefits

In this section, we discuss how tiles can help with the performance of an application and then how they can make some logic more convenient to implement.

Performance

There are several areas where using a tile-based implementation can help you maintain a high level of performance in your game. It allows you to handle world collision detection easily, enables high-performance world scrolling, keeps memory usage low, and gives you a convenient way to store data.

NOTE *All tiles within a tile-based world are the same size.*

Before we look at individual performance benefits, we need to introduce a simple math trick for determining what tile any given point is touching. Consider the following 4x4 grid of tiles, each 40 pixels tall and 40 pixels wide.

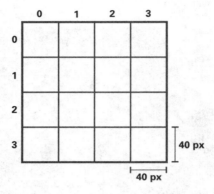

As characters, game items, or enemy opponents move throughout the world, you need to know what tile they are over, to assist with collision detection and game logic. So, given a point within the world, how can you tell which tile it is over? Simple—you look for the column number and the row number of the tile that the point is in.

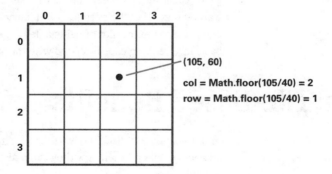

The trick for finding the column number that the point is over is:

```
var column:int = Math.floor(x/tileWidth);
```

And the row the point is over is:

```
var row:int = Math.floor(y/tileHeight);
```

Knowing the column and row that a point is in gives us access to the tile that the point is over.

Now we can move on to look at the other performance benefits of this approach. Most of the benefits are illustrated by comparing them to a non-tile-based approach.

COLLISION DETECTION

Collision detection is used in games to detect when a point is touching an object or when two objects are touching. This can be used to do things like determine when an item should be collected, like a key or a gem, or for determining if a projectile has hit an object. In non-tile-based games, checking for these collisions usually requires a distance check. If you are in a non-tile-based game and there are 1,000 coins to collect, then doing 1,000 distance checks per game loop could become very expensive.

But if you had 1,000 coins in a tile-based game, then checking for a collision is simple:

1   Get the tile that you are currently on.

2   Inspect the tile to see if it contains a coin. If it does, then collect it.

NOTE *This is not always the best way to handle collision detection. For example, you wouldn't handle precise collisions such as those between billiard balls in this fashion.*

This example shows how collision detection can be simplified to such an extent that its impact on the game is negligible.

SCROLLING

Most tile-based games are bigger than a single screen. As the main character moves, the screen scrolls to keep the character within view. If the map was huge—say, 20 times the size of the screen—then you could envision this becoming a performance problem. A level of that size in a non-tile-based game would likely all be rendered at once, even though you can see only one screen's worth at any time. And as the screen scrolls, the Flash player is moving all of that visual information.

In a tile-based game, you could have a similar performance hit if you don't take steps to address it. One of the benefits of the tile-base game is that you have a well-organized grid of visual data. As tiles move into and out of visible range, they can be added to and removed from the display list. If you handle scrolling this way, you are never rendering more than one screen's worth of tiles.

Sometimes programmers take this a step further and just use a single bitmap instance on the screen. All tiles are bitmaps and are drawn onto the main screen bitmap. As the level scrolls, you can use certain tricks to slide the pixels in the direction of scrolling while new pixels are added to the other side. When done properly, this is an extremely high-performance technique.

MEMORY USAGE

Tile-based games are made up of visual elements that are repeated throughout the level. While a level may have 10,000 tiles in it, those tiles are made up of maybe 100 unique pieces of reusable artwork. If handled properly, each time a version of a unique tile is used in the game, the same `BitmapData` class will be used. This allows the application to keep the memory usage low, since the `BitmapData` is a shared resource. Games where every item and occurrence is unique don't have this advantage, and will take up a substantially higher amount of memory.

DATA STORAGE

NOTE *There is no limit to the types of information that can be stored on a tile. Depending on the game, the tile could be used as a spawn point for enemies, a portal to another level, or just to hold collectible items.*

Typically in a tile-based game, there will be a class that represents an individual tile. That class is a convenient place to store information about that tile. It can store things like the image to show, what items are on that tile (such as a coin or other collectible item), and general tile properties. A typical tile property would be `isWalkable`. If the value of `isWalkable` is `true`, then a character can exist on that tile. If `false`, then the character cannot enter that tile. Another common property would be `isHittable`. If `true`, then a fired projectile will stop on that tile. If `false`, it will pass over the tile.

When to Run Logic

NOTE *While it is a good idea to check for collections, levers, etc. when the character hits the center of a tile, that isn't a good time to check if that character is allowed to enter a tile. That check is done before the walk begins.*

How does the application know when your character has collected a coin? We looked earlier at the concept of collision detection, but we didn't discuss *when* that condition should be checked. It is usually checked when the character arrives at the center of a tile. Doing the check at that point allows the application to do a little less work every game loop, and then perform the logic check when it is convenient.

A centrist approach

Many tile-based games make the tiles about the size of the main character that you control, and they only let the character stop at the center of a tile. If your character was at the center of a tile and decided to walk to the right, then the minimum distance it could go is to the center of the tile to the right. This type of control isn't always the case, but it is common. A few of the benefits discussed here are based on this approach.

Enemy AI is another area that benefits from running logic when it hits the center of a tile. AI can be programmed in an unlimited number of ways, but it really boils down to this: either the AI is following a predetermined path, or it is executing a pursuit algorithm. In either case, it only needs to figure out which tile to go to next the moment it hits the center of the tile it is already heading toward.

The final logic advantage I want to discuss is pathfinding. This benefit is not related to a character having to stop at the center of a tile. With a well-organized grid layout, we can logically search for a path between two tiles. If the path is used for moving a character, then A* is the usual choice (and the topic of the next section). If we are looking for a line of sight path (for traveling or shooting), then Bresenham's Line Algorithm is a great choice. Bresenham's Line Algorithm allows you to feed it a starting tile and an end tile, and it returns all tiles that a line drawn between the two would touch. We don't use it anywhere in this book, but it is worth reading about elsewhere!

A* Pathfinding

In some art-based (not tile-based) virtual worlds, such as Club Penguin or Gaia Online, pathfinding is achieved by just walking in a straight line toward wherever the user clicked. Before you jump to the immediate conclusion "that's line of sight!"—don't. The line may pass through an obstacle, yet the avatar walks along it anyway until it hits the obstacle, and then it stops. At that point, the user has to use several shorter paths to walk around the obstacle and continue on the path that was originally intended.

NOTE *While A* is used not only for pathfinding, we use it only for pathfinding, so that is how we'll refer to it for this chapter and the rest of the book—as a pathfinding algorithm.*

If that is the type of pathfinding you want for your world, you'll be happy to know that it is mind-numbingly easy to implement. But personally, I find this approach frustrating. There is another pathfinding approach that uses tiles which is far superior: A*. A* is an algorithm used to find the lowest-cost series of state changes between an initial state of a system and a target state of a system. (We'll discuss what *cost* means soon.)

We'll look at the features of the algorithm, at the pseudo code that represents it, and, finally, at an example.

Concept

As applied to pathfinding in a tile-based world, A* takes a starting tile and a goal tile and then inspects the grid to determine the lowest-cost path of tiles that links the start and end. We'll talk about cost below, but for most purposes, the lowest-cost path is also the shortest-distance path.

The algorithm works by inspecting the tiles surrounding the start tile and then intelligently fanning out in a direction that is most likely going to be part of the end path. This is one of the important differences between A* and other pathfinding algorithms: many of the others don't direct the search in any particular direction; they just stop when they hit the goal.

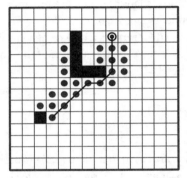

One of the coolest (but rarely used) features of A* is that it can be configured to take terrain into account! The shortest path may not be the best path if it goes through tiles that aren't desirable. We'll dig into this coming up.

As with many technical concepts, the A* algorithm uses a handful of terms you should be familiar with in order to proceed. These terms describe the states, actions, and results that go along with this process:

- A *node* is the tile that you are currently inspecting.

- The act of *expanding* a node means that (in code) you visit each of the node's neighbors.

- A *heuristic*, in A*, is an educated guess, based on a chosen unit of measurement, that yields a number. (Pretty vague, right? We will talk more about heuristics soon.)

- The *cost* is a numeric amount that you assign to the act of moving from one node to another.

- The *score* is made of the sum of the cost and heuristic of every node you visited along the path to the current node.

With these terms in place, let's see how they apply to the algorithm, and more generally, how A* works. As you now know, A* finds the shortest path between two points. But what measurement are we using? Time? Distance? Number of steps? While A* can be used to search according to pretty much any measurement, we choose to use distance. Other measurements might be time (to find the path that takes the shortest time to walk) or the number of tanks of gas used (to find the path that uses the smallest amount of gas in a car). To the cost of moving between one tile and its vertical or horizontal neighbor, we assign a value of 1 (1 foot, 1 mile, 1 tile—it doesn't matter). The cost of moving between one tile and a neighboring diagonal tile is 1.41. The number 1.41 is the distance between the centers of two neighboring diagonal tiles, which is the square root of 2.

The heuristic is the best guess of the cost of moving from the current tile to the goal tile. You can use whatever assumptions and logic that you want to drive this heuristic value, but in A*, used for shortest-path pathfinding, the heuristic is usually the "as the crow flies" distance from the current tile to the goal tile. The heuristic is the best guess of how far is the center of the current tile (that you are inspecting during the search) from the destination tile. You can make this guess fairly easily using simple logic. When visited, each node is assigned a score of f:

$$f = g + h$$

The value h is the heuristic—the best guess of the distance between that tile and the goal. The value g is the sum of the scores of every node visited along the path to the current node. This may be best understood with an analogy. Let's say you are planning a trip from New York to Paris. You are on a tight budget, so you want to find the path that will cost the least. You can think of New York, London, Lisbon, Brussels, Madrid, and Paris as nodes. In the course of your research, you calculate the cost from New York to London and store that. But you also calculate the costs of traveling from Lisbon to New York, London to Paris, and so on. In the end, if you apply other rules (not yet discussed) with A*, you find the best path (for cost). Let's assume that this path turns out to be New York–Madrid–London–Paris. In New York (as in all nodes), $f = g + h$. Remember that g is the sum of all the fs of the previous nodes. Since New York is the starting node, there are no parents, so $g = 0$ in New York. Then you move on to Madrid, where $g \neq 0$, because it was visited from another node. The g value is made up of the f from New York. So g is the running total of cost up to the current

> **NOTE** *The straight-line heuristic calculation here is either precisely the right value, or it is too low (if there are walls in the way). So this type of heuristic is considered to be an underestimation of the cost. If a heuristic is an underestimation, it is guaranteed to lead to the lowest-cost path, but the search might take a while. An overestimation will still lead to a path, and it might do it more quickly than the underestimation, but it might not be the lowest-cost path.*

node. If you were actually on this trip, then g would be the amount of money spent up to your current position.

Remember that A* handles terrain as well as distance. Above, I said that the cost of going from one tile to the next is either 1 or 1.41. That is true if all tiles are equally desirable to become part of the final path. Let's say some of the tiles are made up of water. Chances are you probably don't want to send your character through the water unless it is absolutely necessary. So you then assign a cost of, let's say, 10 to any inter-node transition that involves water. This doesn't guarantee that the path won't go through the water, but it will give extreme preference to paths that don't. If the water is a stream going completely through the map and there is no bridge, then A* will certainly end up giving you a path through the water. However, if there is a bridge, and it is close enough, then A* will give you a path that includes the bridge. Alternatively, if your character is half man and half fish, he may prefer water. In this case, you may give land a lower cost than water. However, in most usages, all tiles are given the same preference, and so the path with the lowest score also happens to be the shortest path.

Pseudo Code

We've discussed the general concept of A* and how it works. But we haven't looked at the detailed decision-making that happens within the algorithm. Below you will find pseudo code for the algorithm. Following that is a line-by-line description of what it is doing.

```
1   AStar.Search
2       create open array
3       create closed array
4       s.g = 0
5       s.h = findHeuristic(s.x, s.y)
6       s.f = s.g + s.h
7       s.parent = null
8       push s into open array
9       set keepSearching to true
10      while keepSearching
11          pop node n from open
12          if n is the goal node
13              build path from start to finish
14              set keepSearching to false
15          for each neighbor m of n
16              newg = n.g + cost(n, newx, newy)
```

```
17                    if m has not been visited
18                        m.g = n.f
19                        m.h = findHeuristic(newx, newy)
20                        m.f = m.g + m.h
21                        m.parent = n
22                        add it to the open array
23                        sort the open array
24                    else
25                        if newg < m.g
26                            m.parent = n
27                            m.g = newg
28                            m.f = m.g + m.h
29                            sort the open array
30              push n into the closed array
31              if search time > max time
32                  set keepSearching to false
33      return path
```

This algorithm makes use of two lists (which are arrays in Flash): open and closed. The open array contains the nodes that have at one time been visited. The closed array contains all nodes that have been expanded (that is, all of its neighbors have been visited). We use the open array as a *priority queue*—not only to store nodes, but also to store them in a certain order. We keep the array sorted from lowest score (*f*) to highest score. Every time we add a node to the open array or change the value of *g* in a node in the open array, we must re-sort the array so that the nodes are in order from lowest to highest score.

In lines 2 and 3 of the pseudo code, we create the (empty) open and closed arrays. In pathfinding we need a starting place and a destination, so that comes next. *S* is an object that represents the starting node. We set s.g to 0, since the starting node has no parents, so the cost (*g*) to get to it is 0 (line 4). Next, we find the heuristic *h* for the start node. (Remember that the heuristic is the estimated cost from the current node to the goal.) We then store the value of *f*, which is the sum of s.g and s.h, on the starting node (line 6). Since s has no parents, we set s.parent to null. Next, we push the s node into the open array (line 8). The s node is now the first and only node in the open array.

In line 9 we set the variable keepSearching to true. While it remains true, we will keep performing the A* search. When we have determined that we have found a path, that no path exists, or that we have been searching for too long, we set `keepSearching` to `false`.

In line 11 we take a node from the priority queue. We then check to see if this node is the goal. If it is, we have reached the goal; we then stop search-ing, and build the path (lines 12–14). If it is not the goal, we expand the node. Expanding the node means that we visit each of the node's neighbors. In line 16 we find the *g* of the neighbor node, *m*, that we are currently looking at. We then check to see if this node has ever been visited. If it has not yet been visited, then we enter the portion of the algorithm in lines 18–23. We set the value of *g* on *m;* it is the *f* from its parent, *n*. Next we calculate and store the heuristic and *f* on *m*. Finally, we set the parent property to be that of the previous node, *n*. If this node has been visited before and now has a lower *g*, then we enter the portion of the algorithm in lines 25–31.

At this point I want to mention something more about *g*. When a node is first visited, it is assigned a *g* based on the path taken to get to that node (as we have already discussed). But it is possible—even likely—that that node will be visited again during the search through another possible path. If the *g* from this new path is lower than the *g* from the previously stored path, then we replace the old *g* with the new *g* (line 27). In line 26 we set the parent property of *m* to be the node that we are coming from. The parent property is what we use at the end of the search to construct the final path. We can move from the goal node all the way back to the starting position by following the parent properties. Next, we recalculate the *f* and then have to re-sort the open array. We do this because we have just updated one of the nodes with a lower *f*, so this node may now take priority over another.

After all of the neighbors of *n* are visited, we move on to line 30. In this line we push *n* onto the closed array because it has been completely expanded. We then check the time to make sure that we haven't been searching for too long. If we have been searching too long, then we set keepSearching to `false`. Otherwise, we move on to the next node in the queue (line 11). If keepSearching is `false`, we stop searching and build the path.

You have now been formally introduced to A*! Don't feel bad if you are hav-ing trouble understanding the algorithm; it is not the easiest thing in the world to grasp. It took me several articles on the Internet before I felt like I fully understood basic A*.

Pathfinding Example

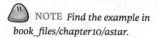 NOTE *Find the example in book_files/chapter10/astar.*

Now it's time to look at an example that uses A*. I created a file that allows you to customize a small 20x15 grid and test the outcome of an A* search on it.

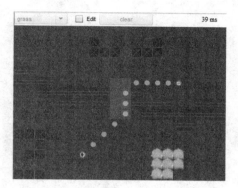

Let's look at the features of the example file before we talk about the code and how to use the A* utility classes.

FEATURES

This example has two modes: Edit and Test. You can switch between them by clicking the Edit checkbox. The example initializes with a predefined layout, in case you want to test but not edit.

To test, simply click on any tile to establish a starting point, and then click on any other tile to establish a goal tile. The application will immediately run the A* search and find the lowest-cost path that links the two tiles. You will also see the search time for the path show up in a text field at the top. Most paths will take between about 10ms and 100ms to find. A* is not super-fast, but that is all right, since in most usages it has to be run only once every few seconds.

Notice that this example contains multiple terrain types. We list them here along with their level of desirability for being used in a path. A little later we'll look at the transition costs for each as well.

- Grass—Most desirable

- Bridge—As desirable as grass

- Water—Less desirable, but OK if necessary

- Fire—Avoid unless it's the only path that exists

- Wall—Avoid unless the it's the only path that exists

A* in action

Look at the following three images to see A* in action.

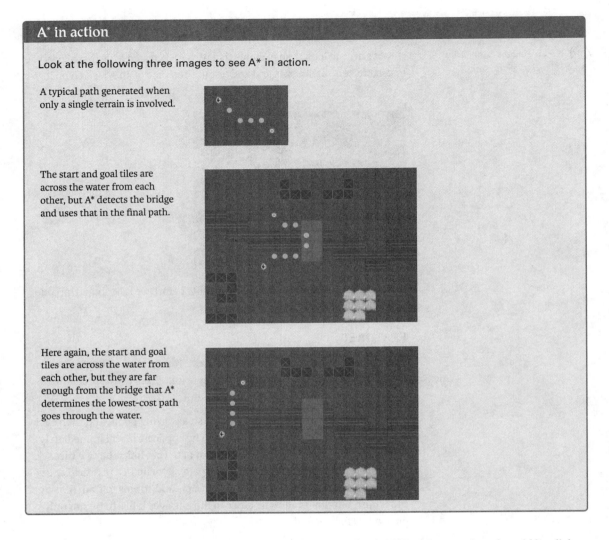

A typical path generated when only a single terrain is involved.

The start and goal tiles are across the water from each other, but A* detects the bridge and uses that in the final path.

Here again, the start and goal tiles are across the water from each other, but they are far enough from the bridge that A* determines the lowest-cost path goes through the water.

To edit the layout, click the Edit checkbox. You can clear the grid by clicking the Clear button. Change tiles by selecting a terrain type from the dropdown list and then clicking on the tile you want to change. After you've configured the grid the way you want, deselect the Edit checkbox, and test.

NOTE *The A* utility code lives in the com.gamebook.utils.astar package.*

THE CODE

Now let's look at some of the code that goes into this example. We will not go through the code that makes up the A* algorithm, rather just how it is used.

For an application to make use of the A* utility code, it must have a class that implements the ISearchable interface, and all tiles must implement the INode interface. The ISearchable interface ensures that certain methods and properties are exposed so that it can be searched by the Astar class. The INode interface ensures that all tiles contain information useful to the search, such as storing a terrain type or the current cost during the search.

When a search is needed, an instance of the Astar class is created, a reference to the class that implements ISearchable is set, and then the search method is called, passing in the start and goal nodes. This method returns an instance of the SearchResults class.

The SearchResults class contains a property indicating if the search returned any path at all. If it did, then it also contains that path, which is an instance of the Path class.

The Path class contains an array of all tiles used in the path, including the end points. It also contains the total cost of the path, which is something you probably won't use.

At a high level, that is what you need to know. Your application implements the two classes ISearchable and INode, then uses the Astar class to perform a search, and finally uses the SearchResults instance returned to apply the results.

So now let's look at what it means to implement INode, and then we'll look at ISearchable. The Tile class in this example implements INode. The INode interface requires that the following methods exist in Tile:

- getCol—Returns the column of the tile

- getRow—Returns the row of the tile

- getNodeType—Returns the terrain type of the tile, such as grass or water

- setHeuristic / getHeuristic—Set and retrieved during a search; you don't need to do anything

- setNodeId / getNodeId—Set and retrieved during a search to allow for quicker tile lookups

- setNeighbors / getNeighbors—Set and retrieved during a search to speed up the process of finding which tiles neighbor the one currently being inspected

The Tile class contains all of the methods listed above. Since it meets the INode interface, it can successfully be used during an A* search.

Now let's look at the ISearchable interface. The Grid class in this example implements ISearchable, which requires the following methods to exist:

- getCols—Returns the total number of columns in the grid

- getRows—Returns the total number of rows in the grid

- getNode—When fed a column and a row, returns the tile (which implements INode) at that location

- getNodeTransitionCost—When fed two INode instances, returns the transition cost

When the Astar class is performing the search, it uses the above methods. The first three are straightforward. The getNodeTransitionCost method is one that deserves some attention. Here is that method in the Grid class:

```
public function getNodeTransitionCost(n1:INode,
n2:INode):Number {
  var cost:Number = costs[n1.getNodeType() + n2.getNodeType()];
  return cost;
}
```

You can see that it accepts two nodes and returns a transition cost for them. For example, if it was given two grass tiles, it would return a very low cost: 1. Notice that it finds the cost by concatenating the two terrain types into a unique key, which is used to look it up on the costs object. Let's look at the full list of terrain transition costs:

```
costs["grassgrass"] = 1;
costs["bridgebridge"] = 1;
costs["bridgegrass"] = 1;
costs["grassbridge"] = 1;
costs["grasswall"] = 1000000;
costs["wallgrass"] = 1000000;
costs["bridgewall"] = 1000000;
costs["wallbridge"] = 1000000;
```

```
costs["watergrass"] = 1;
costs["bridgewater"] = 10;
costs["waterbridge"] = 1000000;
costs["grasswater"] = 10;
costs["waterwater"] = 1;
costs["wallwall"] = 1000000;
costs["firefire"] = 1000000;
costs["firewater"] = 1;
costs["firewall"] = 1000000;
costs["firegrass"] = 1;
costs["firebridge"] = 1;
costs["waterfire"] = 1000000;
costs["wallfire"] = 1000000;
costs["grassfire"] = 1000000;
costs["bridgefire"] = 1000000;
```

In the long list above, we use one of three values. A cost of 1 means the transition is desirable, a cost of 10 means that it is not desirable but can be used if needed, and a cost of 1,000,000 is used when a transition is highly undesirable.

NOTE The values listed for the transition costs are not right or wrong. This is where game design comes in—you're in charge; you can modify the costs to get the behavior you want for your game.

The basic logic behind this list boils down to a few simple facts: The transition of anything to grass is 1. The cost of grass to water is 10 (less desirable but still OK if needed). Water to water is a cost of 1. Once wet, it is OK (low cost) to stay wet until the path goes out of the water. This is unlike fire—a fire-to-fire transition is still very high. No matter what, you want to stop burning. This ensures that in the unlikely event you do have a path through a fire, A* is still going to minimize the time in the fire.

The best path in this situation—that is to say, the lowest-cost path, that gets the guy out of the fire as quickly as possible—is not the shortest path.

The last thing to look at is the code used to actually perform the search. In this example, the `Grid` class also contains a UI and the code to invoke the search and show the results of that search. When start and goal positions are established and a search is to be performed, the search method of the `Grid` class is called. Here is some of the code in that method:

```
var astar:Astar = new Astar(this);
var results:SearchResults = astar.search(INode(startTile),
➝ INode(goalTile));
if (results.getIsSuccess()) {
  var path:Path = results.getPath();
  for (var i:int=0;i<path.getNodes().length;++i) {
      var t:Tile = Tile(path.getNodes()[i]);
      t.showPath();
  }
}
```

The first line creates a new instance of the `Astar` class, passing in `this`, which is a reference to the `ISearchable` class. The next line invokes the search method on the `Astar` class instance by passing in the start and goal tiles. If the search successfully returns a path, then it is iterated over to make it (the path) show up on the screen.

You may wonder why the `SearchResults` class contains a success property—why wouldn't it return a path? A search could take a long time to run. Generally speaking, it should be under 100ms. But if the grid is large and complex, it could take seconds. Since Flash isn't threaded (meaning that it can only do one thing at a time), a multi-second search will freeze the application until it is complete. The `Astar` class lets you specify a timeout value. The default value is 2 seconds. If a search takes longer than 2 seconds, it automatically stops, and returns the `SearchResults` instance with a success property of `false`.

> NOTE *A* is heavily used in games, so there's a lot of information available on the web and in books about making it faster or using it in more unique ways. The book* Artificial Intelligence for Games *by Ian Millington is a good place to learn more on this topic.*

CHAPTER 11

Cooperative Game Play

NOT ALL MULTIPLAYER games pit players against each other. Cooperative game play allows players to work together as teammates to accomplish a common goal. This type of game play can offer challenges that are not possible in single player games or in competitive style multiplayer games.

With few exceptions (like Army of Two), multiplayer games do not offer purely cooperative game play. Instead, cooperative elements are tacked on to the existing game design. For example, an FPS may have a "Capture the Flag" mode in addition to the standard "Deathmatch."

In this chapter, we'll discuss various cooperative game concepts, and look at one example in detail: Super Blob Brothers. In this game, players must act collaboratively in order to reach the end of a level.

Let's get started by inspecting several types of cooperative game play.

Types and Styles of Cooperative Game Play

Cooperative games fall into one of several categories, and sometimes also into different *styles* of game play.

Categories of Cooperation

The category of a cooperative game is based on who or what the players are cooperating against. Each category brings together a set of unique game-play elements and dictates the type of goal needed for that game type. No game has to fall completely within any one of these categories—in fact, it's common for games to employ a mix of these game-play elements. Let's look at the three major categories of cooperative games.

PLAYERS VS. PLAYERS

Many cooperative games offer a variant on competitive game play by allowing teams of players to compete against each other. First Person Shooters (FPS) are a common example of Players vs. Players. Note that this style of game play differs very little from pure competitive game play in terms of game mechanics. Cooperation comes in the form of coordinating attacks to vanquish the opposing players.

Examples of Players vs. Players game play include Quake (players on the same team try to rack up the most kills), Command and Conquer (any one team attacks and defends against any other team), and Wii Tennis (a two-on-two competition for the highest score).

PLAYERS VS. AI

In Players vs. AI, teammates take on artificial enemies controlled by the game. In addition to First Person Shooters, RPGs and platform games fall into this category. Players have to cooperate with each other to attack specific targets in unison or to combat against the sheer volume of enemies. You'll find that many games use some form of Players vs. AI—from Contra to Diablo, players team up to take on hordes of enemies generated by the game itself.

PLAYERS VS. ENVIRONMENT

Players vs. Environment game play allows teammates to tackle challenges created by the very nature of their surroundings. Rather than taking on enemies, players must solve puzzles or manage resources. As an example, players may have to cooperate by standing on two tiles at once to open a locked door. The Legend of Zelda: Four Swords includes elements of this type of cooperation, as well as the example game for this chapter, Super Blob Brothers.

Styles of Cooperation

There are many ways to introduce cooperative game play into multiplayer games. In this section, we attempt to categorize similar styles of game play. Again, remember that most games don't fall entirely into any one category.

SYMMETRIC ABILITIES: MORE OF THE SAME

In this style of game play, players have the exact same abilities. More players mean more power in numbers. Two players with two machine guns deal out twice the damage.

Having extra teammates means that it is easier to take down a really powerful enemy. It would also be easier to tackle swarms of enemies that attack in large numbers.

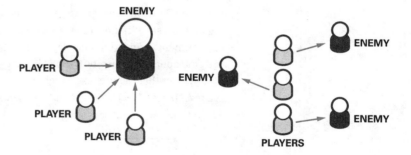

The vast majority of multiplayer coop games fall into this category, including FPSs such as Halo and Quake, shoot-'em-ups such as Metal Slug and Contra, and vertical shooters such as 1942 and Raiden.

ASYMMETRIC ABILITIES: SYMBIOSIS

In this style of cooperative game play, players must support each other through the use of unique abilities. For example, one player may be able to attack at short ranges and deal massive damage, while another player can use ranged weapons that deal less damage but can be used from afar.

Games that exhibit this style of game play are often fully playable without the addition of the supportive teammate. It is rare to find a multiplayer game that truly requires complementing abilities to be used in order to successfully progress through the game.

Games such as Gauntlet and World of Warcraft offer some elements of asymmetric abilities. In these games, players must choose a class that will determine the set of skills at their disposal.

RESOURCE MANAGEMENT: YOU HAVE WHAT I NEED

In this category of game play, players may have the same set of abilities but may have access to differing resources. Players must work together to trade needed resources in order to accomplish a common goal. As an example, imagine Player 1 has access to fuel that can power Player 2's tanks. In turn, Player 2 is positioned near valuable ore that Player 1 needs in order to power generators.

MECHANICAL COMPLEXITY

In this final category, we group games that include challenges requiring an extra set of hands (or claws, or whatever). The layout of the game environment is such that one player alone cannot progress successfully. Imagine doors that must be opened by using two keycards at once, or a dumbwaiter that requires the weight of two players in order to descend to the level below. Mechanical complexity goes hand in hand with Player vs. Environment-type game play.

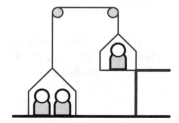

The Game: Super Blob Brothers

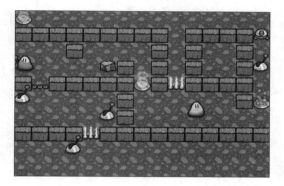 **NOTE** *Find the files for this game in book_files/chapter11/ blob_bros_game.*

Super Blob Brothers is a two-player game of the type Players vs. Environment. Elements of the Mechanical Complexity style are used to force players to work together. Notice how common mechanics that are familiar to players, such as pushing a rock, take on a unique twist when teamwork is required. Old game-play mechanics are now fresh and challenging!

In Super Blob Bros., players must traverse each level in order to reach the Goal Pad. Many obstacles will stand in the way, including gates, rocks, and laser towers (the properties of which we'll discuss below). Both players must stand on the Goal Pad in order to progress to the next level. The game ends in victory when all levels are completed. If either player's number of lives drops to zero, the game ends in defeat.

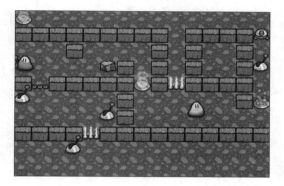

Cooperation is required, since most obstacles can't be overcome by one player alone. For example, players must open gates for each other to clear a path to the goal.

There are two types of players: Defender and Attacker. The server automatically chooses your player type for you. You will always have the opposite type from your teammate. The Defender will automatically transform into a shield when targeted by a laser tower, making himself impervious to laser beams. The Attacker transforms into a sword when placed within striking distance of a laser tower in order to destroy it. In this way, the two player's abilities complement each other. They need to work together to survive and progress.

Each player has three lives. If a player dies with lives remaining, the player will respawn at the beginning of the level or at the last saved respawn point.

In this game, you control one of two blob brothers using the arrow keys on your keyboard. The view is top-down, and the game play is tile based.

Here are the obstacles you and your partner will encounter:

Stasis Gates and Levers—Stasis Gates are impassable when activated. Stasis Gates have corresponding Levers that will deactivate the gate. Place your blob near a Lever in order to pull the lever and toggle the gate. Note that Levers are heavy! Walking away from a Lever will allow it to flip back into its default position, thus reactivating the gate.

Laser Towers—Laser Towers will fire laser beams at your blob if you are unfortunate enough to step on the corresponding glowing red Trigger Pad. Once a laser tower locks on to your blob, its laser beam cannot be avoided. Defenders have the luxury of stepping on Trigger Pads with no fear of damage, but Attackers will be killed.

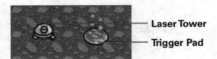

Rocks—Rocks are obstacles that often block a blob's passage or stand in the way of a pad or lever. Luckily, your blobs can move rocks by pushing them. Due to the great weight of rocks, both players must push in unison (and in the same direction) in order to get the rock to budge. Pushing a rock will cause it to slide over one tile at a time.

Save Pad—Glowing yellow Save Pads act as save points. Walking over a Save Pad will update your respawn point so that you won't have to backtrack. Note that only one player needs to reach a save point in order to activate it.

Save Pad (yellow)

Goal Pad—Glowing green Goal Pads mark the end of each level. Reaching this pad is the entire objective. But there's a catch! Both players must be standing on the Goal Pad at the same time in order to progress to the next level. You've got to be really careful to ensure that both you and your teammate have access to the Goal Pad.

Goal pad (green)

Now that you are familiar with the mechanics of the game, notice how Super Blob Bros. compares to other games you may be familiar with. If you have played "Adventures of LoLo" or "The Legend of Zelda," then you are familiar with this style of game play. Again, note how a whole new dimension is added when the game becomes multiplayer! In addition to the traps and puzzles, coordination with your teammate becomes an obstacle.

Server vs. Client: Who's the Boss?

In all multiplayer games, a developer has to make a decision as to what game mechanics are to be managed by the server and what features can be left under the control of the client. This topic was discussed in detail in Chapter 6. Due to the fact that Super Blob Bros. is all about cooperation rather than competition, it is not as critical to put the server in control of every detail. Compare this to a Player vs. Player game, where competition may drive players to resort to any means necessary to gain even the smallest edge. In those cases, it's important for the server to validate moves. In our game, however, cheating isn't so much of a concern, so we use the server only when necessary. Client/server requirements vary from game to game, but you should take care to choose the right balance for a specific game's needs.

With that being said, let's look at how the client and server work together for Super Blob Bros.

Client

The client tells the server:

- Details about level initialization
- My player's location
- When my player dies
- When my player reaches a Save Pad
- When my player reaches the Goal Pad
- When my player reaches a Trigger Pad
- When my player is attempting to toggle a lever
- When my player is attempting to push a rock
- When my player destroys a Laser Tower

Server

The server tells the clients:

- If a lever has been toggled successfully
- The state of Stasis Gates
- If a rock can or cannot be pushed
- When a Laser Tower should fire
- When a level has been completed
- The number of lives remaining for each player
- If the respawn point has been updated
- When and where to respawn
- When the game is over

Understanding the Game Elements

In this section, we'll examine a few of the key game elements and, through them, come to better understand the relationship between the client and the server in this game.

SWITCHES: LEVERS, PADS, AND GATES

The concept of a switch is used to control several game elements that can be toggled on or off. In Super Blob Bros., switches are used to control Levers, Goal Pads, and Trigger Pads. Each of these elements is either off or on. One or more players interacting with a switch toggles it to on.

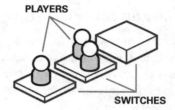

Here's how levers and pads behave as switches:

- Levers: pulled = on, not pulled = off

- Pads: depressed = on, not depressed = off

Stasis Gates are closely tied to Levers. Any Stasis Gate can have zero or more Levers. Pulling one or more Levers will deactivate the corresponding Stasis Gate. Letting go of a Lever will reactivate the Stasis Gate if no other Levers tied to that Stasis Gate are pulled.

> **NOTE** *Remember, as stated previously, a Lever is a type of switch. Pulling a Lever can result in the deactivation of a Stasis Gate. Pulling a subsequent Lever tied to the same gate will result in a successful switch flip, but the state of the gate will remain the same.*

Since a Lever can only be pulled or not pulled, the server needs to keep up with the state of the lever and reflect that state on the screens of both players. If Player 1 pulls a Lever, Player 2 cannot pull it again until all players have released the lever. Player 2 can, however, hold the Lever to keep it toggled while Player 1 walks away.

The server is required to determine if one or more Levers are toggled. If so, the Stasis Gate remains deactivated. Only when all Levers have been released will the server tell the clients to reactivate the Stasis Gate.

ROCKS

Since rocks can only be successfully pushed by two players in unison, the server needs to determine if both players are pushing a rock in the same direction. Each client tells the server that it is pushing a specific rock, along with the direction of the push. If both clients are pushing in the same direction, the server tells the clients that the rock has been moved. If either client tells the server that he or she is no longer pushing, then the rock cannot be moved.

SAVE PADS AND RESPAWN POINTS

Clients tell the server when a Save Pad has been reached. The server saves the location of the Save Pad. Upon a player's death, the server tells the player to respawn after a given time interval. The server sends the location of the Save Pad, along with the respawn message.

GOAL PAD AND LEVEL COMPLETION

Clients tell the server when a Goal Pad has been reached. Since both players are required to stand on the Goal Pad at the same time in order to complete a level, the server keeps up with how many players are on the Goal Pad. When the player count for the Goal Pad reaches 2, a "Level Complete" message is sent to both clients.

Game Messaging

As in other examples, the client and server communicate by sending formatted EsObjects to each other. Each EsObject contains an `ACTION` variable that is used to indicate the purpose of the message, along with any other required data for the message. The following table contains a list of each of Super Blob Brothers' messages and a description of each.

Game Messages and Descriptions for Super Blob Brothers

MESSAGE	DIRECTION	PURPOSE/ACTION
INIT_LEVEL	Client to server / Server to client	When client has joined the room successfully and is ready to receive game data, sends info about board state to the server. Each client sends this information, but only the first set is used.
		Server sends information about board state back to both clients so that both players are working with the same data.
INIT_ME	Client to server	When client has received data about the board state and used that data to initialize the game, client tells server that it is ready to start.
PLAYER_LIST	Server to client	When a client joins the game, server sends list of all previously existing players to the client.

Game Messages and Descriptions for Super Blob Brothers *(continued)*

MESSAGE	DIRECTION	PURPOSE/ACTION
ADD_PLAYER	Server to client	Sent to all clients when a new player joins the game. Also sent for each player at the beginning of each new level.
REMOVE_PLAYER	Server to client	Sent to all clients when a player leaves the game.
POSITION_UPDATE	Client to server / Server to client	When a player uses the arrow keys to move to a new location, the new location is sent to server. Position updates are sent every half-second while player is in motion. Server stores the new position and sends this information back to client so that location of teammates can be matched to the server.
FLIP_SWITCH	Client to server / Server to client	When a player attempts to toggle a switch, the attempt is sent to server. Server validates the attempt against the known state of the switch. Success or failure in flipping the switch is sent back to the client, along with information about what the switch affected.
DESTROY_TOWER	Client to server / Server to client	Client tells server to destroy a Tower. Server validates data and saves new state of Tower. State of Tower is then sent back to clients so that graphics can reflect that Tower is destroyed. Since server stores the fact that Tower is now destroyed, all subsequent messages sent by client to fire the laser will be ignored.
PUSH_ROCK	Client to server / Server to client	Tells server that client is attempting to push a rock, where to push the rock to, and in what direction. Same message is used again by client to tell server when it stops trying to push the rock. Server validates data to see if two players are pushing at same time and in same direction. Server uses this message to report whether or not a rock can be moved successfully and to what new location.
PLAYER_DIED	Client to server / Server to client	Tells server when my player dies. Server tells all clients about the death, and decrements number of lives of deceased player.
REVIVE_ME	Server to client	When a player dies, if there are remaining lives, the player is resurrected after a brief interval. This message tells all clients to respawn client in a specific location on board.
UPDATE_SPAWN_LOCATION	Client to server	When a player walks over a Save Pad, this message is used to tell the server the location of that Save Pad. Server stores the location and uses it for each subsequent respawn of any player.
LEVEL_COMPLETE	Client to server / Server to client	When a player reaches Goal Pad, this message informs server that client is standing on Goal Pad. If the player moves off Goal Pad, the message is resent to server notifying server that player is no longer on Goal Pad. Only when both players are standing on Goal Pad at the same time does server send this message back to all clients informing them that level has been completed.
GAME_OVER	Server to client	When any player's number of lives drops to zero, server tells all clients that game is over. Server also reports who lost the game for everyone.
ERROR	Server to client	Sent to client if something goes wrong.

Client-side Details

As we've determined in the last section, in Super Blob Bros., a lot of the action is happening on the client. Let's take a look at a few noteworthy details.

Level Initialization

Levels are defined via an XML file that is loaded by the client. The XML for each level includes information about the board size, starting position of the players, position of game elements, and relationships between switches and gates.

Player Positions

Super Blob Bros. uses the "Here I am" technique that is presented in Chapter 7. We chose this method because of its ease of use and because the game play doesn't require ultra-precise synchronization. It is OK for clients to show player positions that are slightly out of sync for a moment, as long as they catch up to each other.

 NOTE Game.as *is not the same file as* coopgame.as.

Each client sends its own player's position every half-second, as seen in the following code block, found in Game.as in the enterFrame method. Notice that the position is not sent if a player has not moved, as this would be unnecessary communication with the server.

```
//send a position update every 500ms
if (getTimer() - _lastTimeSent > 500) {
        if (_myPlayer.x != _myPlayer.lastReportedX ||
        ➞ _myPlayer.y != _myPlayer.lastReportedY) {
        dispatchEvent(new PositionUpdateEvent
        ➞  (PositionUpdateEvent.POSITION_UPDATE, _myPlayer.x,
        ➞ _myPlayer.y));
        _myPlayer.lastReportedX = x;
        _myPlayer.lastReportedY = y;
    }
    _lastTimeSent = getTimer();
}
```

Switches, Gates, and Towers

Recall that we are using the concept of a switch for Levers, Trigger Pads, and Goal Pads. When a player enters a tile that contains a switch, that player will automatically attempt to toggle that switch on. When this happens, a message is sent to the server about the attempt.

In order to determine if a tile contains a switch, we store the ID of the switch on the tile when the game is initialized, and call it the "trigger." If a tile has no switch, the value for the `trigger` defaults to `-1`. Any time a player changes tiles, we check for the affected switches.

Not only do we alert the server when we enter a tile with a switch, we also tell the server when we leave that tile. The server will then set the switch back to its default state. Luckily, we can use the same event and send the same message to the server. We pass a Boolean value of `false` to turn a switch off and `true` to turn a switch on. The following code can be found in `Game.as` in the `checkKeys` method:

```
// handle any triggers
if (currentTile.trigger > -1) {
  dispatchEvent(new AttemptToggleSwitchEvent
  ➙ (AttemptToggleSwitchEvent.TOGGLE_SWITCH,
  ➙ currentTile.trigger, false));
}

if (attemptedTile.trigger > -1) {
  dispatchEvent(new AttemptToggleSwitchEvent
  ➙ (AttemptToggleSwitchEvent.TOGGLE_SWITCH,
  ➙ attemptedTile.trigger, true));
  _soundManager.playSound(SoundManager.STRAIN);
}
```

Also note that we play a sound when attempting to toggle a switch into the on position. This trick gives the illusion that the player is straining to pull the Lever. Remember that, because we are using the "Here I am" approach, it is possible for your teammate's position to be slightly out of sync for a short period of time. To avoid any mishaps, the server delays sending the toggle message for one second when a switch is used as a Lever for a Stasis Gate. This allows all players to be in place when the message comes back to the clients.

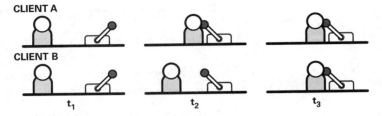

CLIENT A

CLIENT B

t_1 t_2 t_3

Next, we send a message about the switch state to the server. Along with this, we will also pass its ID so that the server can identify which switch we are attempting to toggle. To do so, we use the following function (in CoopGame.as):

```
private function onToggleSwitchAttempt(atse:AttemptToggleSwitch
➤ Event):void {
  trace("onToggleSwitch: " + atse.switchId + ", " + atse.isOn);

  var esob:EsObject = new EsObject();
  esob.setString(PluginConstants.ACTION, PluginConstants.
  ➤ FLIP_SWITCH);
  esob.setInteger(PluginConstants.SWITCH_ID, atse.switchId);
  esob.setInteger(PluginConstants.SWITCH_STATE, atse.isOn ==
true ? 1 : 0);
  sendToPlugin(esob);
}
```

Next, after doing some validation on our attempt to toggle the switch, the server sends back a message with the actual state of the switch. If any Stasis Gate or Tower was tied to the switch, the message will also include information about the state of that item. The function for communicating this information back to the client is located in CoopGame.as:

```
private function handleFlipSwitch(esob:EsObject):void {
  // the switch that was flipped
  var switchId:int = esob.getInteger(PluginConstants.
  ➤ SWITCH_ID);
  var switchState:int = esob.getInteger(PluginConstants.
  ➤ SWITCH_STATE);
  _game.toggleSwitch(switchId, switchState);

  // who fliped it?
  var playerNameWhoFlippedSwitch:String = esob.getString
  ➤ (PluginConstants.NAME);
```

```
// the results of what was flipped
var switchResults:EsObject = esob.getEsObject
➤ (PluginConstants.SWITCH_RESULTS);

// was it a gate or laser tower?
if (switchResults.doesPropertyExist(PluginConstants.GATE_ID)) {

    var gateId:int = switchResults.getInteger
    ➤ (PluginConstants.GATE_ID);
    var gateState:int = switchResults.getInteger
    ➤ (PluginConstants.GATE_STATE);
    _game.toggleGate(gateId, gateState);

} else if (switchResults.doesPropertyExist(PluginConstants.
➤ TOWER_ID)) {

    var towerId:int = switchResults.getInteger
    ➤ (PluginConstants.TOWER_ID);
    var towerState:int = switchResults.getInteger
    ➤ (PluginConstants.TOWER_STATE);
    _game.setTowerState(towerId, towerState,
    ➤ playerNameWhoFlippedSwitch);
}
}
```

Pushing Rocks

Pushing rocks is one of the most interesting game-play mechanics of
Super Blob Bros. As we've said, since the rocks are so heavy, moving them
requires the combined forces of both players. Because of this, each client
must tell the server when it is attempting to push a rock, but the server has
to validate the attempt to ensure that both clients are pushing in unison.

A trick for testing

Testing the mechanics of the rock-pushing on one computer is very tricky! But besides manipulating the code
to alter the behavior for testing, there is a trick you can do with Flash Player to make it a bit easier. Clicking
outside of the standalone player's window will cause it to lose focus. If you are pressing your right arrow
key and walking right, then your character will continue to walk right after the window loses focus. So to test
pushing rocks, simply open two instances of the game in two separate standalone windows, make one player
push the rock, click out of the window, and then make the other player push the rock. Thanks, Flash!

THE LOGIC OF ROCK PLACEMENT

Since Super Blob Bros. is a tile-based game, and since tiles with rocks are unwalkable, rocks must be moved in whole-tile increments. To begin pushing a rock, we simply check to see if the tile we are trying to enter has a rock. If so, we tell the server that we want to push this specific rock, using the following code (in the checkKeys method of Game.as):

```
if (attemptedTile.hasRock) {
  if (!_myPlayer.isPushingRock && !attemptedTile.currentRock.
  ➤ isSliding) {
      _myPlayer.setIsPushingRock(attemptedTile.currentRock.id);
      attemptPushRock(attemptedTile.currentRock, _myPlayer.
  ➤ currentDirection);
      _soundManager.playSound(SoundManager.STRAIN);
  }
}
```

Let's examine the attemptPushRock function. Not only do we need to note the direction of the push, we also need to make sure that the rock is not going to be pushed onto an invalid tile—that is, any tile that is unwalkable or that does not exist. For example, tiles that contain a wall segment are invalid because they are unwalkable. It would not make sense to allow the player to push a rock through a wall. This function is also found in Game.as:

```
private function attemptPushRock(rock:Rock, direction:int):
➤ void {
  var xMove:int = 0;
  var yMove:int = 0;
  var dirName:String;

  switch (direction) {
      case Player.DIR_NORTH :
          yMove = -1;
          dirName = "north";
          break;
      case Player.DIR_SOUTH :
          yMove = 1;
          dirName = "south";
          break;
      case Player.DIR_EAST :
          xMove = 1;
          dirName = "east";
          break;
```

```
        case Player.DIR_WEST :
            xMove = -1;
            dirName = "west";
            break;
    }


    var destinationTile:Tile = _grid.getTile(rock.currentTile.
    ➤ column + xMove, rock.currentTile.row + yMove);


    // is the destination tile ok to push a rock into?
    if (!destinationTile || !destinationTile.isWalkable) {
        trace("can't push rock there!");
    } else {
        dispatchEvent(new AttemptPushRockEvent
            ➤ (AttemptPushRockEvent.PUSH, rock.id, true,
            ➤ destinationTile.column, destinationTile.row,
            ➤ dirName));
    }
}
```

Next, we send the server the ID of the rock we are trying to push, along with the direction and desired x and y tile location. You'll find the onPushRockAttempt function located in Coopgame.as:

```
private function onPushRockAttempt(apre:AttemptPushRockEvent):
➤ void {
  trace("onPushRockAttempt");
  var esob:EsObject = new EsObject();
  esob.setString(PluginConstants.ACTION, PluginConstants.
  ➤ PUSH_ROCK);
  esob.setInteger(PluginConstants.ROCK_ID, apre.rockId);


  // only needed if we are trying to push
  if (apre.isPusing) {
      esob.setInteger(PluginConstants.X, apre.x);
      esob.setInteger(PluginConstants.Y, apre.y);
      esob.setString(PluginConstants.DIRECTION, apre.
      ➤ direction);
  }


  sendToPlugin(esob);
}
```

NOTE *Technically, a rock just "blips" to its destination—not very dramatic. In order to add some eye candy, we slide the image of the rock from its origin to its destination over a small amount of time. (See the move function in* Rock.as.*)*

Finally, the server validates the push attempt and tells the client whether or not the rock could be moved. The attempt will be valid only if the server is aware of two players pushing the same rock in the same direction at the same time. Whew! That's a lot of work for one little rock. The final rock-pushing function is also located in CoopGame.as:

```
private function handlePushRock(esob:EsObject):void {
  trace("handlePushRock");
  var rockId:int = esob.getInteger(PluginConstants.ROCK_ID);

  var tileX:int = esob.getInteger(PluginConstants.X);
  var tileY:int = esob.getInteger(PluginConstants.Y);
  var dirName:String = esob.getString(PluginConstants.
  DIRECTION);

  _game.pushRock(rockId, tileX, tileY, dirName);
}
```

Conclusions and Next Steps

We've discussed several different types of cooperative game play, several styles of cooperation, and we have built a real working game.

Super Blob Bros. serves as an example of Players vs. Environment cooperative game play. Many of these game mechanics can be built upon and improved to create a fully featured game.

Here are a few ideas of how to improve upon the ideas and implementation of Super Blob Bros:

- Use time synchronization for player location so that it is more precisely synchronized.

- Store level data on the server instead of loading it from the client.

- Move control of player death to the server.

- Add more abilities, such as pulling objects.

CHAPTER 12

Isometric View

ISOMETRIC VIEWS HAVE been widely used in video games since the mid 1980s. You may have heard this referred to as "2.5D" or "3/4 view." Whatever you call it, it is a specific view that allows game developers to lay out objects and control things in 3D without having to deal with the computational overhead that comes with other 3D views. Countless popular games make use of this technique, such as Diablo II and Pikmin.

Many of the Flash virtual worlds that I've run across use an isometric view, such as VMTV (virtual.mtv.com) and Sifaka World (sifaka-world.com). A few exceptions use a side view, such as Poptropica (poptropica.com) and Disney's Pixie Hollow (pixiehollow.go.com). But chances are that if you're going to create a virtual world in Flash, it's going to use an isometric view. So pay attention, because this chapter is where you'll learn the fundamentals!

Here, you'll be introduced to the isometric view and the geometry behind it. We'll look at the benefits it brings and see it in use in some examples. While we will be delving into these concepts technically, we won't go through the mathematical derivation of the formulas used to map between 3D coordinates and the screen.

By the end of this chapter, you should know how to use the `Isometric` class provided to assist you in laying out a grid of tiles, and mapping coordinates between the screen and the world, and how to properly depth-sort objects.

Basics and Benefits of Isometrics

In most modern 3D games, there is the concept of a camera, which can move (and rotate) throughout the 3D environment. What the camera sees is mapped to the screen. The isometric view fixes the camera at a specific set of angles (the values of which we'll talk about in the section called "A Technical Look"). This set of angles allows us to view the world and lay out assets in a way that is not only fast to compute, but convenient.

Objects in Isometrics

A perfect cube—aligned with the x, y, and z axis and rendered in an isometric view—looks like this:

Notice that in this view, the cube edges are all the same length; hence the name *isometric*. Now look at the same cube positioned in several places:

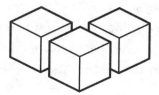

There are two very important things to point out in the diagram above:

- **No perspective change**—As the cube is positioned in different places throughout the scene, it always exposes the same surfaces in the same amount. In a non-isometric view, a cube would show more of one of its sides the further to the left or the right it is moved. The consistency of what you will see in isometric view is great from a content standpoint: objects can be created once and reused in many places without having to be re-rendered at a new perspective.

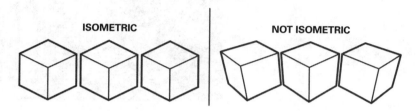

- **No vanishing point**—In isometrics, there is no horizon, or vanishing point, as you can see in the diagram. That means that as objects are positioned on the screen, they don't need to be scaled in size.

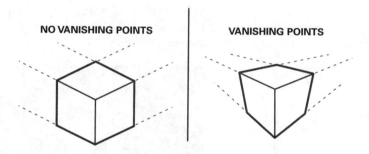

Because of these two major benefits, we can use bitmaps (or vector graphics) as objects to be placed in the world, since they won't scale or need to change perspective. The performance implications are extreme, since objects don't need to be rendered real-time straight from a 3D model.

Tiles

Since the isometric view has the major benefit of allowing reuse of the same object without scaling or making perspective changes, this makes tiling a good option for building a map. Here is a map that is made completely of tiles:

Tiles in an isometric view are diamond shaped. You can easily create such a diamond in Flash or another drawing tool by following these three steps:

1   Draw a square of any size.

2   Rotate the square 45°.

3   Scale the rotated square to 50% the current height.

This diamond is an isometric tile. It can be repeated as many times as you want to create a grid.

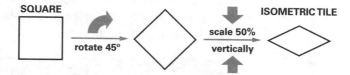

Here are a few more basic facts about tile size that will come up several more times in this chapter and throughout the book. First, the diamond is two times as wide as it is tall. Second, the dimensions of the tile should be some multiple of 2x1. Typical sizes are 64x32 and 128x64. In "A Technical Look" further down, we'll discuss more about the choice of tile size and the implications of making the wrong choice. For now, just know that the dimensions listed above happen to line up nicely on the screen when tiled.

Example Virtual Worlds

In this chapter we focus on isometric environments that are visually built using tiles and objects. In Chapter 10, we mentioned that a hybrid of tile-based and art-based games and worlds is often a good choice. Let's look at two virtual worlds and explain the visual approach of each.

Precious Girls Club

This world is made up completely with tiles—some of the areas have as many as 90,000 of them! As the screen scrolls and the avatar moves, tiles are visually added and removed from the screen.

Faraway Friends

This is hybrid world, using tiles in memory for convenient data storage, but custom art for the backgrounds. The large rich backgrounds are many times the size of the viewable area. Reusable objects exist in the world, but the scene isn't built tile by tile.

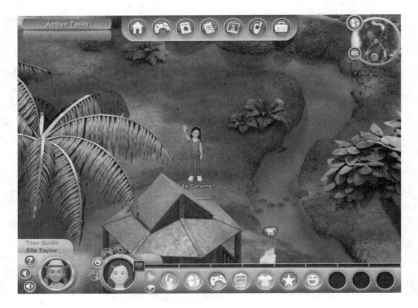

Isometrics Beyond Our Scope

There is a lot more that can be done within the isometric view than we can fit into in this book. We cover enough to handle what you'll see in most virtual worlds. Here are a few things that we *won't* get into:

- Over/under—The ability to have an avatar go over a bridge and then under that same bridge in an isometric view is more difficult to achieve than it sounds. It is an interesting thing to try, though, so give it a shot!

- Ramps—Think Marble Madness. Tiles that are ramps can be used to build character (depth, texture, complexity) into what is usually a flat world.

- Layered sorting—Imagine a floor with a rug on top of it. A chair is placed on top of *part* of the rug, and an avatar can walk over the rug or sit in the chair. This level of sorting is nice to have in a full-featured environment.

A Technical Look

So far we've looked at the major benefits of using an isometric view, but we haven't looked at the coordinate systems or seen how to apply the concepts in ActionScript. It's time to get a little bit more serious about the isometric view. In this section, we'll look at the Flash and isometric coordinate systems as well as learn how to use the `Isometric` class.

After reading this section, you should be able to build a grid of tiles using ActionScript.

The Geometry

Up to this point in the book, we have been seeing the coordinate system as two-dimensional; that is, having an x-axis and a y-axis. Flash does not have a z-axis, but if it did, the positive end would extend out past the back of the computer screen.

The isometric view can be conceptualized (and then treated mathematically) as a second 3D coordinate system sitting inside this Flash coordinate system. Let's call this second system "the isometric system" and the first "the Flash system." The Flash system is stationary; it cannot move, since it is bound to your computer monitor. The isometric system is only isometric when it is oriented in a specific way within the Flash system. Please note that the isometric system does not change when its orientation changes. The only thing that makes it isometric is how it is seen from the Flash system.

Now let's assume that the isometric system is completely aligned with the Flash system. In this case, there is no difference between the Flash system and the isometric system; in fact, it is not yet isometric. What has to happen to this second system to make it appear isometric, as seen from the Flash system? Two things:

1   *It must be rotated 30° around its own x-axis.* The x-axis is treated like an axle, so it stays still while the coordinate system rotates. Before the rotation, all three axes lie along all three of Flash's axes. After the rotation, the isometric system's x-axis still lies along Flash's x-axis, but the other axes are no longer aligned.

NOTE *Find the rotation animation in book_files/chapter12/ rotation_animation/animation.swf.*

2   *It must be rotated 45°around its own y-axis.* During this rotation, the y-axis is treated like an axle, so it stays stationary while the rest of the isometric system rotates around it. When this rotation has been completed, the x and z isometric axes are in different positions from their starting places, and it appears to be an isometric system as seen from the Flash system.

Take a look at the provided animation.swf file. This file was created to help you visualize how these two rotations take place. It shows a straight-on orientation in the Flash system (before it is isometric) and then rotates the cube in two steps. When it is finished animating, you can see the cube in an isometric view.

This is what the final isometric coordinate system orientation looks like as seen from the Flash coordinate system:

In this space, what you would visualize as the floor is the -z, +x quadrant. If something is raised up off of the floor, then it is moving in the -y direction.

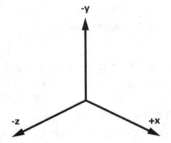

The Isometric Class

We just looked at how the isometric coordinate system looks from the Flash coordinate system. When it comes time to program an isometric game, you'll find you very often have to be able to map coordinates from the isometric system (which we'll now call 3D) to the Flash system (which we'll just call the screen from now on), and from the screen back to 3D. That is where the Isometric class comes in.

NOTE *Find the* Isometric *class in the com.gamebook.utils package.*

The Isometric class was created to allow you to easily take screen coordinates and figure out what 3D point matches up with them, and to take 3D coordinates and determine what screen position that is. Other than calculating a few variables once (for further use later), this class doesn't store any information. It is used like a black box—to take an input and give an output. Let's look at the constructor and then the two methods of the class.

Here is the constructor:

```
public function Isometric() {
  var theta:Number = 30;
  var alpha:Number = 45;
  theta *= Math.PI/180;
  alpha *= Math.PI/180;
  _sinTheta = Math.sin(theta);
  _cosTheta = Math.cos(theta);
  _sinAlpha = Math.sin(alpha);
  _cosAlpha = Math.cos(alpha);
}
```

If you remember from the previous section, the isometric view is achieved by rotating twice, 30° and then 45°. We call those angles theta and alpha respectively. Their values are converted from degrees to radians so they can be used with the trigonometric functions. The next four lines of code calculate and store sine and cosine values of the two angles for future use.

Now let's look at the mapToScreen method:

```
public function mapToScreen(xpp:Number, ypp:Number,
   zpp:Number):Coordinate {
  var yp:Number = ypp;
  var xp:Number = xpp*_cosAlpha+zpp*_sinAlpha;
  var zp:Number = zpp*_cosAlpha-xpp*_sinAlpha;
  var x:Number = xp;
  var y:Number = yp*_cosTheta-zp*_sinTheta;
  return new Coordinate(x, y, 0);
}
```

This method takes a set of 3D coordinates, maps them to the screen, and then returns those screen coordinates. In math, when you deal with multiple coordinate systems, it's common to label the x, y, and z axes for each new system with primes (a superscript) to indicate which coordinate system that variable belongs to. So that is what the p and pp stand for above: "prime" and "prime prime." In the method above, x and y refer to the screen. The variables xpp, ypp, and zpp represent the isometric system. The variables xp, yp, and zp are an in-between mapping to a new temporary system. In other words, we are doing the reverse rotation of the 30° and 45° transform. (We won't look at the mathematical derivation of this transform.) Notice the return result is a new instance of the Coordinate class. That class is just used as a container for x, y, and z coordinates. Also, observe that the z coordinate is set to 0. That is because the screen is only two-dimensional, so z must be 0.

The second and final method of this class is this:

```
public function mapToIsoWorld(screenX:Number,
  screenY:Number):Coordinate {
  var z:Number = (screenX/_cosAlpha-screenY/
  (_sinAlpha*_sinTheta))*(1/(_cosAlpha/_sinAlpha+
  _sinAlpha/_cosAlpha));
  var x:Number = (1/_cosAlpha)*(screenX-z*_sinAlpha);
  return new Coordinate(x, 0, z);
}
```

This method takes a screen coordinate, maps it into the 3D isometric space, and then returns a Coordinate instance containing that information. This is often used for mapping mouse-clicks into the world to figure out what was clicked on. It could also be used for drag-and-drop behavior. The screen x and screen y coordinates are passed in as parameters to the method. Then two lines of code are run to map those into the 3D space. They are complicated-looking lines! Then the Coordinate instance is returned, containing the mapped information. Note that the y variable is marked as 0. Since we are mapping 2D into 3D, we can't generate a new degree of freedom out of thin air. So an assumption is made that the coordinate, once it's mapped from 2D to 3D, will be on the ground, hence y = 0 again.

From an isometric math standpoint, the two methods found in the Isometric class are all you'll need to position objects and move them around. To sort them, you'll need some other code, which will be discussed later in this chapter.

Building a Grid

NOTE *Find the grid files in book_files/chapter12/grid.*

Let's look at an example where you'll learn how to use the Isometric class and tiles to build a 10x10 grid on screen with all tiles positioned properly.

Before we start looking at code, I want to mention something that may not be widely obvious, and is important to understand. When programming an isometric game—or any 3D game, for that matter—you don't have to keep track of your data in any special way. The data is kept in memory, and the way it's treated mathematically is completely irrelevant to how it's going to be seen when rendered to the screen. The only time isometric concepts come into play is at the moment that something has to be added to or updated on the screen. For example, a ball might exist at x = 10, y = 20, and z = 30 in 3D space. It may be affected over time by gravity and other forces that change its position with standard physics code that you're used to using. You worry about how to display it only when you need to update it onscreen, at which time you would take the x, y, and z coordinates and feed them into the mapToScreen method of the Isometric class.

Now that we have that out of way, let's dig into the code! The main class to focus on is Map, which uses the Isometric class to build a grid of 100 tiles.

The constructor of the Map class calls the initialize function. This function does some things that you'll need to do in all applications that use the Isometric class. Here is the initialize function:

```
private function initialize():void{
  _iso = new Isometric();

  //tile dimensions on screen
  _tileWidthOnScreen = 64;
  _tileHeightOnScreen = 32;

  //tile dimensions in 3-space
  _tileWidth = _iso.mapToIsoWorld(64, 0).x;
  _tileHeight = _tileWidth;

  //build the grid of tiles
  buildGrid();
}
```

The first line of code creates a new instance of the Isometric class and stores it as a class-level property. Next, we set two variables to store the width and height of the tile diamond as it should show up on screen to 64 and 32 (we'll talk more about this in a minute). The next two lines of code determine and set the dimensions of the tile as seen in 3D. We do this by taking the width of it on screen and mapping that width into 3D using the `mapToIsoWorld` method. Since within the 3D space the tile is a square, we set `_tileHeight` equal to `_tileWidth`.

Finding the right tile dimensions in 3D

The code above may seem a little odd. We set the dimensions of what we want the rendered tile to be, and then map that back into 3D to figure how big the tile should be so that it would map to the size we want. This seems like the opposite of how it should work. It makes sense that we would just establish some dimensions in 3D and then however it maps to the screen is what we get. (Especially because several paragraphs back I was talking about the data driving the view, not the other way.)

So why do we do it this way? I'll explain by describing what happens if you *don't* do it this way. Until you learn differently, the way that seems to makes sense is to establish tile dimensions in 3D, say, 40x40. You then use those dimensions to figure out the dimensions of the tile to show on screen. A 40x40 tile in 3D maps to the screen as 56.568x28.284. You would then take these dimensions and get an artist to build tiles that match them as closely as possible.

As the grid of tiles is built, they (the tiles) are laid out based on the dimensions 56.568x28.284. But you'll notice that as rows and columns of tiles extend in any direction, there's a slight tear where they should perfectly join. This tear increases and then decreases again. This discrepancy is due to how artwork is drawn to the screen and how positions are rounded to the nearest hundredth place.

Another issue you may run into is that if instead of laying out tiles on the screen as individual display objects you draw them directly to a bitmap, then the positions are rounded to integers. Depending on how you lay things out (using absolute math or relative to the previous tile), you run the risk of that tear constantly increasing, rather than growing and shrinking as the tiles are added.

I'm embarrassed to say that I struggled with this issue for years before I discovered exactly what the problem was and how to fix it. This problem exists on non-Flash platforms as well. The fix is to *play to the screen*: choose tile dimensions that happen to match up perfectly with pixels. In addition, if you choose dimensions that are powers of 2, you can speed up math operations if you need to. That is why it is the most common to see tiles that are 64x32 or 128x64.

Whew! OK, back to the code. The last thing the `initialize` function does is call the `buildGrid` function:

```
private function buildGrid():void {
  _grid = [];

  //establish dimensions
  var cols:int = 10;
  var rows:int = 10;
```

```
//build the grid
for (var i:int = 0; i < cols;++i) {
    _grid[i] = [];
    for (var j:int = 0; j < rows;++j) {
        //create tile
        var t:Tile = new Tile();

        //position it in 3D
        var tx:Number = i * _tileWidth;
        var tz:Number = -j * _tileHeight;

        //map 3D to screen
        var coord:Coordinate = _iso.mapToScreen(tx, 0, tz);

        //position on screen
        t.x = coord.x;
        t.y = coord.y;

        //store tile
        _grid[i][j] = t;

        //add to screen
        addChild(t);
    }
  }
}
```

This function creates all of the tiles and positions them on screen. First a new array called _grid is created. This is used to store all tiles as they are created. They can be retrieved later if needed. We then set the dimensions for the grid that is being created, which is 10x10. Columns extend down and to the right; rows extend down and to the left.

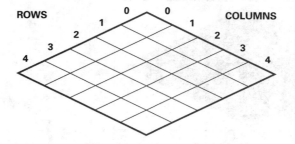

Next, we have a nested loop. The outer loop iterates through all columns needed, and creates a new array on the _grid array for each column. The inner loop iterates through each element in the row for the column it is currently on.

The first thing that happens within the loop is that a new Tile instance is created. This is a display object. We then determine where in 3D this tile should be positioned, based on the loop iterators and the _tileWidth and _tileHeight properties. Notice that the position of the tile is in the +x, -z quadrant. If you remember, that is the floor—y is 0 on the floor.

Now that we know the position in 3D, we map it to the screen using the mapToScreen method on the Isometric class instance. The tile is then positioned on the screen using that information. The tile is stored in the _grid array logically, using its column and row values. Finally, the tile is added to the screen so that we can see it.

Don't be too exact!

Sometimes being too precise has a cost. If you create the tile art to be exactly 64 wide and 32 tall, you may get a very faint line that shows up between all tiles.

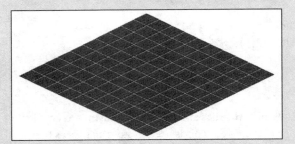

The solution is to make the artwork one pixel bigger in both directions, but still use 64x32 mathematically to place them. By increasing the artwork to 65x33, you can eliminate that faint line.

Selecting a Tile

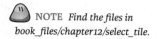 NOTE *Find the files in book_files/chapter12/select_tile.*

Now we can go through an example that shows how to use mouse input to determine precisely which tile it is over by mapping the mouse position into 3D. As the mouse moves, the tile that it is over is selected.

This example is built off of the previous example, so most of the code has already been discussed. We'll look at just what is new. This line of code was added to the `initialize` function:

```
addEventListener(MouseEvent.MOUSE_MOVE, mouseMoved);
```

When the mouse moves over the grid, the `mouseMoved` function is called:

```
private function mouseMoved(e:MouseEvent):void {
  if (_lastTile != null) {
      _lastTile.alpha = 1;
      _lastTile = null;
  }

  var coord:Coordinate = _iso.mapToIsoWorld(mouseX, mouseY);
  var col:int = Math.floor(coord.x / _tileWidth);
  var row:int = Math.floor(Math.abs(coord.z / _tileHeight));

  if (col < _cols && row < _rows) {
      var tile:Tile = getTile(col, row);
      tile.alpha = .5;
      _lastTile = tile;
  }
}
```

If a tile is selected, it is set to the class-level property `_lastTile`. The first thing done in this function is to set the `alpha` property of the last selected tile to `1` and then set `_lastTile` to `null`. This essentially deselects whatever was selected. Next, we map the mouse position into 3D using the `mapToIsoWorld` method. We use the x and z position of the coordinate in 3D to figure out which column and row that point is in. It uses the simple math trick discussed in Chapter 10 to figure out column and row based on a x and y value. You'll notice that for the row value, we take the absolute value of the z coordinate. That is because we are in the +x, -z quadrant, but the column and row are always positive.

If the `col` and `row` values are within the bounds of the grid, then we get the tile that exists at that column and row, and change its alpha value to `.5`. Finally, a reference to that tile is stored as the value of `_lastTile`.

This simple example shows you enough to help you understand how to map user input into the 3D world.

Sorting Algorithm

Now that you've been introduced to isometric techniques and can build a tile map, the logical next step is populating that map with some objects. Placing objects at the correct position in the world isn't difficult, but one thing that has plagued developers for a long time is figuring out how to properly *sort* those objects in an isometric view. The term "sort" in this context means to layer objects based on their position in 3D.

In this example, the bush should show up in front of a tree that (based on its coordinates) should lie behind it.

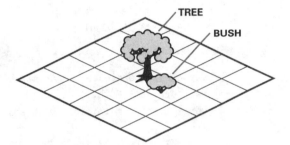

Looking around on Google, I wasn't able to find much good information on how to properly handle sorting in an isometric view. But I did find dozens of forum posts from developers searching for the answer. In this section, I present one solution to the sorting puzzle, and then follow it up with an example that applies it.

Logic

What we want to achieve with a sorting algorithm is the ability to look at the position of all objects, and the number of columns and rows they take up, and sort them appropriately based on how they would look in real life. We make two assumptions here:

1   All items make up a filled rectangle of tiles. That could be as small as just a single tile (which is 1x1), or a dining-room table (which might be 2x4). We won't allow items that make up other shapes, such as an L-shaped couch. An object like that would need to be broken into two objects.

2   Objects cannot overlap each other. Just as in real life you can't have a couch and the dining-room table taking up the same physical space, we won't allow that here.

Here is how the algorithm works. We start with a list of all objects to be sorted. We then create a new empty list that will contain the sorted objects. We loop through the object list and compare it to each object in the sorted list. When a comparison shows that the current object from the object list should be sorted under (aka, behind or below) the object being looked at in the sorted object list, it is inserted before that object. This is done until all items from the original list have been added to the sorted list. If an item doesn't sort behind anything, then it is added to the end of the sorted list. The end result is a list that is properly sorted from lowest sorting value to highest.

The important consideration here is, how is the comparison between the two objects made, to determine if one should be sorted lower than the other? That is what makes this whole process work. Consider the following diagrams.

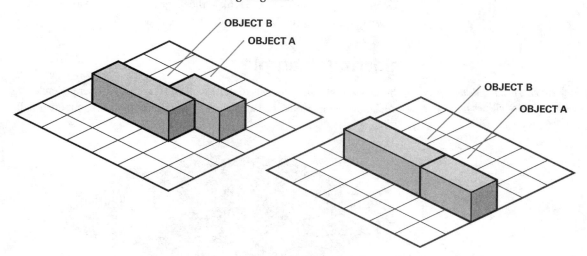

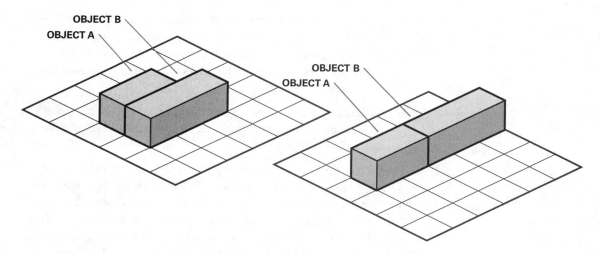

When we perform the comparison to see if Object B should be behind Object A, we ask two questions:

1   Is Object B's starting column less than or equal to the biggest column that Object A extends into?

2   Is Object B's starting row less than or equal to the biggest row that Object A extends into?

If the answer to both of these is yes, then Object B should be sorted behind Object A. Take some time and look at the diagrams above and ask yourself those questions to verify for yourself that the logic works.

Sorting Example

NOTE *Find the files for this example in book_files/chapter12/ sorting.*

In this example, we add items to the screen and sort them properly. Here's what our example looks like with correct positioning of objects, but unsorted:

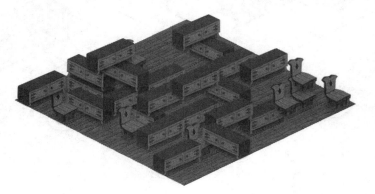

And here's what it looks like sorted:

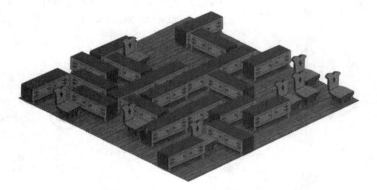

This example was built off of the grid example from earlier in this chapter, so we'll just focus on the relevant new code. All items that will be added to the screen are added to a movie clip called _itemHolder. This movie clip, in turn, is added as part of the initialize function after the grid is built:

```
_itemHolder = new MovieClip();
addChild(_itemHolder);
```

At the bottom of the initialize function, the following code was added:

```
for (var i:int = 0; i < 50;++i) {
  var col:int = Math.floor(_cols * Math.random());
  var row:int = Math.floor(_rows * Math.random());

  var item:Item = new Item();
  item.type = Math.floor(3*Math.random());

  if (testItemPlacement(item, col, row)) {
      addItem(item, col, row);
  }
}
```

```
sortAllItems();
```

This code runs through 50 iterations attempting to add items to random locations. A random column and row are chosen and then a new Item instance is created and given a random type. The item can have a type of 0, 1, or 2. The Item class uses the type value to determine which image to show and how many columns and rows it takes up. Next, there is a conditional statement that tests the intended placement of the item. The placement might not be valid if it goes out of bounds on the map or if it would overlap another item. If the position is valid, then we add it to the screen using the addItem function. Then, the sortAllItems function is called.

Here is the addItem function:

```
private function addItem(itm:Item, col:int, row:int):void {
  for (var i:int = col; i < col + itm.cols;++i) {
      for (var j:int = row; j < row +itm.rows;++j) {
          var tile:Tile = getTile(i, j);
          if (tile != null) {
              tile.addItem(itm);
          }
      }
  }

  var tx:Number = _tileWidth * col + _tileWidth / 2;
  var tz:Number = -(_tileHeight * row + _tileHeight / 2);

  var coord:Coordinate = _iso.mapToScreen(tx, 0, tz);
  itm.x = coord.x;
  itm.y = coord.y;

  itm.col = col;
  itm.row = row;

  _itemHolder.addChild(itm);

  _sortedItems.push(itm);
}
```

The first thing this function does is loop through all tiles that this item will sit on and add itself to that tile. The function that tests for valid item placement, testItemPlacement, will check the tiles to see if they already contain an item, so that is why we add the item to tiles here. After that, we figure out the position of the item in 3D using the same technique as for the tiles, with one difference—a tile is added to the position in both directions. That is done so that the item sits at the center of the tile. The item is then positioned using the coordinates determined using the mapToScreen method. The item is told at what row and column it is placed, and then it is added to the _itemHolder movie clip so it can be seen on screen. The last thing that happens is that the item is stored in the _sortedItems array (even though it is not yet sorted).

Before going on, you should know that all Item instances implement (or meet) an interface called ISortableItem. This is important because it won't be long before you start adding non-items to the screen that need to follow the same sorting logic, like avatars. An avatar would also meet this interface, which would allow it to be sorted just like anything else. The ISortableItem interface simply causes a class to implement the following:

```
function get col():int;
function get row():int;
function get cols():int;
function get rows():int;
```

Now let's look at the sortAllItems function:

```
private function sortAllItems():void{
  var list:Array = _sortedItems.slice(0);

  _sortedItems = [];

  for (var i:int = 0; i < list.length;++i) {
      var nsi:ISortableItem = list[i];

      var added:Boolean = false;
      for (var j:int = 0; j < _sortedItems.length;++j ) {
          var si:ISortableItem = _sortedItems[j];

          if (nsi.col <= si.col+si.cols-1 && nsi.row
          ⟶ <= si.row+si.rows-1) {
              _sortedItems.splice(j, 0, nsi);
              added = true;
              break;
          }
      }
      if (!added) {
          _sortedItems.push(nsi);
      }
  }

  for (i = 0; i < _sortedItems.length;++i) {
```

```
        var disp:DisplayObject = _sortedItems[i] as
    ➤ DisplayObject;
        _itemHolder.addChildAt(disp, i);
    }
}
```

In this function, we follow the algorithm outlined earlier. First, an array called `list` is created by copying the `_sortedItems` list. Next, the `_sortedItems` array is reset to an empty array. We then loop through every item in the `list` array, each of which is called `nsi` ("new sortable item"), and for each of those items, loop through all items in the `_sortedItems` array, each of which are called `si` ("sortable item"). For each `nsi` we set a property called `added` to `false` so that it can be added to the `_sortableItems` array later if it doesn't sort behind anything. The conditional statement contains the two comparison checks that determine if `nsi` should sort behind `si`. If both are `true`, then `nsi` is spliced into the `_sortableItems` array before `si`, `added` is set to `true`, and we break out of this inner loop.

The last thing that happens in this function is that it loops through all items in the newly sorted `_sortedItems` array, and each item is added to the screen at the appropriate depth. You are left with a properly sorted screenful of items!

CHAPTER 13

Avatars

WE NOW START to focus on virtual worlds exclusively, and will do so throughout the remaining chapters. We've created a virtual world for this book, called Old World—a simple place that illustrates many virtual world concepts.

In a virtual world, you are represented by a character called an *avatar*. You can customize the avatar and control it by moving it throughout the world. Avatars are the centerpiece of all virtual worlds.

In this chapter we will discuss what typically constitutes an avatar. We'll look at various rendering techniques, and show an in-depth example of one in particular. Lastly, we'll walk through a simple application that shows how to create a customized avatar, and then we'll log in as that avatar. This application is part of the larger Old World project.

Meet the Avatars

Virtual worlds are social networks, and as such, players interact with each other and form relationships. They can meet and connect with each other in a number of ways, limited only by the creativity of the world designers. Some common interaction points are chatting, playing games, and trading items.

NOTE   *The major pieces of Old World are discussed over the next four chapters and can be found in book_files/old_world.*

As players interact, what they mostly see about each other is the avatar. Since the avatar is such a focal point for initiating interaction and is your virtual representation, it has also become a focal point for expressing one's individuality. One of the core features of all social networks—virtual or otherwise—is self-expression. A player has to have the ability to be unique in some way. If a player doesn't have the ability to be unique, then that player will likely move on to another virtual world.

Players primarily express their individuality through avatar customization. The level of customization made available for an avatar depends on the features provided by the world itself. Here are some example customization areas:

- Clothing—A common type of avatar customization, allowed in most worlds, through clothing options such as shirt, pants, shoes, and hats.

- Skin tone—If the avatar is humanoid, then it is common that skin tone for the avatar can be chosen.

- Hair—Choosing a unique hairstyle can substantially change the overall look of the avatar.

- Body type—This is rare in Flash virtual worlds, due to the content creation implications. But in some cases a body type can be chosen, such as short and stout or tall and thin.

Fully customized avatar in Sifaka World (www.sifakaworld.com).

Another common mode of self expression is through *emotes*. An emote is a special animation that the avatar can perform to convey an emotion; for example, blowing a kiss or doing a belly laugh.

Typically, avatars have an *inventory*—a collection of all items they've acquired. An item can be anything from something that can be used for their own customization, such as a shirt or pants, to something that may be used for entertainment, such as songs. Since customization of an avatar is a huge part of what a player wants to do to be unique, acquiring items in their inventory for customization and uniqueness is an ongoing goal for the player.

Acquiring items is also an area in which the virtual world owners can make money. Players use virtual money to buy these items. An avatar can get virtual money by using real money (for example, purchasing virtual dollars via credit card) or by spending a lot of time in the world doing repeated tasks (such as playing games).

Rendering Approaches

Assembling all of the pieces needed to make up an avatar can be challenging. We'll go over several rendering approaches, each with its pros and cons. First, here are some major considerations to help inform your decision of an approach.

- Business requirements—These are resources or functions that are required to meet the game design, such as the ability for the avatars to change clothes or to hold an item.

- Production pipeline—If there are plans to create a large number of assets for the avatar to wear, for example, then keeping costs down long-term in that area may drive short-term decisions for how to program avatars.

- Available technology—In some cases, a developer may see a superior way to handle assembling and rendering an avatar, but Flash isn't yet fast enough to handle it well (specifically the 3D approach discussed below).

There is no single approach that is best for all virtual worlds. I've worked on nine virtual worlds and have seen or worked with almost every type of avatar assembly and rendering technique that you can think of. I've tried to break them down into some major categories and explain them below. We'll then focus on one of these approaches, sprite sheets, in detail, in its own section, and show an example usage of that method in the "Avatar Creation and Customization" section.

Puppet

This technique is a little difficult to explain in words—those of you who will best understand and recognize this are the Flash developers who have been working with complicated movie clips in Flash hierarchies.

Puppet avatars are pre-animated movie clips in Flash into (or onto) which static images are loaded. Clothing is divided into as many pieces as are needed to have them fit onto an animated avatar without them (the items) having to contain the animation. Imagine the following avatar body:

A pair of pants to go on this avatar would need to contain five pieces: one for the hips area, one for each upper leg portion, and one for each lower leg portion. These static images are loaded in and placed into the appropriate movie clip. The movie clip is animated to form a walk cycle, and the images come along for the ride.

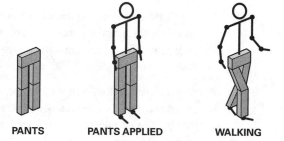

PANTS   PANTS APPLIED   WALKING

Now imagine the same technique used for the pants applied to shirts, hats, hair, and any other accessories that you could imagine.

PROS

- Low file size—The animation data is created just once, and the clothing is loaded into the available slots always as static images—that is, the clothing doesn't have to be animated. For this reason, of all the approaches, the puppet approach usually has the smallest file-size impact.

- Content creation—Since the content that needs to be created is static and not animated, it should take less time for someone who really knows how to do it. (And for that reason, this also appears as a con, below.)

CONS

- Content creation process—There is a high learning curve for artists to work in this way. It isn't something that most are used to. We used this approach at Electrotank on a few projects and found it was difficult to get a new artist up to speed quickly.

- Puppet creation process—Creating the puppet movie-clip structure in the first place can be a lengthy process. It can take weeks to get it right! Generally the avatar structure is drawn and animated for eight directions. Then pieces are cut up and movie clips are named so they can be targeted with code. Then example assets are created to test the positioning of all movie clips.

- Limitations in look—Most of the modern worlds being created have greater demands placed on the look of the avatars than this approach could feasibly allow. The more realistic the avatar, the more moving parts it has, the longer it takes to prepare the puppet (not to mention the time it takes to animate a realistic human walk, by hand, in all eight directions).

WHEN BEST TO USE

Avatars from sites like Club Penguin (www.clubpenguin.com) would fit into this model well. They are simple avatars with few moving parts. They benefit from being easily customizable and having low file size.

Layered Animation

This approach is probably one of the easiest to visualize. Imagine that you have an unclothed avatar walking. Now take a shirt that is pre-animated by itself, and layer it on top of the walking avatar. The end result is a walking avatar that is wearing a shirt.

Throw a skirt, some shoes, and a hair layer into the mix, and you have a fully clothed avatar. (The earrings are part of the hair image.)

If the avatar has an underlying body and then hair, clothes, and shoes all layered on top, then you may wonder how the files are organized. They are generally segmented in one of the following two ways:

- All information for a single item is in the same file. For instance, all animations and rotations of those animations are contained in a single SWF file. That SWF file is loaded and told to play as needed.

- All information for a single item about a single animation is in a file. So, the walking animation for certain hairstyle would be in a single SWF file, but a jumping animation for that hairstyle would be in a second SWF file.

PROS

- If an artist wants to hand-draw an avatar (as opposed to using 3D software), then they will be at home with this method.

- The learning curve for content creation is low. Most animators should be able to pick up this technique easily.

- Easy to program.

CONS

- Limited to hand-drawing. If you want a higher level of realism for your avatars, this approach won't work.

- Since the art here is hand-drawn, that means it's vector. Vector animations can be slow in Flash. Trying to support 20+ avatars on screen at once using a vector approach could cause performance problems.

WHEN BEST TO USE

If you are going for a special cartoony look, or you happen to have access to top-notch animators, then this approach may fit well with your project.

Sprite Sheets

NOTE *We discuss the sprite sheet approach in detail in the next section, and we use it to render avatars in this book.*

A sprite sheet is a large bitmap that contains chunks of graphical information. OK, I realize that's a pretty vague description. As we apply sprite sheets in the context of avatars for a virtual world, the definition will become a little clearer. Suffice it to say for now that a sprite sheet is a grid of frames of an animation. Historically, sprite sheets have been used in games on all platforms.

Customization happens through layering of sprite sheets—similar to that seen in layered animations. We'll look more at that in the next section. For now, just know that the information is laid out in large grids that can be processed by Flash to construct a fully clothed and animated avatar.

PROS

- Can be used to achieve the highest performance avatars in the world.
- Can work well with 3D animation programs that can output to sprite sheets or to a format that can be processed into a sprite sheet.
- Easy to program.

CONS

- Memory footprint can become quite large. We'll look at that calculation in the next section.
- May not work well with UGC (user generated content), which is mentioned in the 3D category below.

WHEN BEST TO USE

Currently, this approach is likely to be the best solution for most existing Flash virtual worlds. The performance benefits are major.

3D

This is potentially one of the best approaches that you can use to render avatars. With a 3D approach, the client loads in a 3D model, textures it, and renders it on the client. Models can be tied to bone animations to animate them.

Recently there has been a lot of progress in 3D rendering speed with Papervision 3D and Away 3D. Unfortunately, the performance isn't yet to the level needed to use this approach for all avatars in Flash. I think the performance is there to render a single, reasonable-quality avatar on a customization screen. But when it comes to jumping into a whole world, I don't think these apps can yet allow for the rendering of 20+ avatars while maintaining a responsive application.

PROS

- Apply the same animation to many models.
- Dynamically texture models.

- Render the avatar from any angle, giving the user more ways to view the avatar during customization.

- Reasonably low file size.

- Works well with UGC (user generated content). A user could create a new pattern for a shirt that becomes a texture that can be dynamically applied.

CONS

- Performance isn't in a good enough place yet to be a feasible option for in-world rendering.

WHEN BEST TO USE

At the moment, this is best to use on an avatar customization screen only. Avatars in the world would have to be handled differently. If the performance of 3D in Flash ever gets to a really good place, then this will become the recommended approach for avatar rendering.

What About Video?

As you can see, there are many approaches to rendering avatars, each with their ups and downs; that is, there is no one right answer. But there's one idea that I've been thinking about for a long time—video. Knowing that 3D doesn't perform well for us yet, and sprite sheets are recommend for most cases, how could we improve on sprite sheets? Flash video (FLV) is a possibility. The sprite sheet contains frames of the same information, slightly changed per frame. Video accounts for that by storing only the difference from one frame to the next. So it is likely that video could contain all of the information of a sprite sheet but at a smaller file size.

I still haven't had the chance to try video in this context, but I do have some questions about it:

- What is a good pipeline for creating FLVs with an alpha channel?

- How will the file size compare to that of a PNG sprite sheet that contains comparable information?

- What performance impact is there in Flash of having 20+ video objects playing at once?

There is no pros-and-cons section here because it is an untested technique. But it would be interesting to try!

Sprite Sheets

Sprite sheets (in the context of avatars) are large bitmaps that contain a grid of animation snapshots. Each snapshot is a frame of animation of that avatar. The file type is usually PNG, so an alpha channel can be used with it. These bitmaps are loaded into Flash, processed, and then used to show animating avatars on the screen.

Animation frames on a sprite sheet

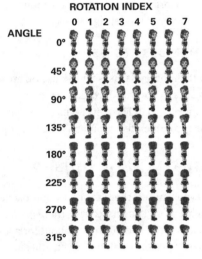

In this section, we'll look at a way to show customized avatars on the client and how sprite sheets can be created in the first place. We'll also talk about rendering performance and memory concerns.

Layering

How do sprite sheets fit in with showing a customized avatar? The example sprite sheet figures you've seen in this chapter show a fully customized avatar. When showing a fully customized avatar using sprite sheets, you have two choices:

- A single sprite sheet that contains the fully customized avatar, or

- Multiple sprite sheets, each of which contains a single customization option (one sheet for the shirt, one for pants, etc.)

To a Flash developer, the former choice is the best—you just load in a single sprite sheet and use it. The potential issue with that first choice is creating all sprite sheet permutations on the file system, to account for all customization possibilities such that you *can* just load a single sprite sheet for a fully customized avatar. (There are some more advanced ways to achieve this, but they are beyond the scope of this book and won't be discussed here.)

The second choice is to layer sprite sheets to create an avatar. With this approach, you start off with a basic, unclothed avatar. Sprite sheets that contain customization options are then layered on top one by one. Here is an example layering order, from lowest to highest layer:

- Body
- Pants
- Shoes
- Shirt
- Hair

NOTE *Usually the unclothed avatar has minimal undergarments that are part of the base image, to avoid bugs that could result in a naked avatar (yes, it happens).*

Single frames from the male avatar sprite sheets used in this book, corresponding with the example layering order stated above.

Performance

When we talk about performance with sprite sheets, we are talking about the technique's impact on frame rate and on memory footprint.

Avatars rendered from sprite sheets have the lowest impact on frame rate of any approach I've ever worked with. We'll look at the code that goes into this in "Avatar Creation and Customization," but for now you just need to know that the sprite sheets are cached into `BitmapData` instances that can be quickly displayed.

NOTE *The memory that a loaded image takes up depends exclusively on the dimensions of that image—originating file type and compression settings are not a factor. A highly compressed JPG and a richly detailed PNG of the same dimensions will have the same memory footprint once loaded into Flash.*

Memory usage is something to keep in mind, be aware of, and plan for. The reason the sprite-sheet approach works so well is that the data taken from the sheet is cached in memory for fast retrieval. But a result of the caching is the potential for consuming large amounts of memory.

Luckily for us, we can easily calculate the memory footprint of any bitmap. Using that calculation along with assumptions about your world, you can estimate how much memory your avatars take up. Here is how you find the memory used for a loaded bitmap:

```
Memory (in bytes) = width * height * 4
```

Applying the above equation to a 200x400 image, you get 320,000 bytes. Divide that by 1024 to convert it to kilobytes, and you get 312.5KB. That is for a single frame of animation. Now assume that the avatar has a walk cycle of 12 frames per direction and walks in 8 directions. That is 96 frames times 312.5KB, which yields 30,000KB or 29.3MB.

Let's round that number up and say it take 30MB of memory for a full walk cycle of an avatar. If you had 20 avatars on screen at once, that's 600MB of memory! If you wanted your avatar to have an idle animation in addition to the walk animation, which many worlds do, then double the memory from 600MB to 1.2GB. Yowch!

NOTE *I use the term "key frame" to mean a frame containing new information.*

You can see how estimations like this can really help in planning early on. Requiring users to have a system that will allow your Flash virtual world to consume 1.2GB of memory is not reasonable. You can look at the above scenario and make a couple of quick adjustments to get things to a better place. For example, if you changed the avatar size from 200x400 to 100x200, then the 1.2GB drops to 293MB. If you cut the key frames down from 12 to 10, it goes from 293MB to 244MB. If you get rid of the idle animation, it drops back to 122MB.

NOTE *Keep in mind that the memory usage doesn't equate to the amount of data that must be downloaded. When we say that avatars may take up 120MB of memory, that might only be a few MB of files to download.*

What is reasonable? I think it is reasonable if the entire virtual world, avatars and everything, takes up 350MB.

Creating sprite sheets

Since I am recommending sprite sheets as a good option for avatars, you probably want to know how to create them. Unfortunately, I don't have a good answer for that; we've used them on several projects now, and each time we've used custom code to take individual images and make sprite sheets out of them. Those individual images are usually scripted output from Autodesk Maya.

I have heard that some 3D tools have plugins to help with exporting images directly into a sprite-sheet format.

Avatar Creation and Customization

NOTE *Find Old World in book_files/old_world. For more information on installing the server extension for Old World, please see the Appendix.*

All our examples from this point on are seen in the larger Old World virtual world project. We cover only a portion of the Old World project in this chapter, focusing on how to use sprite sheets to render and customize an avatar, and how to create a new avatar with ElectroServer. Also, we see how to log in as that avatar and save your avatar customizations.

There are three screens that we use to achieve these avatar creation and customization:

- IntroScreen—To allow the user to log in or click to go to a screen to create a new avatar

- RegistrationScreen—To create a new avatar and login information

- AvatarCustomizationScreen—To customize your avatar after you've logged in

We'll also discuss the general approach taken to handle avatars and the registration system. There is nothing new to point out in the IntroScreen class—it just facilitates the login process, something we've seen throughout the book. The RegistrationScreen class and the AvatarCustomizationScreen classes both make heavy use of the AnimationLoader and SpriteAnimation classes, which are important in seeing how to apply the layered sprite sheet concepts introduced in this chapter. But since both of those screens use these classes in a similar way, we'll just focus on the AvatarCreationScreen class to see how it uses AnimationLoader and SpriteAnimation.

General Description

Old World supports avatars of two types: male and female. There is no advantage to choosing one type over the other. Clothing assets for the male fit only the male, and vice versa. Once created, avatars are stored in a database on the server.

An avatar has the following properties, many of which are self-explanatory:

- Name—Chosen at avatar creation time.

- Gender—Male or female. Also chosen at creation time.

- Money—This is the currency the avatar has. It is defaulted to 1,000 units.

- Hair—Each avatar type has two hairstyles to choose from.

- Top—The shirt the avatar is currently wearing.

- Bottom—The pants or skirt the avatar is currently wearing.

- Shoes—The shoes the avatar is wearing—starting to see a pattern here?

- Clothing—The array of all clothing items owned by the avatar.

- Furniture—The array of all furniture owned by the avatar (used in Chapter 16, *User Homes*).

As you know, you have to log in to ElectroServer to do anything useful with it. Since you create an avatar using ElectroServer, that means you need to be able to log in even without an avatar. We call that type of login a guest login. You log in as a guest to create an avatar, and then log in again as the newly created avatar.

The data that describes all clothing that is possible for any avatar to wear and all furniture that is possible for any avatar to own is loaded from the server on the avatar login response. The images for those items exist on the file system.

The `Avatar`, `Clothing`, and `Furniture` classes represent the entities discussed above. The `AvatarManager`, `ClothingManager`, and `FurnitureManager` classes are used to easily get at all objects that we know about or retrieve them by ID.

The avatar has money because it will be able to buy furniture items. This is discussed in Chapter 16.

AnimationLoader and SpriteAnimation Classes

The avatars in Old World are constructed by layering sprite sheets. The AnimationLoader class handles loading in the needed sprite sheets for a customized avatar and then adding them to the SpriteAnimation class in the right order. When the sprite sheets are finished loading, we don't need the AnimationLoader class anymore, and thereafter only use the SpriteAnimation class. The SpriteAnimation class takes all of the sprite sheets that were added to it and composites them into one master sprite sheet. This composited sprite sheet is then walked through as we grab all of the needed animation frames and store them in arrays. When we are done processing the sprite sheet to cache the individual animation frames, we dispose of the sprite sheet to free up that memory.

NOTE The order in which the files appear in the array dictates the layering order. The first file is at the lowest layer.

Let's look at one method in the AnimationLoader class, and then we'll get into the SpriteAnimation class. A new instance of the AnimationLoader class is created, a SpriteAnimation instance is set in it, and then it is told to load an array of files via the loadFiles method.

When all files are finished loading, the following private method is invoked:

```
private function process():void{
  for (var i:int = 0; i < _loaders.length;++i) {
      var loader:Loader = _loaders[i];
      var b:Bitmap = loader.content as Bitmap;
      _spriteAnimation.layerBitmapData(b.bitmapData);
      b.bitmapData.dispose();
  }
  _spriteAnimation.process();

  _loaders = null;
}
```

A Loader class instance was used to load each sprite sheet. The content property of a Loader points to the display object that it loaded, which in this case is a Bitmap. The BitmapData property of the Bitmap instance is passed to the _spriteAnimation instance via the layerBitmapData method, which applies it as a layer (we'll look at this method below). We then dispose of the BitmapData to free up memory. After all of the Loader instances have been dealt with, we invoke the process method on the _spriteAnimation instance.

Now let's jump into the SpriteAnimation class. Here is the layerBitmapData method used above:

```
public function layerBitmapData(bd:BitmapData):void {
  if (_bitmapData == null) {
      _bitmapData = bd.clone();
  } else {
      _bitmapData.draw(bd);
  }
}
```

This method is called from the AnimationLoader class for every sprite sheet loaded. There is a class-level property called _bitmapData. If it is null, then we set the instance passed in as the value. If it is not null, then we draw the instance passed in onto the _bitmapData instance. The draw method of the BitmapData class has many blend modes. A blend mode specifies how the two BitmapDatas are combined. We use the default blend mode, which allows the instance passed in to just lay on top.

When a new instance of the SpriteAnimation class is created, the width and height of the individual frames in the sprite sheet are passed in to the constructor. They are stored as _frameWidth and _frameHeight. They are used in the process method:

```
public function process():void {
  var cols:int = Math.floor(_bitmapData.width / _frameWidth);
  var rows:int = Math.floor(_bitmapData.height / _frameHeight);

  var rect:Rectangle = new Rectangle(0, 0, _frameWidth,
_frameHeight);

  for (var i:int = 0; i < cols;++i) {
      _grid[i] = [];
      for (var j:int = 0; j < rows;++j) {
          var bd:BitmapData = new BitmapData(_frameWidth,
            _frameHeight, true, 0x990000);
          rect.x = i * _frameWidth;
          rect.y = j * _frameHeight;
          bd.copyPixels(_bitmapData, rect, new Point(0, 0));

          _grid[i][j] = bd;
```

```
      }
    }

  _bitmapData.dispose();
  _bitmapData = new BitmapData(_frameWidth, _frameHeight, true,
    0x990000);
  nextFrame();
}
```

This method takes the large composited `_bitmapData` instance, grabs all of the frames off it, and stores them in an array called `_grid`. First we determine the number of columns and rows contained in the sprite sheet using the `_frameWidth` and `_frameHeight` properties. A new `Rectangle` instance is created at the dimensions of a frame (it will be used a few lines down). We then loop through all columns, creating a new array for each, and loop through all rows in each column to process each frame. A new `BitmapData` instance is created to store that frame's information. The `Rectangle` instance is moved to a position equal to the upper left-hand corner of the frame being processed. Pixels are then copied out of the `_bitmapData` instance and onto the `bd` instance. The `bd` instance now contains one frame of animation. This instance is stored in the `_grid` array. After we are done with the `_bitmapData` instance, we dispose of it to free up memory, and then create a new value for that property. As the animation plays, the `_bitmapData` instance will continually point to the proper animation frame. The last thing done in this method is to call the `nextFrame` method:

```
public function nextFrame():void {
  ++_frameIndex;
  if (_frameIndex == _framesToHold) {
      ++_col;
      _frameIndex = 0;
      if (_col == _grid.length) {
          _col = 0;
      }
  }
  _bitmapData = getFrame(_col, _row);
}
```

Every time this method is called, it determines which animation frame to show. The `_framesToHold` property is defined externally when an instance of this class is created. It tells for how many frames to hold each key frame.

In Old World, each animation is 8 key frames. For the idle animation, we hold it for 6 frames, whereas the walk cycle is held only for 3. The `col` property specifies which key frame in the animation to show. The `row` property specifies the angle of the appropriate frame (each row in the sprite sheet displays a different angle that the avatar is facing).

AvatarCustomizationScreen Class

Once you have created an avatar and then logged in with that avatar, you are presented with an avatar customization screen. The `AvatarCustomizationScreen` class controls that screen, and is created in the `GameFlow` class. An instance of the `Avatar` class that represents your avatar is set in this class, so it has a reference to the avatar it needs to apply customizations to. On this screen you can view all the clothing options that you own. You can equip any of them and see a real-time update of your avatar. As you change what you're wearing, messages are sent to the server to save that information.

The avatar is rendered using a `SpriteAnimation` instance. Let's look at some key lines from the `buildAvatar` method:

```
_avatarLoaded = false;

_spriteAnimation = new SpriteAnimation(220, 400);
_spriteAnimation.framesToHold = 6;

_animationLoader = new AnimationLoader();
_animationLoader.spriteAnimation = _spriteAnimation;
_animationLoader.addEventListener(AnimationLoader.DONE,
onAnimationDoneLoading);

var baseDir:String = "files/avatars/big/" + _avatar.gender +
    "/";
var urls:Array = [baseDir+"base.png", baseDir+_avatar.bottom.
    fileName, baseDir+_avatar.shoes.fileName, baseDir+_avatar.
    top.fileName, baseDir+_avatar.hair.fileName];
_animationLoader.loadFiles(urls);
```

First `_avatarLoaded` is set to `false`. We then create a new instance of the `SpriteAnimation` class, and pass in the frame dimensions of 220x400. The `framesToHold` property is set to 6. An `AnimationLoader` class is

> **NOTE** *The* `buildAvatar` *method is used when this screen is first displayed, and again whenever a clothing option is selected to be worn, at which time it reloads the avatar to reflect the new choice of clothing.*

created, and we listen for its DONE event to know when it is done loading everything. The next few lines construct an array of URLs to pass to the AnimationLoader instance via the loadFiles method. The URLs are constructed using the clothing being worn by your avatar.

The run method is called every frame:

```
private function run(e:Event):void {
  if (_avatarLoaded) {
      _spriteAnimation.nextFrame();
      _avatarBitmap.bitmapData = _spriteAnimation.bitmapData;
      _avatarBitmap.smoothing = true;
  }
}
```

If the files are done loading, then tell the SpriteAnimation instance to go to the next frame, and set its latest BitmapData instance onto the _avatarBitmap. Set smoothing to true, since the avatar is slightly scaled down to fit.

There are user interface elements on the screen that allow you to select different clothing options that your avatar owns. When a new clothing item is selected, two things happen:

- The save method is called, passing in the clothing ID that is being applied to the avatar.

- The buildAvatar method is called again, removing the current avatar and building a new one based on the new clothing being worn.

Here is the save method:

```
private function save(id:int):void {
  var pr:PluginRequest = new PluginRequest();
  pr.setPluginName("WorldPlugin");

  var esob:EsObject = new EsObject();
  esob.setString(PluginConstants.ACTION, PluginConstants.EQUIP);
  esob.setInteger(PluginConstants.CLOTHING_ID, id);

  pr.setEsObject(esob);

  _es.send(pr);
}
```

This method is called whenever you change what an avatar is wearing through the user interface. The clothing ID is passed into the function and then used with the `EQUIP` action to tell the server to save this clothing choice as something your avatar is wearing.

CHAPTER 14

Virtual Worlds

WE HAVE COVERED a lot of ground up to this point, working with time synchronization, tile-based games, A* pathfinding, isometric mapping, and a ton of multiplayer concepts. While most of those concepts stand well on their own, this chapter brings them all together in showing Old World—the virtual world created for this book.

In this chapter, we start by discussing virtual worlds in general and touching on many of their common technical features. After that, we'll get into Old World: what features it has and the map XML format it uses. We then look at some of the code used to render the world, and finish up the chapter by showing how to bring the avatars from Chapter 13 into the world and get them walking around.

Common Features

There are a lot of Flash virtual worlds on the Internet. If you create an avatar and start exploring many of the virtual worlds out there, you'll notice that while they have many unique qualities, they mostly share a set of common features. Some features are not so common, but are becoming more so, such as questing.

In this section, we briefly look at common features that make up a virtual world.

Views—We talked about views in Chapter 12. The *view* of a world is how it is seen on screen, such as top down, side view, isometric, or full 3D. The most common view for Flash virtual worlds is isometric, which gives artists and developers a high-performance, low-production-time way to achieve a 3D look. A small number of worlds opt for a side-view approach. One example of a side-view world is Whirled (www.whirled.com). We'll assume from here on out that the worlds being discussed are isometric.

Tile-based or art-based—Some worlds are tile-based, some are art-based, and some use a little of both. A fully tile-based world is one that is built using diamond-shaped tiles of different types that together form the map. Items in a tile-based map usually take up a certain rectangular area of tiles, making it easier for pathfinding to occur. An art-based world is one that is usually hand-drawn, with hand-drawn items. Typically, the art-based world does not allow for avatars to walk along any path unless it is a straight line.

A combination approach between art-based and tile-based is common as well, and is what we used for Old World. In this hybrid approach, tiles are used for placement of objects and for pathfinding, but we also used large pre-drawn backgrounds, allowing us to show a richly detailed background while retaining most of the flexibility that tiles bring.

Avatars and interaction—It goes without saying that avatars are supported in all virtual worlds. The look of the avatar and level of customization made available changes from world to world. The avatar is used to allow the player to show some individuality through customization, and to interact with other players.

Avatar-to-avatar interaction can take many unique forms, but the most common ones are chatting and becoming buddies. When avatars become buddies, they can usually see when the other one is online and in some cases can tell where they are in the world. Two interaction features that are showing up more frequently are gifting and trading. Gifting is just what it sounds like—one avatar gives another one something, usually an item like clothing. Trading is when two players decide the other has something they want, and they use a trading interface to handle making the trade happen.

Scrolling—Most Flash virtual worlds have a SWF dimension of 800x600 or smaller, but the worlds that players enter are usually larger than those dimensions. This is handled by scrolling—the avatar walks in the world, and code usually tries to keep your avatar near the center of the screen by scrolling the entire world.

The act of scrolling the world can be a very performance-intensive thing for Flash, even if the code to handle it is simple. There are a lot of extremely advanced tricks and techniques that can be used to boost the performance of scrolling; they are another subject for another book.

Interiors—A world is often thought of as being just an outdoor place. But most worlds allow avatars to walk around and find structures such as houses, buildings, and stores. They let the avatar enter these places, usually by standing on a specific tile or by clicking on a door to get in. The avatar leaves the outdoor place, and a new indoor map, called an *interior*, is loaded. Interiors are usually the size of 1 or 2 screens at the most, although they are not limited to that in any way.

It is common in an interior (as seen in an isometric view) that the back walls are visible, the front walls are invisible, and the roof/ceiling is invisible. This is to allow the player to see the avatar without it being blocked out by walls or a roof.

NPCs—A non-player character (NPC) is a character that appears in-world but that is not controlled by a human. In most Flash virtual worlds, NPCs don't walk around. They usually stay in a single position and have a purpose, such as providing information when asked, selling items, or giving a quest to a player (discussed below).

Economy and vendors—All virtual worlds have an economy. Players gain virtual money by using a real-world credit card, or by earning virtual money by doing things in the world (like playing games). Virtual money can be spent on whatever the world creators come up with. At a minimum, this means items. Players like to buy more items for their avatars to wear or to put in their homes.

A spot where items can be purchased is typically called a *vendor*. Sometimes a vendor takes the visual form of a store, and sometimes it takes the form of an NPC.

Questing—While social interaction is an enormous reason that people use virtual worlds, there are many worlds that try to add a gaming slant. Questing gives players something to do that doesn't require interaction with other players. A quest is a series of tasks that the player must complete. When the tasks are complete, the quest is complete, and some reward is given. The reward can be anything, but it is common that the reward is virtual money or an item that can't be acquired any other way.

Quests are usually offered to a player through interaction with an NPC. There are many quest types, but here are some common ones:

- Gather—An NPC might ask your avatar to go find 20 apples and bring them to him.

- Deliver—An NPC might ask your avatar to take an item to another location or NPC.

- Visit—Your avatar might be asked to simply go visit some place. The mere act of visiting that place completes the quest.

Questing can add a whole new dimension of game play and activities to a virtual world. This has been a less common feature, but is starting to show up more frequently.

Playing games—In many Flash virtual worlds, the main activity for a player to do, other than customize their avatar and room, of course, is play games. Some games are single player and some are multiplayer. Most worlds have entry points to these games in places throughout the world. This helps keep the player immersed in the world.

Games are usually accessed through something in the world such as an NPC or simply standing on a specific tile. The games are typically simple and can be played in seconds to minutes. When complete, the player may be rewarded with virtual money or some other kind of prize.

NOTE *The avatar's buddies can visit the room, too. User homes are discussed in detail in Chapter 16.*

User homes—Most virtual worlds give an avatar a place that they can call home. This home is usually a spot that is about the size of one screen. The room is customized using items found in the avatar's inventory— items acquired through purchase or through being rewarded for quests or playing games.

World editors—World editing is a feature generally meant for the developers creating or maintaining the world, not for players. Worlds may have many areas, dozens or even a few hundred. A world editor is a tool that needs to be custom-built and that allows you to easily take pre-made assets, tiles, or world backgrounds and lay them out visually. Building a tool like this is a must for any virtual world—it can be extremely time-consuming to define the layout of a world by hand in XML, so the 2–3 days it takes to create a world editor will be regained several times over by the time saved in map creation and editing down the road.

Old World

As mentioned in Chapter 13, the world created for this book is called Old World. Old World illustrates many virtual world basics. It uses an isometric view and is a hybrid approach of tile-based and art-based. The backgrounds are pre-drawn, but we still make use of tiles for the layout of items in the world and for walking and pathfinding.

Welcome to Old World!

There is an interior and an exterior environment in Old World. The interior can, of course, be accessed from the outside environment. This interior "houses" an NPC that is selling furniture.

Nara encounters an old-world
furniture salesman.

The furniture you buy can then be used in your user home (see Chapter 16).
In the user home, you can place purchased furniture wherever you want,
and save the configuration.

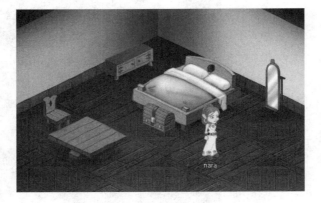

You can chat and become buddies with other avatars by clicking on them
and requesting to be their friend. You can view your friend list at any time,
see who is online or offline, and visit their user homes.

NOTE *Avatar customization code and screens are discussed in Chapter 13.*

You can leave the world to customize your avatar and then go back to the world.

Old World also contains a map editor, allowing you to easily create new maps visually.

Here are some things you will *not* find in Old World (not that any of these things aren't possible to add!):

- Game integration. This would take a few hours to add, but right now you cannot locate and play a game from within the world.

- Questing.

- Trading or gifting.

- Advanced room customization such as rugs, wall colors and patterns, pictures or windows, or rotating items (although Old World does support basic room-layout customization with items such as chairs, beds, and tables).

Map Files

The layout of each area in Old World is defined by (or in) an XML file. That XML file can be created by hand using a text editor like Notepad or can be output using the Old World map editor. In this section, we look at the map XML format in detail, and then look briefly at the map editor itself.

XML Format

Since Old World is a basic virtual world that illustrates basic features, the XML format is also, well, basic. Below we show the smallest amount of XML that we can while illustrating all features of the format. The lines are numbered so that we can refer to them below.

```
1.      <map>
2.          <background file="floor2.png" x_offset="-510"
            y_offset="-5" cols="15" rows="15"/>
3.          <ItemDefinitions>
4.              <ItemDefinition id="chair2_a" file="chair2_a.
                png" x_offset="-40" y_offset="-40"
                rows="1" cols="1" walkable="true"
                overlap="false"/>
```

```
5.              <ItemDefinition id="nightstand1_a" file=
                → "nightstand1_a.png" x_offset="-75"
                → y_offset="-25" rows="2" cols="1" walkable=
                → "true" overlap="false"/>
6.          </ItemDefinitions>
7.          <Items>
8.              <Item source="chair2_a" col="2" row="1"/>
9.              <Item source="chair2_a" col="1" row="2"/>
10.             <Item source="nightstand1_a" col="3"
                → row="7"/>
11.         </Items>
12.         <Tiles>
13.             <Tile col="4" row="2" walkability="false"
                → placeability="false"/>
14.             <Tile col="7" row="3" walkability="true"
                → placeability="false"/>
15.             <Tile col="11" row="4" walkability="false"
                → placeability="true"/>
16.         </Tiles>
17.     </map>
```

BACKGROUND NODE

We see the `<background>` node on line 2. It defines the background image file to be used for this map. As with all images defined in this XML file, it can point to either a PNG or a JPG image. This node has the following parameters:

- `file`—The name of the file to be loaded. This file must exist in the /assets directory relative to the Old World SWF file.

- `x_offset`—Along with `y_offset`, defines how much the image must be offset in the x direction such that the 0, 0 point in isometric is aligned with the image in the correct spot.

- `y_offset`—Works with the `x_offset`.

- `cols`—Number of columns the entire map takes up.

- `rows`—Number of rows the entire map takes up.

ITEMDEFINITIONS / ITEMDEFINITION NODE

The `<ItemDefinitions>` node contains as many `<ItemDefinition>` nodes as are needed. (Yes, these really *are* two different node names.) Each

<ItemDefinition> node defines everything about an item that could appear in the world. For example, the same tree could be used in a world 50 times. We just need to define what makes up a tree item once in an <ItemDefinition>, and then use the <Item> node (discussed next) to place instances of it. There are example <ItemDefinition> nodes on lines 4 and 5 in the XML above. One of them describes a chair that takes up only a single tile, and the other one describes a nightstand that takes up two tiles.

Each <ItemDefinition> node has the following parameters:

- id—Used by the <Item> node to specify which <ItemDefinition> node to use.

- file—Points to an image file.

- x_offset—Used with y_offset to offset the image with respect to the tile position so that it is properly placed.

- y_offset—Used with x_offset.

- cols—The number of columns the item should take up.

- rows—The number of rows the item should take up.

- walkable—A Boolean value. If true and placed on a tile that has a walkable property of true, then an avatar can walk on this tile.

- overlap—A Boolean value. If true, then the item can exist on the same tile as another item.

ITEMS / ITEM NODE

The <Items> node contains as many <Item> nodes as are needed to represent all items that are placed in the world. An <Item> node defines an instance of an <ItemDefinition> and specifies which tile it should be positioned on. Lines 8 and 9 show two <Item> nodes that point to the same item definition ID.

Each <Item> node has the following parameters:

- source—A string value that points to an id parameter found in an <ItemDefinition> node.

- col—The column in which to place the item.

- row—The row in which to place the item.

- onStop—An optional parameter. If it exists and has a value, that value should be the path to another XML file to load. If an avatar stops while standing on this item, then a new world is loaded.

- onClick—An optional parameter. If it exists, then a click event is fired off if a player clicks on it, and the value of the parameter is passed into the event. This is used to make items interactive, such as NPCs.

TILES / TILE NODE

When the map file is loaded into Old World, it creates a number of tiles equal to the rows value times the cols value found in the <Background> node. So if there are 10 rows and 10 columns, then 100 tiles are represented in memory. They all have default values that allow items to be placed on them and allowing avatars to walk on them.

This area of the XML gives you a chance to identify specific tiles that should not have the default behavior. The <Tiles> node contains as many <Tile> nodes as needed to specify all unique tiles. Lines 13, 14, and 15 override default properties of 3 different tiles. Each <Tile> node has the following parameters:

- col—The column of the tile to specify.

- row—The row of the tile to specify.

- walkability—A Boolean value. The default value is true. If false, an avatar cannot walk on this tile.

- placeability—A Boolean value. If false, an item cannot be placed on this tile. This is particularly useful in defining the XML format for a user home.

Map Editor

NOTE *Find the map editor in book_files/old_world/editor. Double-click it to install the application. If you don't already have Adobe AIR installed, download it from http://get.adobe.com/air/.*

We created a basic map editor for Old World. The editor is an Adobe AIR application.

After the editor is installed, launch it, and then choose Options > Change Source Directory. You'll be prompted to browse for a directory. The directory that you browse to should contain an assets folder and a data folder, just like the bin directory for Old World. The data folder should contain a file called Asset List.xml. The editor uses this file to determine which items to make available for placement in the world.

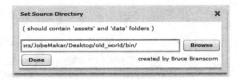

Editor limitations

Using the editor, you can do nearly everything you need to for building a world. What you *can't* do in the editor is:

- Specify an item as being able to teleport.

- Specify an item as being interactive, such as an NPC.

You can adjust the item offset through the panel at the bottom of the editor window.

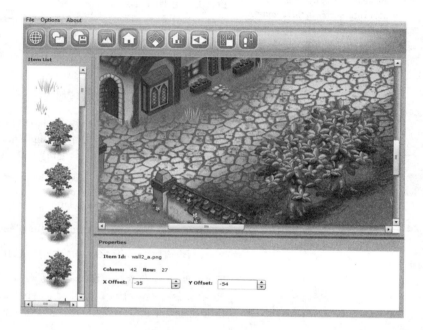

To add items to the world, just drag them out of the list on the left and drop them into the world. To move an item, click to pick it up, and then click somewhere else to place it again.

When you're ready to save your map, just click the Save button.

Map Rendering

In Chapters 12 and 13, we covered tile concepts as well as isometric concepts. We looked at how to lay out objects on the screen using the Isometric class and the sorting algorithm. In this section, we will review how Old World uses concepts we've already learned to build a scene and render it.

Map Class

To render a map, Old World loads a map XML file, parses it, loads all of the items defined in the XML file, and then draws the map background and lays the items on top. The Map class controls most of this.

NOTE *Sorting was covered in Chapter 12, but we'll look at how it is handled here with dynamically moving avatars later in this chapter. For now, just know that sorting is handled in the* Map *class.*

The loadMap method is used to make the Map class load a map XML file. An event, Map.READY, is fired from this class when all items are loaded and rendered. The Map class has a property called isEditable, which is a Boolean that defaults to false. If set to true, the Map class allows items to be added, removed, and moved from outside of the class. It exposes methods and events to allow this to happen (discussed in Chapter 16).

ISortable Interface

Anything that will need to be sorted in the world (which in this case means the Item and Avatar classes) must implement the ISortable interface. This interface simply requires that the following properties exist:

- col—The column the object is in.

- row—The row the object is in.

- cols—The number of columns the object takes up.

- rows—The number of rows the object takes up.

The sorting algorithm is the same as what was introduced in Chapter 12. However, when sorting is applied and how the sort list is managed are a little different, and are both discussed later in this chapter.

ItemDefinition Class

Earlier in this chapter we introduced a node in the XML file called <ItemDefinition>. The ItemDefinition class is the ActionScript analog to that node. It stores the walkable and overlap properties, as well as the number of columns and rows the object occupies.

In addition to the data mentioned above, the ItemDefinition class also contains the image information. The image is loaded by the ItemManager, and then the BitmapData instance is stored in the appropriate ItemDefinition instance.

Item Class

The map XML contains an `<Item>` node, and the `Item` class is the ActionScript equivalent to that. Each `Item` class instance specifies an `ItemDefinition` to use and where in the map it should go. Since the `ItemDefinition` contains the `BitmapData` for that visual item, all `Item` instances use that same `BitmapData`. This keeps memory usage low. For example, if an `ItemDefinition` that represents a tree is used 100 times in a map, then the tree image still just exists a single time in memory.

There is a useful method in this class called `checkPointCollision`. It is used for determining if a point is touching a non-alpha portion of the item. If you want to interact with an item via mouse click, then using typical click events is not the way to go. A normal click event is fired even if the mouse clicks on an area of the item that is fully transparent. However, the `checkPointCollision` method helps us solve that problem by firing a click event only for non-alpha areas of the item.

```
public function checkPointCollision(tx:int, ty:int):Boolean {
  var collision:Boolean =
_bitmap.bitmapData.getPixel32(tx - _bitmap.x, ty - _bitmap.y)
➤ != 0;
  return collision;
}
```

This method uses the point passed in with the `BitmapData` instance to inspect the value of the pixel it is over. If the pixel value is 0, then it's alpha, and that means the point is not over a visible part of the image.

ItemManager Class

The `ItemManager` class handles loading all of the images specified in the `ItemDefinition` instances, and then associates `Item` instances with the right `ItemDefinition` instance. This class also stores all `Item` and `ItemDefinition` instances in arrays and by their IDs, and provides ways to conveniently look them up.

The World

In Chapter 13, we discussed the application up to the point where you can customize your avatar. There is a button on that screen that says Enter World. If you click that button, the avatar customization screen goes away, and your avatar enters the exterior portion of the world.

When you click Enter World, the following function is invoked in the GameFlow class:

```actionscript
private function onEnterWorldClicked(e:Event):void {
  removeAvatarCustomizationScreen();
  createWorld("data/world.xml");
}
```

It removes the avatar customization screen, and then calls the createWorld method, which handles setting up a world that you are going to join:

```actionscript
private function createWorld(url:String, home:Boolean=false,
  owner:String=null):void{
  _world = new World();
  _world.addEventListener(World.TELEPORT, onTeleport);
  _world.addEventListener(World.GO_TO_HOME, onGoToHome);
  _world.es = _es;
```

```
    _world.clock = _clock;
    _world.clothingManager = _clothingManager;
    _world.furnitureManager = _furnitureManager;
    _world.buddyList = _buddyList;
    _world.initialize(url, home, owner);

    addChild(_world);
}
```

There are three parameters passed into this method. The first one, url, specifies the path to the XML file that is used for the world you're joining. The second parameter, home, defaults to false. If true, that means the world being joined is a user home, and the third parameter must have a value. The third parameter, owner, is the name of the avatar that owns the user home being joined.

The first thing done in this method is that a new World instance is created. Earlier, we looked at the Map class and how it handles rendering a world. The World instance wraps the Map instance, and handles all of the user interface code and client-server communication. We then add two event listeners to handle when an avatar walks onto a teleport spot or when they click a button in the user interface to go to their own home.

The next several lines just give the World class access to several things that the GameFlow class keeps track of, most of which have been discussed before. The _buddyList property is an AvatarManager instance that contains a list of all of your buddies (which we will cover in Chapter 15). The _world.initialize method is called while passing on the three parameters received by this function.

Jumping into the World class, let's talk about the initialize method. This method is called from the GameFlow class after all properties that have to be set externally are set, such as the ElectroServer instance. This method creates the new Map instance, listens for some events on it, and tells it to load the map. In this method we also create an Astar class instance (used for pathfinding), and add the user interface elements.

When the map is fully loaded, the onMapReady event handler is fired, which in turn joins the player to a room. Here is the familiar-looking code that does this:

```
private function joinRoom():void{
  var crr:CreateRoomRequest = new CreateRoomRequest();
  crr.setRoomName(_mapUrl);
```

```
crr.setZoneName("world zone");

var pl:Plugin = new Plugin();
pl.setPluginHandle("AreaPlugin");
pl.setPluginName("AreaPlugin");
pl.setExtensionName("GameBook");

if (_isHome) {
    crr.setRoomName(_owner);
    pl.getData().setString(PluginConstants.ROOM_OWNER,
    ➤ _owner);
}

crr.setPlugins([pl]);

_es.send(crr);
}
```

Entering a world means joining a room. Using the map URL as the room name is a convenient way to group people together. Remember that the CreateRoomRequest by default will join you to a room of the name you specify (if it already exists) or will create it (if it doesn't). So by using the URL as the room name, you end up joining a room with others who are viewing the same map. A plugin on the server is associated with this room so that it can control the avatar list and walking. If the room you are joining is a user home, then we change the name of the room to that of the room owner, and pass that name into the plugin.

Just like we've done with previous examples in this book, when the JoinRoomEvent occurs, the client sends an INIT_ME message to the plugin. The plugin will then recognize that client as being part of the world and will send an avatar list, avatar add/remove events, and walk events as they occur.

Managing Avatars

After a client joins the room, the client will receive an avatar list. This list contains information about all avatars currently in that world, such as what clothes they are wearing and their latest walk path. This event, and all server events while in a world, are received and parsed by the World class. The World class calls the addAvatar and removeAvatar methods on the Map class as needed.

The addAvatar method adds an avatar to the AvatarManager. The avatar is also added as a sortable display object by passing the avatar reference into the placeSortableItem method (discussed below in the "Sorting" section). All sortable items are added to the same display object, called _ground. Some items we want to always have on top, such as chat bubbles and the nameplate for an avatar. The nameplate is the text field containing the avatar's name, seen under the avatar's feet. The chat bubble and nameplate for the avatar are added as children to the _topLayer display object, which is always on top of the _ground display object.

The avatar is sorted behind a tree, while the nameplate and chat bubble are sorted in front of the tree.

The removeAvatar method takes just an avatar name. It finds the avatar of that name, and removes it from the avatar manager and also as a display object. It then removes the chat bubble and nameplate for that avatar.

Walking

Getting an avatar to walk on the screen is not that difficult, but it does use a lot of concepts learned throughout this book, such as server communication, A*, time-based movement, and sprite sheet avatar rendering. Here is the general process, and then we'll look at the code that handles it.

First we listen for clicks on the map. If a tile is clicked, then an event is fired by the Map class and captured by the World class. We perform an A* search from the tile your avatar is currently on to the tile you clicked on. The resultant path is then formatted and sent to the server, with a time stamp pulled from the _clock instance. Everyone in the world (including you) receives a walk event for your avatar. The path is parsed into Tile instances, and then wrapped as WayPoint class instances (discussed below). We then move the avatar from point to point in a time-based way. The avatar plays a walk animation and shows the correct rotation as it moves.

Here is the event handler found in the World class that handles the tile click event:

```
private function onTileClicked(e:TileEvent):void {
  var startNode:INode = _map.getTile(_map.avatarManager.me.col,
  ➤ _map.avatarManager.me.row);
  var goalNode:INode = e.tile;

  var results:SearchResults = _astar.search(startNode,
  ➤ goalNode);
  if (results.getIsSuccess()) {
      sendWalkPath(results.getPath());
  }
}
```

All Tile class instances meet the INode interface so that they work with an A* search. The starting node is where the avatar is currently standing, and the goal node is where it wants to go—the tile that was clicked. We use the two nodes in the search with the _astar Astar class instance. If the search is successful, then the Path instance is passed into the sendWalkPath method to format before being sent to the server, along with a time stamp.

When the client receives a walk event, it is captured and parsed by the World class. The World class calls the walkAvatar method in the Map class:

```
public function walkAvatar(name:String, time:Number,
➤ tiles:Array):void {
  var avatar:Avatar = _avatarManager.avatarByName(name);
  var wpIndex:int = 0;
  var wayPoints:Array = [];

  for (var i:int = 0; i < tiles.length;++i) {
      var tile:Tile = tiles[i];
      var dis:Number;
      if (i != 0) {
          dis = getDistance(tile, tiles[i - 1]);
          time += dis / avatar.walkSpeed;
      }

      var wp:WayPoint = new WayPoint();
      wp.time = Math.round(time);
      wp.tile = tile;

      if (_clock.time > wp.time) {
```

```
            wpIndex = i;
        }
        wayPoints.push(wp);
    }
    avatar.walk(wayPoints);
    avatar.wayPointIndex = wpIndex;
}
```

This method has a few parameters: the avatar name, the time the walking began, and an array of Tile instances that form the path. The purpose of this method is to create a WayPoint class instance to represent each spot along the path. All the WayPoint class does is wrap a Tile reference and the time the avatar should arrive at that Tile. We build the array of waypoints by looping through the array of tiles. For each tile, we calculate the distance between the previous tile and the current one we are looking at, and based on the avatar's walk speed we determine what time the avatar should arrive. The Tile class instance and the time are grouped together in a new WayPoint instance and added to an array. Since walking is time-based and we can't control latency, and since a new player could join while another avatar is halfway through a path, we check to see at which WayPoint the avatar should currently be positioned by comparing the WayPoint time with the current time. The last two lines of this method tell the avatar to walk by passing the waypoints into the walk method, and then setting the current wayPointIndex, which specifies which waypoint the avatar is currently on.

On every frame, the moveAvatars method in the Map class is called:

```
private function moveAvatars():void{
  for each (var avatar:Avatar in _avatarManager.avatars) {
      if (avatar.state == Avatar.WALKING) {
          stepAvatar(avatar);
      }
      avatar.run();
  }
}
```

An avatar is always in one of two possible states: idle or walking. In this method, we loop through all avatars. If an avatar is walking, then we pass it into the stepAvatar method, which we'll discuss in a moment. Either way, we then call the run method on the avatar, which the avatar uses to make sure it is showing the correct angle and to move to the next frame of the idle or walk animation. The run method also makes sure that the nameplate and chat bubble are positioned at the appropriate relative spots.

Here is the stepAvatar method:

```
private function stepAvatar(avatar:Avatar):void{
  var time:Number = _clock.time;
  var wp:WayPoint;
  var ind:int = avatar.wayPointIndex;

  //is it time for the next waypoint?
  if (ind < avatar.wayPoints.length - 1) {
      wp = avatar.wayPoints[ind + 1];
      if (time > wp.time) {
          avatar.wayPointIndex = ind + 1;
          ind = ind +1;
      }
  }

  //current way point
  wp = avatar.wayPoints[ind];

  var x:Number;
  var y:Number = 0;
  var z:Number;

  //position in isometric space
  x = _tileWidth * wp.tile.col;
  z = _tileHeight * wp.tile.row;

  var elapsed:Number = _clock.time - wp.time;

  if (ind == avatar.wayPoints.length - 1) {
      avatar.changeState(Avatar.IDLE);
      checkForOnStopEvent();
  } else {
      x += elapsed * avatar.walkSpeed * avatar.cosAngle;
      z += elapsed * avatar.walkSpeed * avatar.sinAngle;
  }

  var coord:Coordinate = _iso.mapToScreen(x, y, -z);
  avatar.x = coord.x;
  avatar.y = coord.y;
}
```

This method is called every frame for any walking avatar, moving an avatar along the path from the current waypoint to the next waypoint based on the elapsed time since the avatar arrived at the current waypoint. If the time lapse is great enough, we change the current waypoint to the next waypoint. The x and z variables are initialized to represent the position of the current waypoint. We add to those values based on the elapsed time walking since arriving at this waypoint. We then use the mapToScreen method of the Isometric class instance to map those coordinates to the screen and update the avatar's screen x and y position.

Sorting

The sorting comparison logic that was discussed in Chapter 12 is used in this project as well. But here, we keep track of the things to sort a little differently. In a world there are static items, and there are moving items. There could be hundreds of static items such as trees, bushes, and houses. There are probably going to be only a few moving items—avatars, in our case. The static items need to be sorted only once, since they don't move with respect to each other. In this project we keep track of an array of sortable static items. Then, every frame we just sort the avatars into this array.

The placeSortableItem method is called when adding anything to the screen that is sortable, such as an avatar or a house:

```
private function placeSortableItem(sortable:ISortable,
 insert:Boolean = true):void{
  //add to display list
  _ground.addChild(sortable as DisplayObject);

  if (insert) {
      //add to sortable items list
      _sortables.push(sortable);
  }

  //find 3D coordinates
  var iso_x:Number = sortable.col * _tileWidth;
  var iso_z:Number = -sortable.row * _tileHeight;

  //map 3D coordinates to the screen
  var screenCoord:Coordinate = _iso.mapToScreen(iso_x, 0,
 iso_z);
```

```
//update display object with screen coordinates
(sortable as DisplayObject).x = screenCoord.x;
(sortable as DisplayObject).y = screenCoord.y;
}
```

All sortable items must implement the ISortable interface. If you remember from Chapter 12, that just means that it must expose col, row, cols, and rows. If the insert parameter is true, then you add this item to the _sortables array. When avatar instances are passed into this method, insert is set to false. The next few lines of code position it on the screen on the appropriate tile.

Every frame, the sortMovableItems method is called:

```
private function sortMovableItems():void {
  var list:Array = _sortables.slice(0);
  var moving_arr:Array = _avatarManager.avatars;

  for (var i:int = 0; i < moving_arr.length;++i) {
      var nsi:ISortable = moving_arr[i];
      var added:Boolean = false;
      for (var j:int = 0; j < list.length;++j ) {
            var si:ISortable = list[j];

            if (nsi.col <= si.col + si.cols - 1 && nsi.row <=
            ➝ si.row + si.rows - 1) {
                list.splice(j, 0, nsi);
                added = true;
                break;
            }
      }
      if (!added) {
            list.push(nsi);
      }
  }

  for (i = 0; i < list.length;++i) {
      var disp:DisplayObject = list[i] as DisplayObject;
      _ground.addChildAt(disp, i);
  }
}
```

The sortMovableItems method sorts all avatars into the array of static items, which is then copied into a new array called list. We create a local variable called moving_arr that contains all avatars. We iterate through the moving_arr array, and use the sorting logic to determine where the avatar should be inserted into the list array. We then loop through the list array and add each sorted display object at the right index.

Buying Items

There is an NPC in Old World, selling furniture at the inn.

Enter the inn by walking on top of the teleport spot by the front door.

Click on the NPC to see the user interface elements that allow you to browse the items for sale.

You cannot buy clothing in Old World, only furniture.

⚇ NOTE *Since you can use the furniture items that you own only when you are in your own user home, they are only loaded when you join your user home. We'll see more about that in the User Homes chapter.*

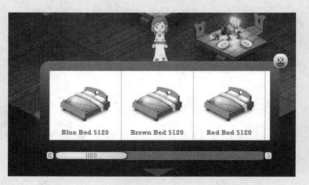

Scroll through the available furniture and click on what you want to purchase. When you confirm the purchase, then a BUY_ITEM request is sent to the server.

The items that are available for purchase are found in the FurnitureManager instance. They were loaded as part of the login response.

CHAPTER 15

Buddies

VIRTUAL WORLDS ARE social networks. Their popularity relies heavily on the ability of avatars to interact and form bonds. The most common type of bond formed between avatars is becoming buddies, also known as *friending*. Once you have a bond with another avatar, the virtual world gives you ways to interact directly with that avatar, whether through private chatting, playing games, or other unique interactions.

In this chapter, we will do the following:

- Discuss the concept of relationships and describe a few types.

- Go over different ways a relationship can be formed.

- Look at buddies as they exist in Old World and walk through some relevant code.

Relationships

The ability for a person to form a connection with another person, and then have some level of interaction with that person, is the foundation for social networks. At their core, applications like Facebook, MySpace, and Old World are very similar—they provide a novel way for users to find each other, establish a relationship, and allow for interaction between people who have relationships.

Relationship Types

I refer to bonds between people as *relationships* instead of using the term friends or buddies because there are many types of relationships. There is no limit to the type of relationships that can exist. Here are a few that I've seen in virtual worlds or other social networks.

FRIENDS / BUDDIES

This is the most common type of a relationship—allowing players to add other players their buddy list. How you interact with the buddies after they are added to the list depends on the virtual world you are dealing with. At a minimum, it usually means that you can do the following:

- Tell whether they are online or offline.

- Send them private messages.

- See where they are in the world.

In many worlds, you can also do the following with people in your buddy list:

- Challenge them (or invite them) to a game.

- Give them a gift. This is usually an item from the inventory, such as a hat or shirt.

- Send them an in-game email. This is a way to send messages to players who may not currently be online. If the mail supports attachments, this can be another way to give an item.

IGNORE / BLOCK

This might not sound like a relationship, but it is. When players have the ability to interact with each other, there is always the chance for abuse. Abuse can take many forms, but it usually occurs through chatting. If a player is bad-mouthing or otherwise bothering another player, then the victim can just add the abuser to an ignore list. A player will not see chat messages or other events from a player in the ignore list.

PARENT / FAMILY

Most Flash virtual worlds target kids 8–12 years old. With security being a big concern, some virtual worlds allow parents to view information about what their child is doing and even control times when the child can access the world. A special parent/child relationship is established for that.

In some worlds, a family member is treated the same as a buddy, but with an extra parameter indicating that the buddy is a family member.

CO-WORKER / COLLEAGUE

This type of a relationship is rare in virtual worlds, but common in other social networks like Facebook or LinkedIn. A relationship can be formed between people who have worked together professionally. Often, information about how long they worked together and in what capacity is stored with the relationship.

ENEMIES / FOES

Social networking is a huge part of virtual worlds, but it isn't the only part. Many virtual worlds are adding game elements, such as questing or battling, to give the players other things to do. One type of relationship that can exist in a virtual world that has competitive gaming elements is enemies—enemies in the context of the game, though; not people that you would truly dislike.

Forming the Relationship

In virtual worlds, a relationship is usually created when you see another avatar in the world, click on the avatar to bring up a context menu, and then select an option to form a relationship (such as adding him as a buddy or to the ignore list). But just because you want a relationship to exist doesn't mean that it will. Each relationship has two properties that define how it is established.

SYMMETRY

The symmetry of a relationship says if it goes both ways or not. For example, if Player A ignores Player B, that doesn't mean that Player B has to ignore Player A. Ignoring is an asymmetric relationship. But in most cases, buddy relationships are symmetric: if Player A has Player B as a buddy, then Player B also has Player A as a buddy.

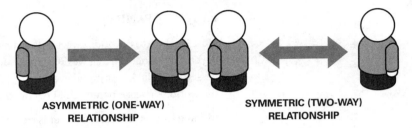

ASYMMETRIC (ONE-WAY) RELATIONSHIP   **SYMMETRIC (TWO-WAY) RELATIONSHIP**

AUTHORIZATION

Authorizing relationships can be handled in a lot of different ways; we'll describe the most common one here. When Player A attempts to establish a relationship with Player B, Player B is informed of this, and can authorize and accept this relationship or decline it. If the relationship is accepted, then both players are informed that the relationship now exists. If the relationship was declined, then Player A is informed that it was declined, and no relationship is made.

In most cases, symmetric relationships require authorization, whereas asymmetric ones do not. For example, Player A shouldn't require Player B's authorization to ignore.

Buddies in Old World

The buddy system in Old World is very simplistic. For ease of programming and explanation, buddies are asymmetric. Below we'll explain all of the features of buddies in Old World and show some of the code behind the buddy relationship.

ElectroServer has the concept of buddies built in. Clients in a world use the WorldPlugin to add and remove buddies in the database. Just after a player logs in and before he joins a world, he loads his complete buddy list from the WorldPlugin. This is just done a single time. The list contains the names and avatar IDs of all his buddies, as well as a Boolean value indicating if they are online or not. From that point forward, the online/offline status for buddies is updated through the use of the ElectroServer event called the BuddyStatusUpdatedEvent. This event is fired whenever someone in your buddy list logs in or logs out. ElectroServer knows when your buddies log in and log out because that is a built-in feature of ElectroServer. When the WorldPlugin loads the buddy list for a player, it registers each of those avatars as a buddy in memory, which allows ElectroServer to fire off the BuddyStatusUpdatedEvent at the correct times.

Loading the Buddy List

To reiterate from the previous paragraph, after a player logs in but before he goes to join a world, his buddy list is loaded. This is done in the GameFlow class. The following function is called in the onLoginResponse event handler:

```
private function loadBuddies():void {
  var esob:EsObject = new EsObject();
  esob.setString(PluginConstants.ACTION, PluginConstants.
  ➞ LOAD_BUDDIES);

  sendToWorldPlugin(esob);
}
```

An EsObject is formatted with the LOAD_BUDDIES action. The WorldPlugin receives this request, loads the buddies for that avatar, and responds with a LOAD_BUDDIES response, which is handled in the handleLoadBuddies method in the GameFlow class:

```
private function handleLoadBuddies(esob:EsObject):void{
  var list:Array = esob.getEsObjectArray(PluginConstants.
  ➞ BUDDY_LIST);
  for each (var buddyOb:EsObject in list) {
      var avatar:Avatar = new Avatar();
      avatar.avatarName = buddyOb.getString(PluginConstants.
      ➞ BUDDY_NAME);
      avatar.avatarId = buddyOb.getInteger(PluginConstants.
      ➞ BUDDY_ID);
```

```
                 avatar.isOnline = buddyOb.getBoolean(PluginConstants.
              ➤ LOGGED_IN);

                 _buddyList.addAvatar(avatar);
         }
}
```

NOTE *Each buddy has three properties: a name, an ID, and a Boolean value indicating if they are online or not.*

The buddy list is managed using an instance of the AvatarManager, called (ready for this?) _buddyList. In the function above, we iterate through the list of buddy EsObjects sent from the server, and parse each one of them into an Avatar instance, which is then added to the _buddyList. The _buddyList instance is set in the World instance whenever a new one is created. This is so the World instance has access to the buddy list to show it in the user interface.

Showing If a Buddy Is Online

In the buddy list user interface discussed in the next section, there is a color indicator for each buddy that indicates if that buddy is online or not. If the isOnline property of that buddy (which is an Avatar instance) has a value of true, then the buddy is online and the color indicator will show yellow. That value is initially set when the buddy list is loaded. But as time goes on and buddies log in and log out, we want the isOnline property to stay current. We do this by listening to the ElectroServer event called BuddyStatusUpdatedEvent. That event is fired whenever a buddy in your buddy list logs in or logs out. Here is the event handler in the GameFlow class:

```
public function onBuddyStatusUpdatedEvent
➤ (e:BuddyStatusUpdatedEvent):void {
  var name:String = e.getUserName();
  var isOnline:Boolean = e.getActionId() ==
  ➤ BuddyStatusUpdatedEvent.LoggedIn;

  if (_buddyList.avatarByName(name) != null) {
       _buddyList.avatarByName(name).isOnline = isOnline;
  }
}
```

This event handler grabs the appropriate buddy from the _buddyList, and then it updates the isOnline property based on the getActionId value in the event. If the value of getActionId is the same as that of BuddyStatusUpdatedEvent.LoggedIn, then the buddy has just logged in. Otherwise, the buddy has just logged out.

Adding a Buddy

Most of the code that goes into adding a buddy is user interface code. We'll talk about which functions are used to drive the user interface, but only look at the code that talks to ElectroServer to add the buddy.

When you see another avatar in the world, you can click on it. This click is handled in the `World` class method called `onAvatarClicked`. As long as you didn't click on yourself, you are given a popup asking if you'd like to add this avatar as a buddy.

If you click No, the popup just goes away. If you click Yes, the `onBuddyConfirmYes` event handler is invoked. This function sends a request to ElectroServer to add the buddy, adds the buddy directly to the buddy list, and removes the popup:

```
private function onBuddyConfirmYes(e:Event):void {
  var pop:BuddyConfirmationPopup = e.target as
  ➞ BuddyConfirmationPopup;

  var avatar:Avatar = pop.avatar;

  var esob:EsObject = new EsObject();
  esob.setString(PluginConstants.ACTION, PluginConstants.
  ➞ ADD_BUDDY);
  esob.setInteger(PluginConstants.BUDDY_ID, avatar.avatarId);

  sendToWorldPlugin(esob);

  _buddyList.addAvatar(avatar);

  removeBuddyConfirmPopup(pop);
}
```

The avatar reference is pulled from the popup. An EsObject is formatted with an ADD_BUDDY request and sent to the WorldPlugin. Next, we add the avatar directly to the buddy list. The popup UI element is then removed from the screen.

Removing a Buddy

Removing a buddy is done through the buddy list. If you select a buddy in the buddy list, two buttons are enabled: Remove and Home.

If the Remove button is clicked, then the buddy is removed. Here is the function in the World class invoked as a result of clicking Remove:

```
private function removeBuddy(avatar:Avatar):void {
  var esob:EsObject = new EsObject();
  esob.setString(PluginConstants.ACTION, PluginConstants.
  ➝ REMOVE_BUDDY);
  esob.setInteger(PluginConstants.BUDDY_ID, avatar.avatarId);

  sendToWorldPlugin(esob);

  _buddyList.removeAvatar(avatar.avatarName);
}
```

An EsObject is formatted with the REMOVE_BUDDY action and sent to the WorldPlugin, which then removes the buddy from the database and unregisters it as your buddy with ElectroServer. The last line of this function removes the avatar directly from the buddy list.

Viewing the Buddy List

Viewing the buddy list uses straightforward user interface code. The button with the heart icon  in the bottom-right area of the screen is the buddy list button.

When the buddy list button is clicked, the onBuddyListClicked event handler is invoked in the World class, which in turn calls createBuddyListUI. The createBuddyListUI function creates a new BuddyList class instance. The BuddyList class is a display object that shows the list of all buddies.

When the BuddyList instance is created, it is passed the array of Avatar instances that represent your buddies. There is a colored circle to the right of the buddy name, indicating if that buddy is online or offline. Red means offline, yellow means online. If a buddy is selected in the list, as you learned above in "Removing a Buddy," then the Remove and Home buttons are enabled. When the Remove button is clicked, the buddy is removed from the buddy list and a REMOVE_BUDDY request is sent to the WorldPlugin. By clicking the Home button, you are taken to that buddy's user home. We'll look at user homes in Chapter 16.

If the X button is clicked in the buddy list, then the list is removed from the screen.

Ways to Improve

If all of this buddy-related code were to be used in a virtual world intended for public use, there are a few additions that would help make it a more useful feature:

- **Make buddies symmetric**—In the example here, you can add anyone you want as a buddy without their approval, and you are not their buddy unless they manually add you. Enhancing this so that the avatar you select must authorize you as a buddy, but when done you are both each other's buddies, would make this similar to other worlds.

- **Show where your buddies are**—We currently show if each buddy is online or offline. But it would help with finding and interacting with your buddies if you could see exactly where they are in the world or have the ability to teleport directly to their location.

- **Private chat**—It would be nice to include this common feature so that you can carry on a private chat with buddies. This would be initiated through the buddy list. There is already complete server support for this feature, with no code modifications necessary. The only code required would be to add user interface elements that support private chatting on the client.

Since the interaction between players is one of the primary reasons players stay and come back, it makes sense to spend time working on features that support those interactions.

CHAPTER 16

User Homes

AS HAS BEEN discussed in previous chapters, virtual worlds are social networks. At their core, they allow for player-to-player interaction and self-expression. We've outlined how players can interact in worlds and establish relationships, and we've seen how they can express their individuality through the customization of their own avatars. There is another feature common to most virtual worlds that allows for self expression: user homes.

An avatar's user home is their own space in the world, customizable using the items found in that avatar's inventory. Avatars can also invite buddies into their homes to show off the items they've either purchased or received for completing a quest or for playing games. Unlike the customized avatar itself, the user's home is always viewable by others, whether the "owner" is logged in or out.

In this chapter, we'll discuss all of the things that are possible with user homes, and then discuss a limited user-homes feature that was programmed as part of Old World.

"Open House"

In this overview section, we'll look at common features found in user homes—checking it out as a user, if you want to think of it that way. User homes can take advantage of all the same features that a world can have—avatars can enter the home, walk around, and interact with other avatars. What makes user homes special are the additional features that are not found in a typical world area. Most of these features are focused on the customization of the home by the specific player who owns that home.

Carpets, curtains, pictures—custom décor makes this not your everyday world environment.

In most virtual worlds, each player gets a single user home. They can customize the room by adding or moving items, changing the wall color or patterns, or even by changing the layout (size and wall placement) of the home itself. As changes to the room are made, they are saved to a database. The player can leave the world and come back later to find all of the customizations still applied.

Players can enter other player's homes. How (and whether) this is done varies from world to world. It is common that a player can visit only the home of a buddy. It is also common that a buddy doesn't need to already be online or in that room for someone to visit that buddy's user home. However, some worlds do disallow visitors when the owner is not online or in the home already.

Items in User Homes

Most of the customization that can occur in a user home is through item placement. Avatars acquire items in a virtual world by buying them, getting awarded them for completing quests, or through gifting and trading. Most acquired items are meant to be used to customize either the avatar or their user home.

Each item that can be used in a user home can fall into one of the following categories:

- **Furniture item**—This item type is the most common environmental item found in a user's home. Furniture includes items such as chairs, tables, boxes, and beds.

- **Wall item**—This type of item exists only on walls. Common wall items are posters, clocks, doors, and windows.

- **Floor item**—These items are floor-bound and allow for furniture items to be placed on top of them. A rug is a common floor item.

Examples of Furniture, Wall, and Floor items.

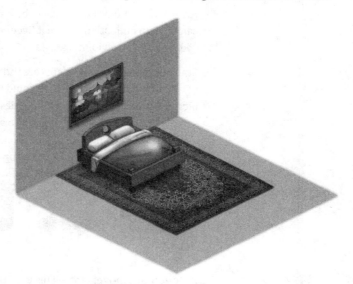

NOTE *It is common to create multiple visual rotations of an item. That way, the player can choose which view of an item to show when placing it in the world.*

These items can be visually placed in the world by the player. Typically, the player will see a list of all of the items they own in an inventory list. The player can drag an item out of the user interface and into their user home. The behavior that the item exhibits while being dragged may depend on the item. For instance, a furniture item would typically match the mouse position as it was dragged, whereas as a wall item would move along a wall as it was dragged.

The items and customization abilities mentioned so far in this chapter give players a lot of freedom to make their homes unique. But there are more advanced customization features that can be employed to give players even more freedom in that area. Here are some additional features that items can exhibit:

- **States**—Items can be created with the ability to show different states. For instance, a lamp in the room could be on or off. The state of this example item could be linked to the time of the day, for instance, or it could be changed through user interaction.

- **Animation**—Items don't have to be a static image, like a chair. They can contain animation to give it liveliness. For instance, a fish tank could show fish swimming.

- **Stackability**—Stackable items are those which can be placed on top of other items. A stackable item could be a TV, table lamp, vase, or picture frame. Only some items are designated as stackable, and only some items are designated to allow for items to be stacked on them. For example, you wouldn't want to stack an item on top of a coffee cup, but you might want to stack the coffee cup on top of a night stand.

- **Autonomous movement**—This item understands the user home's map and directs its own movement through it based on custom logic. This could be anything from a remote-control car to a hands-free vacuum cleaner like a Roomba®.

User Homes in Old World

Now that you've become familiar with user homes and many features that can be found in them, we can look at an example user home implementation programmed in Old World.

Visiting and Decorating

In this example, you can enter another player's home only if they are in your buddy list. To do that, bring up the buddy list, and then select a buddy in the list. You'll see that the Home button becomes enabled. Click that button to enter that buddy's home.

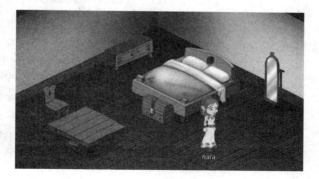

To enter your own home, simply click the Home button 🏠 found on the bottom-right side of the screen.

Once you are in your own home, you'll be able to customize it. The home can be in one of two states: design or normal. When it's in design state, you can customize it but not walk around. When it's in the normal state, you can walk around but not customize.

To customize your home, click the hammer button 🔨 on the bottom-right side of the screen.

When you enter design mode, you will see a user interface that contains all of the furniture items that you own that aren't yet placed in the home. If you don't own anything, you can purchase items from the NPC found in the Inn (discussed in Chapter 14). To bring an item out of the user interface and into your home, click the item once. Then, when you move your mouse, you'll see the item follow under your mouse. Click another time in an available spot in the home to place the item.

To move an item, click it once to pick it up, move your mouse to move the item on the screen, and click to place the item. You can remove the item by picking it up and moving your mouse over the Recycle button and clicking. The item will be removed from the home and placed back in the inventory.

Don't worry—when you recycle an item, it won't go to the dump; it will be placed back in inventory.

Now that you know how user homes behave in Old World, we can move on to look at some of these behaviors from a technical standpoint.

Data and Transactions

In this section, we'll look at how the client knows about all furniture that exists and how it (the client) finds out what furniture an avatar owns when joining their user home. In addition, we'll see how the client tells the server that an item has been moved from one location to another.

In the login response handled in the `GameFlow` class, there is extra information sent to the client. In Chapter 13 we saw that there was clothing information here, which was parsed in the `parseClothing` method. There is also furniture information found here in the EsObject that comes in the onLoginResponse event handler. All furniture that exists in the system (not necessarily anything that an avatar owns) is sent to the client this time. It is parsed in a method called parseFurnitureItems. We'll look at that method in a little while, but first, a let's have little furniture review and a little new information.

First, the quick review of the Furniture, FurnitureDefinition, Item, and ItemDefinition classes: Item and ItemDefinition were introduced in Chapter 14. You may recall that the ItemDefinition class contains the visual information for an item and its offset. The Item class is used to contain the positional information of an ItemDefinition. For instance, you could have 20 Item instances in various locations that all use the same ItemDefinition instance.

With all that in mind, you should also know that the Furniture class is instanced for every item that an avatar owns. A Furniture class instance contains a pointer to an Item class instance, which is used for placing the furniture in the world, and which contains a FurnitureDefinition instance. The FurnitureDefinition holds information about that furniture item that was purchased, such as its filename, its cost, and the ID of that furniture type.

The NPC that sells furniture uses the list of all FurnitureDefinitions to display what items are available for sale. The inventory of items that a player can place in the home are all Furniture class instances.

Now that we've got that all settled, let's get back to the parseFurnitureItems method, which is called in the onLoginResponse event handler in the GameFlow class:

```
private function parseFurnitureItems(items:Array):void{
  for (var i:int = 0; i < items.length;++i) {
      var furni:FurnitureDefinition =
      new FurnitureDefinition();

      var furniOb:EsObject = items[i];
      furni.name = furniOb.getString(PluginConstants.
      FURNITURE_NAME);
      furni.fileName = furniOb.getString(PluginConstants.
      FURNITURE_FILE_NAME);
      furni.id = furniOb.getInteger(PluginConstants.
      FURNITURE_ID);
```

```
        furni.cost = furniOb.getInteger(PluginConstants.
      ➤ FURNITURE_COST);

        _furnitureManager.addFurnitureDefinition(furni);
    }
}
```

This is a list of all furniture available for sale in the system. What is passed into this method is an array of EsObjects. Each EsObject contains formatted information that is parsed into a FurnitureDefinition instance and then stored in the _furnitureManager, which is an instance of the FurnitureManager class.

The rest of the client-server transactions for user homes are handled in the World class. As you know from Chapter 14, when entering a new area, a new instance of the World class is created to manage the user interface, create a Map instance, and load the XML layout as well as all images. As part of the initialize method in the World class, there is a class-level Boolean value called _isHome that is set to true if this is a home that's being joined. We'll see that property used in a moment, and again in the next section, "User Interface."

In Chapter 14 we saw that the avatar list for the area being joined is sent to the client immediately after joining. It is processed in a method in the World class called handleAvatarList. Here's an if statement at the bottom of that method, which wasn't discussed at that time:

```
if (_isHome) {
  parseHomeFurniture(esob);
}
```

If this is a user home, then the EsObject sent to the client also contains all of the furniture owned by the client and its positional information. That is handled in the parseHomeFurniture method. That method parses EsObjects into Furniture instances and stores them for convenient access in three ways. They are stored in a typical indexed array called _furniture. They are stored by ID in a Dictionary instance called _furnitureByEntryId. And they are stored by Item instance in another Dictionary instance called _furnitureByItem. Storing the Furniture instances in these various ways allows us to easily access them later. For instance, if an item is clicked in the world, we can look up the Furniture instance by using the Item instance.

The last client-server communication issue for us to talk about concerns moving items. An item can be moved from the user interface into the

world; from one position to another position in the world; or from the
world back to the user interface. Whenever any of those three things
occurs, the following method is called:

```
private function moveFurniture(item:Item, inWorld:Boolean):
 void {
  var furni:Furniture = _furnitureByItem[item];

  var esob:EsObject = new EsObject();
  esob.setString(PluginConstants.ACTION, PluginConstants.
 MOVE_FURNITURE);
  esob.setInteger(PluginConstants.FURNITURE_ENTRY_ID, furni.
 entryId);
  esob.setInteger(PluginConstants.PLACEMENT_ROW, item.row);
  esob.setInteger(PluginConstants.PLACEMENT_COLUMN, item.col);
  esob.setBoolean(PluginConstants.FURNITURE_IN_WORLD, inWorld);

  sendToAreaPlugin(esob);
}
```

This method takes two parameters: item and inWorld. The item parameter
contains the Item instance that was moved. The inWorld parameter is a
Boolean value specifying whether or not the item is in the world. If inWorld
is true, then the item is in the world; otherwise it is back in the inventory.

The rest of this method formats the item information onto an EsObject,
and then sends that EsObject to the server. The information sent is the ID
of the item being moved, its column and row position, and the Boolean
value specifying whether or not it is in the world.

In summary, all FurnitureDefinitions are loaded as part of the login
response, you are given all Furniture instances owned by a player when
entering their home, and the moveFurniture method is used to inform the
server that a piece of furniture has moved to a new location.

User Interface

In this section, we'll look at some of the code used to drive the user interface, such as how we know when to allow a client to edit a room and when
not to, and how we use the user home selection window to move an
unplaced item from inventory into the space. Look at the following line of
code (taken from the createWorld method in the GameFlow class):

```
_world.initialize(url, home, owner);
```

After the `World` class instance is created, the `initialize` method on it is called, as you just saw. The `url` parameter points to the location of the XML file that defines the static world layout. The `home` parameter is a Boolean value which if `true` means this area is a user home. The `owner` property contains a value only if `home` is `true`, and if so it contains the name of the avatar that owns the home.

Here are the top several lines of the `initialize` method found in the `World` class:

```
public function initialize(url:String, home:Boolean,
→ owner:String):void {
  _mapUrl = url;
  _isHome = home;
  _owner = owner;
  _isMyHome = _es.getUserManager().getMe().getUserName() ==
→ owner;
```

You can see that it stores the parameters passed in. In addition, if the owner value is equivalent to the avatar name of the client running this code, then `_isMyHome` is set to `true`. The `_isMyHome` property is used to determine if the client should be able to edit this specific room. That is done in the `onMapReady` event handler in the `World` class. Let's look at that now:

```
if (_isMyHome) {

  // Alter Bottom UI "Home Buttom" => World Button
  _bottomUI.home_btn.visible = false;
  _bottomUI.worldButton.visible = true;
  _bottomUI.addEventListener(UserHomesEvent.EXIT_HOMES,
→ onHomesExited);

  // Add Bottom UI for Homes
  _homesBottomUI = new HomesUI();
  _homesBottomUI.addEventListener(UserHomesEvent.EDIT_MODE_
→ TOGGLE, onEditModeToggle);
  _homesBottomUI.addEventListener(UserHomesEvent.ITEM_RECYCLED,
→ onItemRecycled);
  _homesBottomUI.x = 687.5;
  _homesBottomUI.y = 550;
  addChild(_homesBottomUI);

  // Create Furniture Selection UI
```

```
_furnitureList = new UserHomesItemList();
_furnitureList.addEventListener(UserHomesEvent.ITEM_SELECTED,
    onListItemSelected);
_furnitureList.visible = false;
addChild(_furnitureList);

// Add Listeners to Map for in-world Item Interaction
_map.addEventListener(ItemInteractionEvent.ITEM_SELECTED,
    onItemSelected);
_map.addEventListener(ItemInteractionEvent.ITEM_PLACED,
    onItemPlaced);
}
```

If _isMyHome is found to be true, we add the specific user homes interface
to the screen in the function above. As you can see, there are many state
changes that take place: the home button is made invisible, and the globe
button is made visible and listens for the event to exit the home. There are
two additional buttons added to the list of buttons found at the bottom-
right of the screen. One of them—the hammer button—controls the
normal and customization modes of the user home. The other (leftmost)
button is used to recycle items back into inventory. Next, a new instance
of UserHomesItemList is created and stored as _furnitureList. This user
interface element shows a list of all furniture items owned that are not currently in the world. It allows you to select an item to bring into the world.
The last two lines in this function add event listeners to the Map class
instance, to capture when an item is selected in the world and when it is
placed in the map.

We initially set the visibility property of _furnitureList to false, due to
the fact that the default mode is normal. Once the user clicks the hammer
icon and enters customization mode, _furnitureList will display, and the
user's furniture will appear within that window.

Once an item is chosen from the _furnitureList, the onListItemSelected event handler is invoked:

```
private function onListItemSelected(e:UserHomesEvent):void {
  _map.startDraggingItem(e.item);
  e.item.filters = [new GlowFilter(0x009900)];
}
```

The item that was selected is found on the event object and then passed into the startDraggingItem method on the Map class instance. Calling this method adds the item visually to the map, sorted above everything else, and allows it to follow the mouse as the mouse moves. The item is also given a glow effect, to indicate that it is selected.

When the item is actually placed in the world, the onItemPlaced event handler is invoked:

```
private function onItemPlaced(e:ItemInteractionEvent):void {
  e.item.filters = [];
  moveFurniture(e.item, true);
}
```

This event handler removes the selection filter from the item and then calls the moveFurniture method (discussed earlier in this chapter). It communicates with the server to update the database to store the new position of the item.

If the player should decide to place the item back into inventory, they may do so by picking up the item and clicking the recycle button. When the recycle button is selected, the onItemRecycled event handler is invoked:

```
private function onItemRecycled(e:UserHomesEvent = null):void {
  var item:Item = _map.itemBeingDragged;
  if (!item) {
      return;
  }
  if (_furnitureList) {
      _furnitureList.add(item);
  }
  _map.stopDraggingItem();
  moveFurniture(item, false);
}
```

This event handler takes the item that was being dragged, adds it back to the `_furnitureList` instance, tells the `Map` instance to stop dragging it, and then calls the `moveFurniture` method to have the new position stored in the database.

That's it! We've looked at all of the relevant code that goes into handling the client-server interactions and displaying and placing furniture items. If this example were to be taken further, a good next step would be to add item rotations. But that's up to you—the ball is now in your court. Enjoy the game!

Setting Up the
Sample Extension

THE ZIP FILE that you downloaded to go with this book contains
an extension that you can deploy in your ElectroServer installation
without needing to be able to compile Java. In the book_files/
examples_extension/extension folder, find and copy the GameBook
subfolder. Paste this into your ES4 installation folder/server/
extensions. Reboot the ES4, and then add the server-level
components.

Server-Level Components

After deploying the extension, restart ElectroServer and open the administration panel. If you are running ElectroServer locally, this is typically done by opening a web browser to https://localhost:8080/admin. After logging on as administrator, go to the Extensions tab. You should see every extension that is installed on your ElectroServer on this screen. Click the plus button (+) for GameBook, and then click the New Server-Level Component button. The next screen should show the Extension name of GameBook. Choose TimeStampPlugin from the Plugin Handle drop-down menu, and then type **TimeStampPlugin** into the Plugin Name field.

Repeat this process with GMSInitializer, and then restart ElectroServer again.

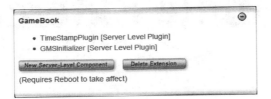

Old World

The GameBook extension discussed above doesn't include OldWorld, because that requires an authenticated login. The zip file that you downloaded for this book contains an extension that *does* include OldWorld, that you can drop into your ES4 in the same way as the extension for all of the other the examples. Find the book_files/old_world/server_extension/ oldWorldExtension folder, and, again, copy the GameBook folder. Paste this into your ES4 installation folder/server/extensions. It is OK to just merge the two extensions—that is, the contents of the two folders. Reboot the ES4, and then add the extra server-level components. When you've finished, your set of server-level components will include all of these:

- GMSInitializer (not required for OldWorld)
- TimeStampPlugin
- WorldPlugin
- LoginEventHandler
- LogoutEventHandler

You will also need to deploy the database for OldWorld. Find book_files/ old_world/server_extension/server/db. Copy the BookWorld folder, and then paste it into your ES4 installation folder/server/db.

Reboot Electroserver one more time, and OldWorld will be ready to use.

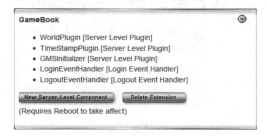

Configuring the Logging

If you wish to set the server logging to DEBUG level so that you can more easily diagnose problems, look in your ES4 installation folder/server/config and edit the log4j.properties file. Add the following two lines:

```
log4j.logger.com.gamebook=debug
log4j.logger.Extensions.GameBook=debug
```

After rebooting Electroserver, you should be able to see each plugin message in the server log. Note that this should not be done in the production environment, but it is extremely useful for development.

Setting up the Server-side Development Environment

The remainder of this appendix is for readers who are interested in modifying the Java source code provided, or creating their own plugins.

Install Java and NetBeans

Both Java and NetBeans are free downloads. Other IDEs are available with Java, but this appendix will assume that you are using NetBeans.

Download and install the latest version of the Java SE Development Kit (JDK) from http://java.sun.com/. If you did not get NetBeans bundled with Java, you may download it from www.netbeans.org.

Create the NetBeans Project

After installing both Java and NetBeans, it is easy to set up a NetBeans project for the GameBook extension.

1   Copy the Java source code found in the book_files/examples_extension/ server folder. We will assume that your copy is placed in C:/GameBook/ server.

2   Open NetBeans, and choose File > New Project.

3   In the Categories list, choose Java. In the Projects list, choose Java Free-Form Project. Click Next.

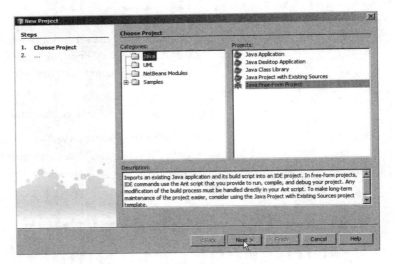

4   Browse to find the GameBook folder that has the build.xml file in it, such as C:/GameBook/server. NetBeans will fill in the rest of the fields, and you may take the defaults or specify other locations. Click Next.

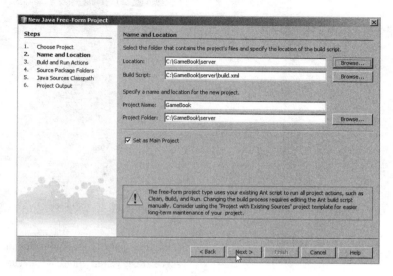

5   On the next screen, just take the defaults, and click Next.

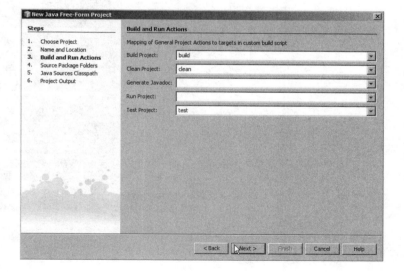

6 On the Source Package Folders screen, click the Add Folder button on the top right, and browse to C:/GameBook/server/src.

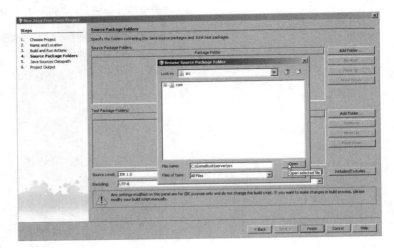

7 Click the second Add Folder button, and browse to C:/GameBook/server/test. When you're done, the screen should look like this:

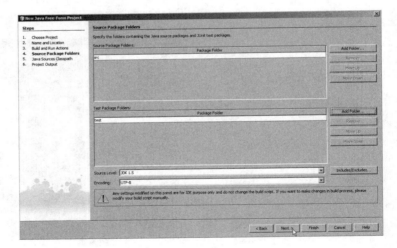

8   Click Next to get the Java Sources Classpath screen. Click Add Jar/
     Folder, and then browse to C:/GameBook/server/lib.

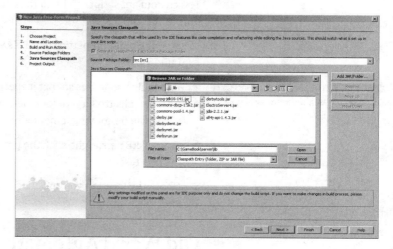

9   Add each of the jars in that folder. When you're done, it should look
     like this:

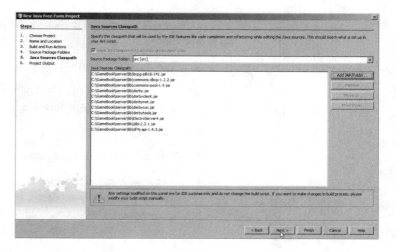

10   Click Finish. The NetBeans project is now ready. To compile, right-click
     the project name (GameBook), and choose Build.

Automatic Deployment

The custom ant script can build the entire extension for you at the same time as it compiles.

1   Find the build.properties file. This will be in the same folder as the build.xml file.

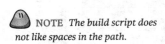

NOTE   *The build script does not like spaces in the path.*

2   Edit build.properties so that it specifies the location of your locally installed ElectroServer4 (or where you prefer to place the extension if you will be copying it manually).

3   From NetBeans, right-click the project name (GameBook), and choose Test.

4   Check the location you specified in build.properties to see if the extension magically appeared.

Old World Automatic Deployment

When you start working on the Old World chapters, you will need to change your automatic deployment and the server-level components.

1   From NetBeans, right-click on the project name (GameBook), and choose Properties.

2   Click Build And Run.

3   If you don't see an ant target named oldWorldTest, click Add, click the empty field under Ant Target, and select oldWorldTest.

4   Click OK.

5   Right-click on the project name (GameBook), and select oldWorldTest.

6   Check the location you specified in build.properties to see if the extension magically appeared. You can tell it is not the same as before because there should be a config folder inside GameBook that was not there before.

See the previous Old World section of this appendix for deploying the database and setting the server-level components.

CREDITS

We thank the following companies for generously allowing us to use images from their websites. Please patronize their sites!

CHAPTER 4

Pages 32 and 33—Faraway Friends, www.farawayfriends.com

CHAPTER 5

Page 53—Comedy Central, www.comedycentral.com

Page 54—Sifaka Productions, www.sifakaworld.com

Page 55—Faraway Friends, www.farawayfriends.com

CHAPTER 8

Page 118, 120, 121, and 122—Comedy Central, www.comedycentral.com

CHAPTER 10

Page 153—Precious Moments, Inc., www.preciousgirlsclub.com.

CHAPTER 12

Page 190, bottom image—Precious Moments, Inc., www.preciousgirlsclub.com.

Page 191—Precious Moments, Inc., www.preciousgirlsclub.com.

Page 192—Faraway Friends, www.farawayfriends.com

CHAPTER 13

Page 210—Sifaka Productions, www.sifakaworld.com

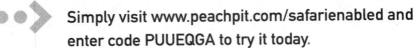